Thucydides
on
International Law and Political Theory

Thucydides
on
International Law and Political Theory

Iacovos Kareklas

LEXINGTON BOOKS
Lanham • Boulder • New York • London

Published by Lexington Books
An imprint of The Rowman & Littlefield Publishing Group, Inc.
4501 Forbes Boulevard, Suite 200, Lanham, Maryland 20706
www.rowman.com

6 Tinworth Street, London SE11 5AL

British Library Cataloguing in Publication Information Available

Library of Congress Cataloging-in-Publication Data

Names: Kareklas, Iakōvos, 1976- author.
Title: Thucydides on international law and political theory / Iacovos Kareklas.
Description: Lanham : Lexington Books, [2020] | Includes bibliographical references and index.
Identifiers: LCCN 2019050612 (print) | LCCN 2019050613 (ebook) | ISBN 9781498599580 (cloth) |
    ISBN 9781498599603 (paper) | ISBN 9781498599597 (epub)
Subjects: LCSH: International law--History--To 1500. | Greece--Politics and government--To 146
    B.C. | Thucydides--Influence.
Classification: LCC KL4384.2 .K37 2020 (print) | LCC KL4384.2 (ebook) | DDC 341--dc23
LC record available at https://lccn.loc.gov/2019050612
LC ebook record available at https://lccn.loc.gov/2019050613

Contents

Preface

Thucydidean scholarship has always been rich. The present monograph is the product of two and a half decades of study and research on Thucydides and well over twelve years of teaching in the context of my course, international law. The originality of this work lies in the fact that it proves, on the one hand, that in classical times, certainly in the era of the Peloponnesian War, international law and strategy existed in an advanced form among the city-states of ancient Greece. On the other hand, this book shows how the work of Thucydides, and, in fact, classical Greek international law and politics, have influenced some aspects of modern international law and international politics, in particular the following.

Firstly, Thucydidean political realism is analyzed extensively and it is indicated how it differs from realist and neo-realist theories of politics in the modern era. Simultaneously, the role of ethics in international politics is especially stressed, a factor notable in the work of Thucydides, which follows in this regard a diametrically different approach than the Machiavellian.

Secondly, the monograph unearths the grounds of just war in classical Greece. It indicates that neither the causes nor the grounds of the Peloponnesian War in the *History of the Peloponnesian War* by Thucydides are in conformity with previously established grounds of warfare. It proves that the grounds of war in Thucydides, as distinct from the causes of that war, have formed the legal and political basis of contemporary kinds of military intervention in international law. In this context, the contribution of Thucydides in the international law of war is duly presented.

Thirdly, the warfare practices which were developed in the time of Thucydides prove that in classical Greece there existed in a systematic form a corpus of law with regard to armed conflict; that is, legal rules governing the conduct of opponents in the field of battle, which were not of a rudimentary form, but, in fact, sufficiently developed. If it cannot be said that these rules have influenced the formation of equivalent rules in modern international humanitarian law, it could certainly be deduced that they stood firmly in their own right as an aspect of classical Greek international law.

Fourthly, some representative and most important treaties referred to by Thucydides are presented and examined. In this way documentation is provided for the fact that the historian is a pioneer in preserving with accuracy the diplomatic practices of ancient Greece. Also, the conventions surveyed testify to the great diplomatic activity of the Greek people and their tendency to bring about as far as possible regularization of international or inter-state relations.

Fifthly, some notable personalities and their role in the politics of the Peloponnesian War are analyzed throughout the text (Cleon, Hermocrates, Pericles, Alcibiades) and in a chapter drafted especially for this purpose. It is submitted that Alcibiades at all stages of his career knew exactly what he was doing and did it with deliberation, and that he should not be regarded as a traitor, as some contemporary philologists have characterized him, but, instead, as a patriot who deep down cared for the benefit and interest of his city-state, Athens. It is not doubted, however, that occasionally he acted on the basis of self-interest. Further, the personality of Pericles is examined in detail, not only with regard to policy making or strategy, but through his funeral oration. Any thoroughgoing analysis of Thucydides would be inadequate if it does not include an overview of this famous oration and the corresponding ramifications of the Periclean personality.

Sixthly, political intelligence and its role in the work of Thucydides are extensively exposited in a separate chapter.

Seventhly, the contribution of Thucydides in strategic studies is preeminent in the book, due to the fact that the historian analyzed, for the first time in history, the most important forms of strategy. A subchapter on the grand strategy of Sparta is further provided.

Eighthly, in a very analytical chapter it is proved that reports of gods, oracles, and natural phenomena in the work of Thucydides are significant, because they prove the historian's convictions. It is submitted that his stance was favorable toward traditional Greek religion. Also, in contrast, to Thucydides, against whom unfair criticisms have been raised as to his stance toward religion, Herodotus has always been regarded by modern scholarships in the classics as a historian who not only firmly accepted traditional Greek religion, but was deeply influenced by it. In a final chapter, by means of a comparative perspective and method I purport to present a few cases whereby the religious convictions of Herodotus are particularly evident.

Let me express my deepest thanks and gratitude to the Faculty of Classics in the University of Cambridge. The magnificent holdings of the Classics Faculty Library, where sustained research for this monograph has predominantly been done, have been extremely useful. Also, I am grateful to Cambridge University Press for permission to publish excerpts from Jeremy Mynott's *Thucydides: The War of the Peloponnesians and the Athenians: Cambridge Texts in the History of Political Thought* (Cambridge: Cambridge University Press, 2013). Further, I would really like to thank the Philological Journal *Parnassos* for permission to reprint my article published in volume NE' [2013-2014], Athens: 2018, which here sees the light as chapter 2, "Grounds of Lawful War in Classical Greek International Law and Causes of War in Thucydides."

Last, but certainly not least, I would like to give my warmest thanks to Rowman and Littlefield and all the members of the editorial team for so willingly and diligently publishing my book on Thucydides.

It is hoped that this work, like the one of Thucydides, shall be κτῆμα ἐς αἰεὶ μᾶλλον ἢ ἀγώνισμα ἐς τὸ παραχρῆμα ἀκούειν.

—Dr. Iacovos Kareklas

Chapter One

Thucydidean Political Realism

ATHENIAN GREAT POWER AND IMPERIALISM

Political realism as a theory of international politics features impressively in the *History of the Peloponnesian War* by Thucydides, particularly in the context of Athenian imperialism.[1] The tension between nature and justice is the most overt characteristic of this theory. The exploration of this very tension is evident in Book I in the speech of the Athenian envoys at Sparta.[2] These ambassadors, who remain anonymous, in town on other business, step forward, themselves having requested it, to reply to the complaints of the Corinthians.

The Corinthians had already offered contrasting views of the cities of Athens and Sparta. Athens had been presented as a city which is in constant motion, whereas Sparta as a city which wishes only to remain at rest. What is stressed in particular is the restlessness of Athenian injustice.

> And so they pass all the days of their lives in toils and perils of every description, enjoying far less than others what is already theirs, so busy are they adding to it; the only holiday they observe is to do whatever requires to be done, and they think unremitting toil a lesser misfortune than the tranquility of a quiet life. In short they were born (or it is their nature) neither to enjoy and rest nor to leave any to others.[3]

This extract almost denotes that the Athenians are victims of their own empire, their thirst for which deprives them of all repose. This, in fact, serves as a defense against the very charge of injustice. This defense would plead an overwhelming internal compulsion, which removes from the actor's shoulders all responsibility for what would otherwise be regarded as injustice. And this is precisely what the Athenian envoys put forward with a remarkably

sophistic twist. Not just as Athenians but as human beings are they congeni-
tally unable to leave their neighbors in peace. Such a defense of the empire
diverges from that of the Funeral Oration with its celebration of Athenian
exceptionalism.[4]

The Athenian speech is too bold to have been publicly uttered before a
powerful opponent, so that this opponent might be inclined to peace. The
speech, however, is lucid. Both Thucydides and the speakers themselves
deem it necessary to inform us of their intentions. In accordance with Thucydides, the intentions of the Athenians were to show the Spartans that the
matter before them should not be decided in haste, and simultaneously to
exhibit the power of Athens.[5] According to the Athenian envoys, they have
not come forward to refute the charges of the other cities, as they neither
have a mandate from home to do so nor recognize the authority of the
tribunal. They hope to prevent the Spartans from following the counsel of
their allies. They also aim to demonstrate that their city holds her empire not
unjustly and that Athens is "one to be reckoned with" (ἄξια λόγου).

The ambassadors begin their speech with reference to the Athenian empire by stressing its coming into being through the magnificent accomplishments of their city during the Persian Wars. This counts clearly as a reminder
of power, which was very likely to have been the main intention of the
ambassadors. They discuss their imperialism, which manages, in their expression, "to be frank." They do not deny that their subjects are not capable
of administrating their own cities. They confess that they exert power and
rule strictly for their own purposes. The envoys, though, do not say that right
is a consequence of might, or, to put the matter somewhat differently, that
righteousness depends upon power. They openly admit that their rule rests
upon superior strength, which they aptly ascribe to virtue, which is superior
to the one held by their allies,[6] and assert that the stronger will inevitably
exert power and rule. However, they seem to insist that Athens is an empire
not ruled unfairly, if not justly, by claiming that no people has ever been so
just as to resist the temptation to be a ruler. Athens did not become an empire
by the use of force, the envoys assert, but by victoriously fighting the Persians. Conversely, they say, Sparta's lack of friendliness had driven city-
states into the Athenian alliance. So the argument is that the noble actions
and stance of Athens are the grounds to which she owes her empire:

> And it followed from this very action (that is, our acceptance of the allied
> command) that we were compelled in the first place to advance our empire to
> its present state, swayed first of all by fear, though later by honour too and
> lastly also by profit.[7]

The envoys go on to expound upon the compulsions of obtaining an empire:

> So we have done nothing to be wondered at, or off the beaten track for human beings, in accepting an empire that was offered us and in not relinquishing it, overcome by the greatest things, honour and fear and profit.[8]

They imply that it does not matter on which of these compulsions their empire rests, because all are among the greatest things, honor, profit, and fear, all being equally irresistible. Thus, the distinction among necessity and political expediency is erased effectively.

No society has ever been shown to resist the inclinations to empire is the argument further employed by the ambassadors:

> Or have we innovated in this: it has ever been the case that the weaker have been subjected by the stronger. We held ourselves, moreover, worthy of this role, as indeed did you, until now for reasons of interest you raise the argument from justice—which none has ever adduced to his loss when he stood to gain something by force.[9]

Their second excuse for accepting to run an empire is that in their manner of ruling their superiority is manifestly asserted:

> And praise is due to all who, while so far subject to human nature is to rule others, yet are juster than they need be considering their power.[10]

Athens practices rule by law. In her disputes with her subjects, she pursues the path of litigation, at the city of Athens or in the subject city. She continues to preserve the appearance of equality. The envoys claim that Athens treats her subjects with restraint (μετριάζομεν), taking but little from them, and this is conducted judicially (δικάζεσθαι) rather than by force (βιάζεσθαι). It is apparent that the ambassadors mistakenly equate justice with the judicial process, which is not enough per se to implement what is just in each case:

> Our subjects, however, are used to associating with us as equals, so that if they are crossed in any way in something, whether by a legal verdict or by the power that the empire confers on us, and their opinion as to what is called for does not prevail, they give us no thanks for leaving them with most of their possessions, but resent their losses more bitterly than if we had from the first cast law aside and openly gratified our rapacity. In that case even they would not have disputed that the weaker must make way for the stronger. As is only likely, people get angrier at an unjust verdict than at being constrained by force, for the former seems like being cheated by an equal, the latter like being compelled by a superior.[11]

At the end of their speech the ambassadors refer to the unforeseeable fortunes of war.[12] They make reference to the thirty years' treaty, which they stand accused of transgressing. Although the envoys talk about justice, their strategy depends on fear—of chance, and of themselves. Most of the Spartans, though, vote with the ephor Sthenelaidas for war "not so much because they were persuaded by the speeches of the allies as because they feared the rising power of the Athenians, seeing that most of Greece was already subject to them."[13]

In order to survive in the international system but also to safeguard and pursue their political expediencies, states long for power. Thucydides may be regarded as the founder of the long tradition of political realism, according to which power is a central theme in international politics. The *History of the Peloponnesian War* is essentially a historical, political, and philosophical analysis of the problem of power in international affairs. It attempts to provide a definition of state and inter-state power, to explain its development and importance in inter-state affairs, to explore the moral dilemmas which stem from its use, and to discuss whether power should, in certain circumstances, be legally limited. The interpretation of power, as provided for by Thucydides, has come to be seen as the basis of contemporary political realism.

At the very outset of his book,[14] Thucydides creates a theoretical picture which explains the birth and further development of state power. He divides power into three main categories, which still firmly survive in the theoretical discourses of international politics: diplomatic power, military power, and economic power, which, to a certain extent, interact, so that the preeminence of a state is secured internationally.[15]

Thucydides employs these very categories of power, so that he may interpret the rise of Athenian hegemony. Athenian naval power was the one due to which the empire came into being. In turn, the Athenian empire brought about wealth, and, therefore, economic power. Subsequently, economic power stood as a pillar to military power (practically the navy) and so forth. So Thucydides is interested in exploring what may be termed "real power," or what modern political realists call "hard power," the term being a synopsis of the aforementioned three main categories of power.

Firstly, diplomatic power, according to the analysis of Thucydides, mainly means the effort made by a state to build up alliances with other city-states. These alliances potentially succeed in furthering the state's wealth and eventually its military power. Particularly for Sparta, making alliances was considered as a main factor which secured military power for her. On the other hand, to Athens, alliances were really a major source of economic benefits. In the Mytilenaean debate, Cleon argues as to the basis of alliances, stressing that making allies is a safe strategy for Athens to retain and strengthen its economic capability. Similarly, Pericles urges his fellow citizens not only to strengthen ties with allied city-states, but also to make sure that hard economic measures are imposed upon them as these were regarded as the main source of Athenian naval power.

Secondly, military power is analyzed by Thucydides in its two main established facets, namely land power and naval power. As regards the city of Athens, Thucydides obviously concludes that naval power is the more important one, given that the Athenian empire was largely the outcome of expeditions by the city's navy. It should not be surprising that Thucydides depicts Pericles saying that the ramifications of sea power are, indeed, huge (μέγα τὸ τῆς θαλάσσης κράτος).[16]

Thucydides, also ascribes a further dimension to military power. He considers that military power, aside from being tangible, is also a matter of human decision-making. Thus, he presents Pericles counseling his citizens that they should never let fear overwhelm their decision-making process.

Thirdly, expounding on economic power, Thucydides poses the argument of King Archidamus, perhaps by far the most important one spelled out by him to the Spartans, that war is carried out less on the basis of weapons and more on the basis of economic resources. Therefore, King Archidamus argued that Sparta was unlikely to be capable of meeting the needs and vicissitudes of war since she did not acquire enough economic power.[17]

In his discussion of the various categories of power, Thucydides also gives emphasis to the notion of balance of power. In an international system of the modern world, where states struggle to promote their political interests, retaining peace is not easy. The safest way to retain peace, according to political realists, is the existence of a balance of power system. In practice, this means that states need to take measures necessary for their security and well-being and also to make steps deemed to be indispensable for the maintenance of international balance of power. This issue is significant in the analysis of Thucydides and manifests itself when Corinth began making preparations for war against Corcyra. The Corcyreans immediately ran to the Athenians seeking their help.[18] The argument of the citizens of Corfu was that they could, in their own right, maintain the balance of power adequately to deter or repel the manifestation of military power on part of the Corinthians, and that not being able to do so would lead to total disaster.[19] Furthermore, it may be noted that the tensions of political realism appear in the issue of Corcyra in another form too. Thucydides, in his analysis of the Corcyraean Sedition, is no longer a defender of Athenian imperialism, if he has been at all, in the "Archaeology" of his *History of the Peloponnesian War*. During that insurrection, all forms of order gave way, words changed their meaning, and human beings reverted to the worst in themselves.[20] Thucydides writes:

> The causes of this were the desire to rule on account of greed and love of honor, from which they were put into a state of zealous love of victory. . . . As they were struggling by every means to gain an advantage over each other, they dared to do the most terrible things and executed still greater acts of vengeance. For they did not propose anything up to the limit of what was

expedient for the city, but defined the limits by what was pleasing to either faction at any instant. . . . Thus, life in the city was thrown into confusion at this critical time. Once human nature prevailed over the laws by becoming accustomed to do injustice against the laws, it manifested delight in being unrestrained passion, stronger than justice and an enemy to its superior.[21]

The balance of power issue appears also in the speech of Hermocrates at Gela in the face of the imminent attack of the Athenians. As soon as the leader of Syracuse realizes that the Athenians are ready to launch war against Sicily, he proposes before his fellow citizens and the rest of the Sicilian tribes a number of political measures aiming at bringing about a balance of power and virtually preventing the Athenians from taking hold of their homeland.[22]

Balance of (military) power may be achieved in two ways: internally and externally. King Archidamus lucidly spells out these two forms in his speech towards the Spartans.[23]

In modern international politics, preparations made for war in the interior of a state, mobilization of the masses, education and military training, expenditure on military equipment, and so on, form part of internal efforts made by a state to achieve a balance of power in inter-state and international affairs. On the other hand, making of alliances is a conspicuous example of external ways of achieving balance of power in states' affairs. Alliances are formed on the basis of common interests. This is the position taken by the Corinthians in the *History of the Peloponnesian War*, who proclaim that no bond is more important among cities or citizens than common interests.[24] In turn, common interests are themselves divided into two subcategories: the need for threat balancing and the need of power balancing in view of an up-and-coming military power.

As regards the former subcategory, one could indicate the speech of the citizens of Corfu as an example. They made efforts to secure the military alliance and assistance of the Athenians by stressing the fact that the Corinthians were their common enemy, namely opponents both of the Athenians and the people of Corcyra.

With regard to the latter subcategory, emphasis is placed, not on the intentions of the opponent, but on his capability to form a threat to the interests of a state. The Spartan policy, for instance, aimed at balancing the power of the rising Athenian empire. In order to achieve this aim, Sparta did not hesitate to call on Persia to succor her struggle. Persia, on its part, also pursued this very same goal, that is, to weaken the power of Athens. In the first instance, however, the Persians used the power balancing method in such a manner so as to weaken both antagonists in the hegemony of Greece, Athens and Sparta alike. The principle of divide and rule is particularly revealing of the intentions of the Persian satrap Tissaphernes, as presented by Thucydides:

To me, however, it seems perfectly clear that the reasons for not bringing the fleet were to wear out and immobilize the Greek forces: this was a process both of attrition—while he was making the journey there and wasting time, and of equalization—in making neither side stronger than the other by lending his support to it. Had he actually wanted to, he could have brought the war to an end by making a decisive appearance on the scene.[25]

To the same effect, Alcibiades advised Tissaphernes on another occasion:

Alcibiades further advised Tissaphernes not to be too keen to bring the war to an end. Nor should he want to give the same people control of both land and sea, either by bringing up the Phoenician ships he was equipping or by providing pay to a larger number of Greeks. Instead he should let the two sides divide power between them and so make it possible for the King always to turn the other side against whichever of them was proving troublesome to him.[26]

In the end, the Persians took the plunge to militarily support the Lacedaemonians, an eventuality which yielded the balance of power to the favor of the Spartans.

Many preeminent scholars of political science and classics have insisted on the importance that the book of Thucydides bears on modern international politics. Conspicuous examples of these are Robert Gilpin, professor of international affairs, and Clifford Orwin, professor of political philosophy—to name but a few.

Gilpin believes that "an underlying continuity characterizes world politics. The history of Thucydides provides insights today as it did when it was written in the fifth century B.C."[27]

Stressing the international system, Gilpin quotes Thucydides:

Indeed, frequently, one power fails to play its necessary role in duopolistic balance. This was the case when Sparta failed to arrest the growth of Athenian power. Enumerating Athenian preparations for war, Sparta's Corinthian allies delivered the charge that Sparta failed to arrest Athenian expansion and permitted the balance to shift in Athens' favour:

For all this you are responsible. You it was who first allowed them to fortify their city after the Median war, and afterwards to erect the long walls, you who, then and now, are always depriving of freedom not only those whom they have enslaved, but also those who have as yet been your allies. For the true author of the subjugation of a people is not so much the immediate agent, as the power which permits it having the means to prevent it; particularly if that power aspires to the glory of being the liberator of Hellas. . . . We ought not to be still inquiring into the fact of our wrongs, but into the means of our defense. For the aggressors with matured plans to oppose our indecision have cast threats aside and been taken themselves to action. And we know what are the paths by which Athenian aggression travels, and how insidious is its progress. A degree of confidence she may feel from the idea that your bluntness of perception prevents your noticing her; but it is nothing to the impulse which her advance will receive from the knowledge that you see, but do not care to interfere. You, Lacedaemonians, of all the Hellenes are alone inactive, and defend yourselves not by doing anything but by looking as if you would do something; you alone wait till the power of an enemy is becoming twice its original size, instead of crashing it in in its infancy. And yet the world used to say that you were to be depended upon; but in your case, we fear, it said more than truth. . . against Athens you prefer to act on the defensive instead of on the offensive, and to make it an affair of chances by deferring the struggle till she has grown far stronger than at first. . . if our present enemy Athens has not again and again annihilated us, we owe more to her blunders than to your protection. Indeed, expectations from you have been the ruin of some, whose faith induced them to omit preparation. [28]

Considering political realism, he states that "this theory explains the most important aspects of international relations (war, imperialism, and change) as consequences of the uneven growth of power among States." Thucydides was perhaps the first political scientist to take note of this relationship when he wrote that "the growth of power of Athens, and the alarm which this inspired in Lacedaemon, made war inevitable." [29]

The great wars of history—we have had a world war about every hundred years for the last four centuries—are the outcome, direct or indirect, of the unequal growth of nations.

Referring especially to hegemonic war, Gilpin notes, as Thucydides told us, the issue in the great war between Sparta and Athens was hegemony over Hellas, not the more limited matters in contention between the opposing states. Although politicians on both sides regarded the conflicts limited and hence negotiable, Pericles went to the heart of the issue in response to those Athenian politicians willing to accept Sparta's seemingly limited demands:

They order us to raise the siege of Potidea, to let Aegina be independent, to revoke the Megara decree; and they conclude with an ultimatum warning us to leave the Hellenes independent. I hope that you will none of you think that we shall be going to war for trifle if we refuse to revoke the Megara decree, which appears in front of their complaints, and the revocation of which is to save us from war, or let any feeling of self-reproach linger in your minds, if you went to war for slight cause. Why, this trifle contains the whole seal and trial of your resolution. If you give way, you will instantly have to meet some greater demand, as having been frightened into obedience in the first instance; while firm refusal will make them clearly understand that they must treat you more as equals. Make your decision therefore at once, either to submit before you are harmed, or if we are to go to war, as I for one think we ought, to do so without caring whether the ostensible cause be great or small, resolved against making concessions or consenting to precarious tenure of our possessions. For all claims from an equal, urged upon neighbor as commands, before any attempt at legal settlement, be they great or be they small, have only one meaning, and this is slavery.[30]

The correlation between Thucydides and the international relations discipline is, indeed, a great one. Just as Hobbes, who translated the work of Thucydides, found it to be relevant to the seventeenth century, current scholars believe the *History of the Peloponnesian War* has something important to contribute to our understanding of international relations in the twentieth and twenty-first centuries. The *History of the Peloponnesian War* is of interest to international relations as well as international law scholars, because the work can help stimulate the development of a number of basic concepts and propositions on the causes and dynamics of war. After long studies in the aforementioned fields, one may feel inclined to agree with Robert Gilpin's observation that "in honesty, one must inquire whether or not twentieth-century students of International Relations know anything that Thucydides and his fifth-century campatriots did not know about the behavior of States."[31] Thucydides provides us with what appears to be explicit propositions and axioms of international politics.

HEGEMONIC WAR: SIMILARITIES BETWEEN THE PELOPONNESIAN WAR AND THE COLD WAR

It has been said that one should be interested in the past only as a guide to the future. I do not fully concur with this. One usually emerges from an intimate understanding of the past, with its lessons and its wisdom, with convictions which put fire in the soul. I doubt seriously whether a man can think with full wisdom and with deep convictions regarding certain of the basic international issues of today who has not at least reviewed in his mind the period of the Peloponnesian War and the fall of Athens.[32]

Scholars and statesmen have seen similarities between the war of Athens and Sparta and their own era: Rome against Carthage, Great Britain versus France, Great Britain against Germany.

The similarities between the Peloponnesian War and the Cold War are particularly evident and striking. Two former allies, having defeated the common enemy (like Athens and Sparta that had defeated the Persians in the fifth century B.C.), turn on one another. On one side, the United States (like Athens) is democratic, commercial, and mostly a sea power. On the other side, the Soviet Union (much like Sparta) is totalitarian and predominantly a land power.

In this subchapter, these similarities will be specifically explored. However, I shall argue that, in spite of these very similarities, there are important differences. In brief, whereas the first great power confrontation, which took place in classical times, escalated into a long and devastating war, the second appears to take place in a larger global framework as military and economic power diffuses to the rising states in the system. Whereas in fifth-century Greece a bipolar structure took shape that created the necessary conditions for the war, in the closing decades of the twentieth century the American-Soviet antagonism is being overtaken by the emergence of a multipolar system. The dangers facing mankind in the present world due to the continuing antagonism between the United States and the former Soviet Union are no less than those of the time of Thucydides. In fact, they are no doubt greater.

Thucydides may be termed as the father or the originator of hegemonic war. A hegemonic war involves a military crisis of the entire international political order. According to Thucydides, the Peloponnesian War was the result of the uneven and unprecedented growth of power in the international system of fifth-century B.C. Greece and the creation of an unstable international structure. The effects of the growth of Athenian power on the distribution of power in the system constituted the cause of the armed conflict.

The fifth century in Greece was a time of political, economic, and military growth. The basis of the economy was being transformed with the rise of commerce and the increasing importance of money as a source of economic and military power. Military affairs were undergoing significant change with the introduction into Greek life of new military technologies such as the trireme and fortifications. Sea power in particular was of great importance.

Athens had undergone a domestic social and political revolution. It experienced a change in the class system as the traditional aristocracy was replaced by a class which laid emphasis on wealth and power. This development also meant that the democratic constitution of the city-state was strengthened all the more. The Athenians built a wall to protect themselves from Spartan land power and also built a fleet of war triremes. As a commercial and sea power, Athens subjugated its former allies and established a vast sea empire, the members of which eventually resented the loss of their liberty and sought revenge against Athenian domination.

On the contrary, Sparta remained isolated, though she retained, to a great extent, the solidarity of the Peloponnesian League. Sparta faced a serious Helot revolt, which was suppressed by force with the help of the Athenians. Thus, the Spartans realized that, if Athenian influence could extend into the Peloponnese to assist them, it could as easily favor the Helots and threaten Spartan security.

Against this background of the uneven growth of power between the two great powers, of their mutual suspicion, and of differing vital interests, diplomatic events took place that would bring Athens and Sparta into mortal conflict. Beginning with the Corcyrean dispute and culminating in the Megarian Decree, the Spartan ultimatum, and the actual outbreak of the war, the two protagonists became locked into action/reaction that escalated until it eventually threatened the vital interests of both sides. Once the vital interests of Athens and Sparta were at stake, options narrowed and a compromise solution of their political differences became increasingly unlikely.[33]

When one turns to the sufficient causes of the war, the place to begin is the incident at Corcyra. The effect of this dispute was to set in motion events that would greatly escalate the developing conflict. Corcyra itself was important because of its strategic location alongside the sea route to the western Mediterranean and its possession of the third-largest fleet in the system. Because of its potential significance for the balance of power between Athens and Sparta, its neutrality was an important stabilizing factor in the system. The instigation of the dispute by Corinth and the implications of the independence of Corcyra thus threatened to overturn the balance of power in favor of Sparta and its allies. The Athenian response was cautious and prudent. Through forming a defensive alliance with Corcyra, the Athenians sought to deter Corinth. Deterrence failed, and the subsequent defeat of Corinth by the combined forces of Corcyra and Athens greatly inflamed Corinthian hatred of Athens and stirred in them a powerful desire to avenge their humiliating defeat.[34]

Athens and Corinth escalated the conflict even further by their subsequent actions with respect to Potidaea, a colony of Corinth but a member of the Athenian empire. Athens initiated the confrontation over Potidaea. Thereafter the Corinthians encouraged Potidaea to overthrow its Athenian masters and sent troops to assist in the revolt. This attack on the integrity of the Athenian empire and the accompanying Corinthian appeal for ethnic conflict between Dorians and Ionians aroused an intense fear among the Athenians of an imperial revolt. The Corinthian actions thus posed a direct and serious threat to Athenian security. Potidaea was of economic and strategic importance, but also its successful defiance of Athenian imperial rule would have severely undermined the empire. This Corinthian escalation of the struggle engaged a vital interest of the Athenians for the first time, and they felt compelled to take action to remove the growing threat to their empire.[35]

Whereas in the earlier confrontations at Corcyra and Potidaea, the Athenians had acted defensively, and the issuance of the Megarian Decree was a provocative action. Megara was strategically located on the isthmus connecting the Peloponnesus to the rest of Greece, and the political status of the city was of crucial significance to both Sparta and Corinth. Because of its geopolitical importance in controlling access to the Peloponnesus, the Spartans, as part of the Thirty Years' Peace, had forced its return to their sphere of influence. Thus, the Athenian use of economic sanctions against Megara, sanctions the purpose of which was undoubtedly to dislodge that city from its alliance with Sparta and bring it back under Athenian control, posed a direct threat to Spartan and Corinthian security. [36]

The Cold War between the United States and the Soviet Union has been one of rapid escalation. Following an initial effort to preserve the spirit of the wartime alliance and prevent the type of split that occurred following the Persian Wars, the conflict between the United States and the Soviet Union intensified and reached its zenith in the Cuban missile crisis of 1962. The sobering effect of this potentially devastating confrontation between the two nuclear powers led to the first successful effort to deescalate the Cold War (i.e., the limited nuclear test ban treaty [1963]). Other and more significant agreements have followed intense and difficult negotiations. While the conflict between these two states has important parallels with the period prior to the outbreak of the Peloponnesian War, the differences are equally striking. [37]

The origins and causes of what is loosely called the Cold War are matters of intense scholarly dispute. The outbreak of the conflict was in Western Europe, and Europe continues to be the primary focus of their differences. Some scholars emphasize the ideological conflict that began with the intervention of the Western powers in the Russian civil war. Ideology by itself cannot explain such an intense conflict. Most writers, therefore, stress political differences arising out of World War II and date the origins of the conflict to the earlier postwar period. They differ, however, in assessing responsibility for the collapse of the wartime alliance and the emergence of two hostile ideological and military blocs. [38]

In analyzing the nature and dynamics of the postwar conflict between the United States and the Soviet Union, its political, ideological, and strategic components must be kept clearly in mind. The history of the conflict is essentially one of succeeding phases during which these three distinguishable features of the conflict emerge and become intimately fused. [39]

The Cold War was a direct outgrowth of World War II. It originated in the unwillingness of the two former allies to accept the consequences of the war and the inability of each side to accept the other's conception of the postwar international order. Subsequently, what originally had been a geographically restricted conflict of political interest centered almost exclusively on Western Europe, expanded into a global conflict between two hostile ideologies. This interest and ideological struggle, then, quickly escalated into a power struggle and an unprecedented arms race between the two military alliance systems. [40]

Roosevelt's Grand Design was a universal political and economic order. The political order, based on the principle of collective security, was embodied in the United Nations and the idea that the victorious allies would work together to keep the peace; the basic democratic and human rights of all people would be respected, and exclusive spheres of influence would not exist. The foundations of the postwar economic order were established in

1944 by the United States and Great Britain at the Bretton Woods Conference. As the two leading economic powers, they wanted to create an open world economy of liberalized trade in which all nations would participate.[41]

With regard to the Soviet postwar objectives, at a minimum, the Soviets certainly wanted to eliminate their historical security concerns emanating from central Europe and East Asia. This meant the incorporation of some parts of Eastern Europe directly into the Soviet Union, as in the case of the Baltic States and eastern Poland, and bringing the whole of Eastern Europe into a Soviet sphere of influence. In Asia, it meant an alliance with a friendly, communist China and the extension of Soviet influence into Korea. Beyond these minimal objectives, the Soviet Union wished to extend its influence, particularly with the assistance of indigenous communist parties, into Western Europe and other areas in its periphery. In short, the behavior of the Soviet Union in the postwar period revealed a desire to enlarge its domination over the Eurasian continent and to eliminate all potential enemies from its borders.[42]

As early as 1945, the United States thwarted the efforts of the Soviet Union to extend its influence into Western Europe and Iran. Despite Soviet behavior, however, the desire to prevent a breakdown of the wartime collaboration and to preserve the peace was uppermost in American thinking.[43]

The Cold War may be said to have begun in 1947 when the United States took the necessary economic and political actions to prevent the collapse of the West European economies and committed itself to the containment of Soviet expansion beyond the boundaries laid down at Yalta. The principal initiatives taken in that year by the United States need only be enumerated to underline the importance of this decisive shift in American policy: the Marshall Plan and European recovery program, the enunciation of the containment policy, the Truman Doctrine, and the beginning of the effort to incorporate West Germany into what would become the Western system of military and political alliances.[44]

The Red Army had advanced far beyond the Soviet borders into Western Europe and northeast Asia. The whole Eurasian continent seemed to lie within its grasp. Nothing prevented Soviet domination of the continent except for the continued presence of the Americans, who the Russians firmly believed had no historical right to be there.

In effect, the Cold War arose as a conflict of American and Soviet political interests. This geopolitical struggle would become greatly exacerbated by ideological differences and domestic American political groups hostile to the Soviet Union and by Soviet suspicions and intense hatred of the West.[45]

The reformulation of the American-Soviet conflict as essentially one between two hostile ways of life and alliance systems took place in the period 1948 through 1950. The revelations of Soviet spying, the Western decision to revive the West German economy, the Czech coup, the Berlin blockade, the creation of the North Atlantic Treaty Organization (NATO), and, above all else, the Soviet explosion of an atomic bomb in October 1949 greatly intensified the evolving conflict and converted it into a struggle between irreconcilable political, social, and economic systems. The crucial American response to these developments is contained in NSC-68, a study conducted by the National Security Council, which foresaw a protracted global clash between the free world and a totalitarian enemy and called for extensive rearmament.[46]

The outbreak of the Korean War increased significantly the stakes in the contest. It led to an arms race and a massive increase in the American military budget. Although both antagonists in this global struggle sought to expand their influence, it was the United States that was the most successful expansionist power. In response to its intense fear of the Soviet Union and in the pursuit of its containment policy of the Soviet Union, the United States, much like fifth-century Athens, became the most expansive power in the system. American influence expanded rapidly in Europe, Asia, and the Middle East.[47]

During the presidency of Richard Nixon, American expansionism ceased in response to the defeat in Vietnam, and the assumptions underlying American foreign policy began to be significantly modified. The Nixon administration deemphasized the ideological interpretation of the Cold War and redefined the foremost challenge to American interests to be the Soviet Union itself and its desire to dominate the Eurasian continent. Diplomatic efforts culminated in two significant agreements. The first was the SALT I Treaty (1972) and an associated protocol, which restricted the development of missile defensives and placed a limit on the number of offensive weapons. Efforts toward pacification collapsed in the late 1970s due to conflicting interpretations of such pacification. It is noteworthy that Soviet leader Leonid Brezhnev stated that efforts leading to the path of pacification should not interfere with the objectives of Soviet foreign policy, that is, strengthening of socialist-bloc solidarity and support of national and social liberation movements.[48] He further stated that the laws of the class struggle cannot be abolished and that no one should expect that the communists would reconcile themselves with capitalist exploitation or that monopolists would become followers of the revolution. During the Brezhnev years, the Soviet Union reached the zenith of its power at the same time that the United States was in a state of disarray and its power was in relative decline. Taking advantage of the American defeat in Vietnam and the confusion of Watergate, the Soviet Union rapidly increased its military power and began to assert its influence more aggressively around the world.[49]

However, after the collapse of the Soviet Union, when the Cold War did not really end, but became an ongoing political and military process, the United States has regained its might and influence. The NATO intervention in Kosovo in 1999 and effectively the creation of a NATO protectorate in the Balkans, despite the legal objections to the military action, have strengthened the role and military influence of the United States in the region. Also, the 2016 intervention in Syria and the current political conflict with Iran clearly denote that the Cold War is not really over and that the United States is reasserting its position of domination in the Middle East.

Yet, in spite of the above striking similarities between the Peloponnesian War and the Cold War, there exist important differences. The most important difference between the era of the Peloponnesian War and that of the Cold War is clearly the existence of nuclear weapons. While there is no way to prove that nuclear weapons have prevented war between the superpowers, they certainly have had a restraining influence, notably in the Cuban missile crisis of 1962. Both superpowers appear to believe that they could not escape destruction in a nuclear war, and mutual deterrence has become an uneasy basis of the international political order. Yet one should not be overly sanguine about the stability of this peace. As Thucydides tells us, events can easily get out of control and escalate into a war that no one really predicted or wanted. This danger will continue to exist as long as the political interests of the superpowers conflict and they remain antagonistic to one another.[50]

Secondly, in contrast to Athens and Sparta, both the United States and the Soviet Union, with the exception of the Cuban missile crisis, have respected the vital interests of the other and have worked out important rules of peaceful coexistence. They have tended to avoid offensive actions, and, if one excludes the American intervention in Vietnam and the Soviet invasion of Afghanistan, neither has attempted by the use of force to change the status quo established at Yalta. Therefore, neither superpower has been tempted to pursue dangerous actions such as the Megarian Decree or the Spartan ultimatum.

The third important difference between the two wars is to be found in the structures of the international system. Although it is appropriate to refer to both systems as bipolar, the distribution of power in the contemporary system has been more diffuse than in fifth-century B.C. Greece, and the political interrelationships have been more stabilizing. Today, the majority of states (the so-called Third World) are nonaligned and have remained largely outside the superpower conflict. The existence of strategically located neutral states, for example Austria and Sweden, has contributed to the stability of the system. However, the realignment of any of these neutrals, as occurred in the case of Corcyra, would have significantly altered the balance of power between the superpowers.[51]

In sum, the nuclear revolution, the conservative behavior of the superpowers, and the structure of the Cold War international system are the main differences between the Cold War and the Peloponnesian War.

THEORY OF FOREIGN POLICY

In contrast to contemporary structural realists (proponents of the theory called structural realism or merely structuralism), who attempt to interpret foreign policy of states sometimes focusing almost exclusively on the analysis of the international system, Thucydides adopts a more complicated and certainly more effective approach. This very approach combines three levels of analysis: the systemic level, the state level, and the personal level.[52]

Thucydides, much like modern political theorists and international politics scientists, commences his analysis from the systemic level. He examines the structure and nature of the international and inter-state system of classical Greece, the balance of power,[53] and the degree to which threats are extended on the part of the various city-states at various times of history.

Immediately afterwards, however, he proceeds to a different level of analysis, exploring the internal structures of states as, for example, the character of the constitution. Thucydides makes pointed parallels among the foreign policy of powerful Sparta and the stability of its internal structures, namely its ancient and admirable constitution, itself a mixture of kingship, aristocracy, and limited democracy.[54] Contrary to the stable foreign policy of Sparta, the foreign policy of Athens was pretty much subject to changes. This was partly due to the fact that foreign policy decision-making in Sparta was much more rigid and based on traditional structures of aristocracy and monarchy as opposed to the democratic Athens, where influential demagogues occasionally led the mob towards rather disastrous choices and military enterprises. Thucydides vividly describes how the internal political situation in Athens after the death of Pericles negatively influenced the foreign policy of that city-state.

Pericles. . . and after he died his foresight about the war became still more fully recognized. He told them that if they held back, looked after their navy, did not try to extend their empire during the war, and did not expose the city to risk, then they would prevail. But they did just the opposite of this in every way, and in other respects apparently unconnected with the war they were led by private ambition and personal greed to pursue policies that proved harmful both to themselves and to their allies; for when these policies succeeded they brought honor and benefit just to individuals but when they failed they were detrimental to the city in its war effort. The explanation for this was that Pericles, through his personal ability, his judgment, and his evident integrity could freely restrain the masses. He led them more than he was led by them. That is, he did not say things just to please them in an unseemly pursuit of power, but owed his influence to his personal distinction and so could face their anger and contradict them (καί πρός ὀργὴν τί ἀντειπεῖν).[55]

Also, it is worth noting that Thucydides places emphasis upon national character, the ethnic element or ethnicity, in the formation and implementation of foreign policy. This becomes evident in particular in the words of Hermocrates, leader of Syracuse, who exhorts his comrades to unite against Athens, and no doubt in the famous oration of Pericles, who notoriously declares that Athens is a model of education for the whole of Hellas and that the Athenians should never underestimate and set aside the perils of a potential war, but rather fight courageously protecting their own city.[56]

Furthermore, Thucydides is perhaps the first political scientist to analyze authoritatively and genuinely the role played by personalities in the formulation and execution of policies in the Greek city-states of classical Greece. The role of the statesman is hugely important, since he not only expresses or is supposed to express the will and visions of the people, but also leads the people at crucial moments.[57] The contribution of Pericles, for example, in the making and legitimization of his rather unpopular policy forms a conspicuous example in this regard.

The political leadership analysis, though, becomes the more significant and even decisive at the point where the statesman or politician acts on his own right; that is, his strategic choices and policies are based entirely on personal convictions and opinions. Such a case appears in the personality of Alcibiades, who does not hesitate to confess at a conference before the Spartan assembly that his motives of his policy (and, therefore, succor towards the city-state of Sparta) have to do more with his own troubled political career.[58]

Effectively, Thucydides presents an accurate and complete analysis of foreign policy theory. Accordingly, it, with the causes of the states' policy and attitude, may be interpreted on three levels of analysis: the international system, the state level, and the level of persons or more accurately political personalities.

INTERNATIONAL LAW AND ETHICS IN WORLD POLITICS

Classical paradigm of definition of political realism is the dialogue of the Melians. In 415 B.C., the sixteenth year of the Peloponnesian War, the Athenians set sail against the island of Melos, a colony of the Lacedaemonians, which, until then, remained neutral in the war, aiming at forcing her to join the Athenian League. The conservative foreign policy of Sparta, fearing an eruption of Helot revolt in the interior of the state, did not send forces to succor the Melians in time, despite the constant calls of the latter. A Spartan fleet was dispatched, however, but was nevertheless called back to Lacedaemon halfway through the journey. The Athenian ambassadors laid down before the islanders of Melos a dilemma, which in fact constituted a clear threat: subjugation or war.

Surprisingly, the Athenian ambassadors, not the Melians, are the first to evoke the divine:

> Nor must you behave just like the many, who while human means of deliver-
> ance are yet at hand, when they are in distress and manifest grounds of hope
> are lacking to them, turn to immanifest ones, divination and oracles and that
> sort of thing, which crash with hopes. [59]

The Melians exhibit trust, however (πιστεύομεν), that "as blameless men standing against unjust ones" (ὅτι ὅσιοι πρὸς οὐ δικαίους), "they will not be at a disadvantage in the fortune that is from the divine" (τῇ τύχει ἐκ τοῦ θείου).

The Athenians, in turn, take into account the divine:

> Well now, as far as the divine is concerned, neither do we suppose that we
> shall fall short of you in its regard. For there is nothing that we claim
> (δικαιοῦμεν) or that departs from what human beings believe of the gods or
> from how they regard one another. From what is reputed (δόξει) of the divine
> and what is manifest (σαφῶς) of human beings, we conclude that always, by
> necessity of nature, they rule to the limits of their power. And it was not we
> who made this law, nor were we the first who finding it in force have submit-
> ted to it, but having found it in being, will leave it in being for all time to come.
> And so we do submit to it, knowing that you and anyone else, coming into the
> same power as we have, would do the very same thing. As regards the divine,
> then, the likelihood is that we need not fear being at a disadvantage. [60]

No worse sophistry could have been articulated on part of the Athenians. They flagrantly violated bonds of religion; they twisted the meaning of words. It goes without saying that these are manipulations, not what nature dictates.

The Melians, on the other hand, take the respectable view that the gods favor those who are blameless toward them, against those who are unjust; that is, injustice toward human beings, by which they mean aggression in archaic and contemporary international law terms, incurs blame also with the gods. This the Athenians reject, all the while denying that they innovate in the approach to the divine. [61] Though they do not claim accurate knowledge of the gods as they do of human beings, their notions of them stem from received opinion. From it they have concluded that the gods, too, are in the habit of ruling wherever they can.

The Athenians subsequently exhort the Melians to show "moderation" in view of the circumstances:

> For surely you will not resort to that notion of disgrace which in those dangers
> that while disgraceful are lin to see, so often destroys human beings. For many,
> even as they foresee the sort of things toward which they are being borne, are

so led on by the thing called disgrace and the seductive power of name, that, worsted by word, they quite gratuitously (ἕκοντας) sink into incurable disasters in deed, thus incurring disgrace the more disgraceful due to folly rather than bad fortune. This, if you deliberate properly, you will guard against and not deem it unbecoming to be worsted by the greatest of cities, when it offers you mild (μέτρια) terms: to become its allies, retaining the country that is yours while paying tribute—nor, having been offered the choice between war and security, will you hold out for the worse of the two. It is those who do not yield to equals, who bear themselves with dignity (or nobly, καλῶς) toward superiors, and who are mild (μέτριοι) toward inferiors, who most often prosper.[62]

As Bagby put it,

It is easy to conclude that the Melians foolishly refused the Athenians' offer, naively trusting in divine or Spartan intervention. One can accuse the Melian oligarchs of irresponsibly deciding the fate of so many "behind closed doors." But even if these conclusions and accusations were to be largely accurate, the Melians' assessment of the Athenians might still be seriously considered. The Athenians easily reduced the remaining Melians to slavery, with no immediate consequences to themselves. Yet the Athenians were soon to experience grave political and strategic reversals due to their increasingly extreme ideology. The Sicilian expedition, launched with such grandiose hopes and hubristic impulses, is placed by Thucydides immediately after the Melian Dialogue. The Melians' disaster is followed by the internal political chaos and the eventual military defeat of Athens.[63]

"Δυνατοί πράσσουσι, ἀδύνατοι δέ ξυγχωροῦσι,"[64] the Athenians further exclaim.[65] This phrase is often presented as representative of the implications of political realism and the corresponding stance to be taken by states in such given circumstances. It is forgotten, inadvertently misunderstood, or perhaps on purpose misinterpreted, that these are words which are spelled out in arrogance on part of the ambassadors of Athens, the superpower of the fifth century B.C.[66]

"Χρήσιμον ὑμᾶς μή καταλύειν τό κοινόν ἀγαθόν,"[67] the Melians respond. Which is the common good? What is meant by this expression? Clearly here the Melians imply the common law, the international and inter-state law of ancient Greece. It is meant that the weak or weaker state also has the right to evoke international law and demand its implementation. It is noteworthy that the Melians do not use the word πρέπον (must), but χρήσιμον (it is useful). The utilitarian character that they ascribe to law is surely not accidental. They express themselves in the language of interest and political expediency, the only language that could potentially have persuaded the Athenians. Here, Thucydides remarkably identifies law (δίκαιον) with interest (ξυμφέρον). Law is the only real interest to the Athenians and the Melians alike. The monumental book of Thucydides constitutes a blend of international law and

international politics. International law and international politics should be
seen as forming part of one and the same order.[68]

The Melians were in the end massacred. The population of men was
exterminated almost in its entirety. But the Melian propositions had and still
have their deep meaning. On the one hand, the Melians chose to sacrifice
themselves, instead of choosing enslavement. They proved that dignified
death is much more important than life itself. Their sacrifice is an archaic
exclamation of "freedom or death." On the other hand, the Melians warned
that the chance of war someday might force the Athenians themselves to
evoke international law. This war incident denoted the end of the Athenian
empire. Indeed, ten years later, after Athens had been defeated at the Aigospotamoi of Hellespont, the Athenian ambassadors evoked legal, and more
accurately juridical arguments, in order to save what was left of the dignity
and glory of the city of Athens, the superpower of the day.

The inhabitants of the island of Melos, the areas which were called by the
Athenians as islets (νησίδια), crudely but frankly put, gave to the Athenians
lessons of international law and international justice. Years and centuries
have passed since then, and yet this famous common good, inter-state law,
has not become the basis of international politics. Nevertheless, Thucydides,
in his peculiar political realism, and in a vein of optimism, declares from the
very outset of his book that humans can be taught from the past thus avoiding
committing similar mistakes in the future.

"Όσοι δὲ τῶν τε γενομένων τὸ σαφὲς σκοπεῖν, καὶ τῶν μελλόντων, ποτὲ
αὖθις κατὰ τὸ ἀνθρώπειον τοιούτων καὶ παραπλησίων ἔσεσθαι, ὠφέλιμα
κρίνειν ταῦτα, ἀρκούντως ἕξει. Κτῆμά τε ἐς αἰεί, μᾶλλον ἢ ἀγώνισμα ἐς τὸ
παραχρῆμα ἀκούειν ξύγκειται."[69]

In view of the above analysis, it is proved that the realism of Thucydides
is not compatible with modern forms of realism, and certainly not with
Machiavellian realism. Certain scholars in international relations and international law, quite correctly, draw a line between neo-realism and the "classical
realism" of Thucydides and perhaps that of Hans Morgenthau.[70]

Let us briefly survey the elements of the modern forms of political realism. *Minimalism* portrays a worldview or explanation of inter-state politics
as a state of war. It is premised on three views. First, the international scene
is properly described as an anarchy—a multiplicity of powers without a
government. Second, the primary actors are independent states whose domestic hierarchy (sovereignty) complements international anarchy. Third, no
restraint—whether moral, social, cultural, economic, or political—is sufficiently strong to eliminate or to guarantee the resolution of conflicts of interest, prestige, or value.[71] *Fundamentalism* accepts the anarchy assumption of
minimalism, but questions the differentiation between domestic and inter-
state politics. Fundamentalism specifies both the means and preferences
(both power) left open by the minimalist. Rooted in human nature itself, the

drive for power leaves statesmen no choice other than power politics.[72] *Structuralism* also explains the state of war. Like minimalism, structuralism assumes international anarchy and the predominance of state actors. Unlike the minimalists, structuralists assume that state actors differ in capabilities but not ends, as Kenneth Waltz noted in the *Theory of International Politics*.[73]

Thucydides's political realism is different. It is hereby submitted that Thucydidean realism is linked with morals and the view of Thucydides as an "amoral realist"[74] is firmly rejected.

If we define realism as "might makes right," then we cannot interpret that debate between Cleon and Diodotus as a simple triumph of Diodotus's realist prudence over Cleon's legal vengeance. The Athenian assembly decided to reconsider its harsh decision to execute all the Mytileneans as a punishment for the Mytilenean rebellion against Athens. Cleon demanded that the assembly adhere to its harsh sentence as a just punishment for the rebellious criminals he claimed the Mytileneans were. Diodotus then told the Athenians that their assembly was a political body, not a court of law. Athenian self-interest—the stable acceptance of their imperial rule by their colonies—required moderation in his view. Although it was probably true that Diodotus had to speak deceptively so as to persuade the Athenians, deception did not require him to cater the assembly's self-interest, disguising his moral repugnance at Cleon's legal defense of vengeance.

At the outset of the Peloponnesian War, Thucydides did approve of the Athenian assembly's rejection of Corinth's legal condemnation of Corcyra's actions and endorsed the strategic reasons the Corcyreans offered as to why the Athenians should support their cause against Corinth. Thucydides seemed to disapprove of all the simple formulas. He rejected the "might makes right" doctrine, but did not seem to reject outright those who, like Cleon, argued that "right makes might," that the moral course of action inherently builds strategic support or strength.

Minimalist realism has also been challenged by scholars who dispute the state-as-actor assumption underlying realist considerations of foreign policy. Francis Cornford[75] has challenged the realist emphasis on state-as-actor in favor of an interpretation of war, stressing that an aggressive policy had been forced on Pericles by the domestic commercial faction within Athens that sought to promote its private business prospects overseas. The merchants were the group with most to benefit from an imperialist policy in the West and from the destruction of their Megarian commercial rivals.

Cornford rejected the strategic rivalry between Athens and Sparta as a sufficient explanation of the Peloponnesian War, because, in his view, neither state was best served by an aggressive policy.

According to Hobbes, one should interpret Thucydides in the narration.[76] Thucydides himself did not formulate general laws (other than perhaps impliedly), though the speakers whose words he recounts often did. He did, however, seek the truest causes and the exact truth, an accurate view. He reported competing explanations, but he only offered multiple interpretations of the same event in his own voice when he could offer nothing better. His own method was a combination of different explanations of the truest cause and indirect explanations implied by his placing events in multiple contexts—interstate, domestic, and personal.

Power versus Justice Struggle:
The Speech of Hermocrates at Sicily

One of the most spectacular speeches in the *History of the Peloponnesian War* is that of Hermocrates, both in terms of style as well as content.[77] Thucydides places emphasis on it, as events in Sicily, so far marginal, for the first time acquire a central role through the authoritative speech of Hermocrates. This is not an apology of imperialism, but, as it will be proved straightaway, a hymn to peace and liberty. In presenting and defending Syracuse at the pan-Sicilian conference at Gela, Hermocrates faces complicated circumstances. Sicily is divided into Greeks and barbarians and the Greeks are divided among themselves into many cities and two races, Dorian and Ionian.[78] These are hostile, and allies of Athens and Sparta, respectively. All Sicilian cities fear Dorian Syracuse, which was then the most powerful. This is the very factor which ostensibly justified the Athenian military intervention. Athens appeared to be the protector against hometown menace, though the preparations in Athens and the supporters of the Sicilian campaign seemed to rely on different, rather imperialist, arguments.

Hermocrates proves to be the great peacemaker in Thucydides.[79] He begins his speech, however, by noting that Syracuse is not the city suffering most from the war. In fact, he never discusses what she particularly has to gain from not getting involved in war. In order to show that the cities have gone to war rather hastily, he distinguishes among their special interests and those shared by the whole of Sicily. The Sicilian cities run the risk of being subjugated to Athens.[80] Hermocrates does not deny the importance and primacy of special interests and political expediencies, as the city needs to consider broader ones only to the extent that its own interests demand it.[81] Although he makes reference to the hostility among Dorians and Ionians, his argument stresses that every city seems to be the enemy of every other. Therefore, he calls upon them not to set aside their particular expediencies for the sake of a broader aim, but he only urges them to carry out their former objectives in a peculiar manner. He urges them to call themselves allies only to the extent that such a practice supplements their particular interest and simultaneously benefits Sicily as whole. Not only has Hermocrates linked the particular interests of the various Sicilian cities with the broader objective that appeared at the time, that is to wage defensive war against Athenian imperialism, but he also claimed that the cities would be guilty of *stasis* (i.e., subversion of the existing constitution) had they gone on safeguarding and pursuing only their own expediencies.[82] In 4.61.2. he firmly cried, "we must be reconciled, individual with individual, and city with city, and try in common to save the whole of Sicily." The threat of an Athenian expedition against Sicily, should in the words of Hermocrates, unite the Sicilian cities and transform them from foes into allies in view of instant danger. The common good which Hermocrates addressed is not separate from the special goods and interests of the cities.[83] Here, the so-called law of the stronger (in terms of crude political realism) becomes an injunction for the weaker to unite forces, fight hard, repel the opponent, and live in freedom.[84]

Nevertheless, Hermocrates, apart from the above-mentioned considerations, proceeds to praise peace. He proclaims a point of universal agreement, that peace is excellent in its own right. He lays down some of its obvious advantages as opposed to the pitfalls, perils, and disadvantages of war. Is this stance not in contradiction with his previously stated position? Not at all. Quite impressively, he succeeds in demonstrating to his fellow citizens and to the citizens of other tribes that they should make peace only in so far as this serves the interests of the Sicilian cities, but should be wary and prepared for launching war against Athens in the event of a campaign on part of the latter against the whole of Sicily. Hermocrates does not suppose that he has persuaded his listeners of the desirability of permanent peace, as he has suggested that no one is deterred by the perils and drawbacks of war.[85]

In his concluding remarks, Hermocrates applies his argument to his own case, as the representative of a very great city, more used to attacking others than to defending itself.[86] One more time, through emphasizing the drawbacks of war campaigns, he openly states that he is prepared to make concessions and urges the representatives of the rest of the Sicilian cities to follow suit. He smooths down their warlike passions by arguing that it is essential for themselves to make peace and that the future will present opportunities for going to war, but that war should be launched without involvement of foreign and hostile parties.[87]

Hermocrates eventually is successful in persuading the cities and tribes of Sicily to accept his offer of truce and to unite against Athens. It is clear from what he said that the cities of Sicily will soon face a Syracusan threat and that peace among Sicilians will certainly be short lived without prospects of permanent tranquility. He faced Athenian imperialism by placing emphasis on the ethnic characteristics of the Sicilians, which should, in his opinion, supersede any foreign connection of the tribes and cities of Magna Graecia. Hermocrates persuades the citizens of wider Sicily that they can have a portion in the administration of Syracusan power. And, that the Athenians are always ready to militarily intervene, even uninvited,[88] or they can always be invited to return. [89] He effectively acts in persuasion by establishing that Syracuse is not yet ready to materialize its military expansionist aims. [90] Further, and more importantly, he succeeds in establishing two things: firstly, that the incalculability of the future (τό ἀστάθμητον τοῦ μέλλοντος), though the most powerful of everything, is also the most useful (χρησιμότατον), since everyone is vulnerable to it and so may equally enjoy the benefits from fear of it (δεδιότες, [91] δέος διά τό ἀστάθμητον [92]). Against hope, Hermocrates invokes fear, insofar as it lessens our hopes. [93] He speaks not of φόβος, though, but of δέος.

It remains that the most important part of his speech, it must be stressed, is his exhortation to his fellow citizens and the Greek tribes to unite together and fight against the danger of the common Athenian enemy. [94] This passage is, in my opinion, the most important statement of Thucydidean political realism. Given the friendly relations that Thucydides is confirmed to have kept with Hermocrates, it may be inferred that he also shared the sayings and convictions of Hermocrates. The words of Hermocrates describe and establish a peculiar and political realism that differs fundamentally from harsh Machiavellian realism and certainly neo-realism.

> That the Athenians should covet and scheme for these things is only too pardonable, and I blame not those who wish to rule—to extend their power—but those who too readily serve. For it is ever men's nature to rule those who submit, just as it is to resist those who attack. [95]

This, I regard as a statement of a statesman who would never allow his state to surrender, never yield to any menace of foreign imperial powers, who recognizes the bitter reality of military expansionism, but simultaneously regards it as his national duty to resist and fight for freedom to the end.

Notes

1. Power in economic terms nowadays.
2. Thucydides, *History of the Peloponnesian War*, 4 vols., *Loeb Classical Library* 108, 109, 110, and 169, trans. C. Forster Smith (Cambridge: Harvard University Press, 1919–1923) (hereafter cited as Thucydides), 1.72–78.
3. Thucydides, 1.70.8–9.
4. Clifford Orwin, *The Humanity of Thucydides* (Princeton: Princeton University Press, 1997), 44.
5. Thucydides, 1.72.1.
6. Thucydides, 1.74, 1.75.
7. Thucydides, 1.75.3.
8. Thucydides, 1.76.2.
9. Thucydides, 1.76.2.
10. Thucydides, 1.76.3.
11. Thucydides, 1.77.3–4.
12. Thucydides, 1.80.
13. Thucydides, 1.88.
14. Thucydides, 1.1–23.
15. Thucydides, 1.4–8.
16. Thucydides, 2.62.
17. Thucydides, 1.41.
18. Thucydides, 1.31.
19. Thucydides, 1.32.
20. Thucydides, 3.82, 3.83.
21. Thucydides, 3.83, 3.84.
22. Thucydides, 6.34.
23. Thucydides, 1.82.
24. Thucydides, 1.124
25. Thucydides, 8.87.
26. Thucydides, *The War of the Peloponnesians and the Athenians, Cambridge Texts in the History of Political Thought*, ed. Jeremy Mynott (Cambridge: Cambridge University Press, 2013), 537.
27. Robert Gilpin, *War and Change in World Politics* (Cambridge: Cambridge University Press, 1981), 211.
28. Thucydides, 1.69.1, quoted in Gilpin, *War and Change in World Politics*, 211.
29. Thucydides, 1.23.6., quoted in Gilpin, *War and Change in World Politics*, 211.
30. Thucydides, 1.141.4.
31. Gilpin, *War and Change in World Politics*, 227.
32. General George C. Marshall in a speech delivered in 1947 at Princeton University.
33. Robert Gilpin, "Peloponnesian War and Cold War," in *Hegemonic Rivalry from Thucydides to the Nuclear Age*, ed. Richard Ned Lebow and Barry S. Strauss (Boulder: Westview Press, 1991), 34.
34. Gilpin, "Peloponnesian War and Cold War," 34.
35. Gilpin, "Peloponnesian War and Cold War," 35.
36. Gilpin, "Peloponnesian War and Cold War," 35.
37. Gilpin, "Peloponnesian War and Cold War," 37.
38. Gilpin, "Peloponnesian War and Cold War," 38.
39. Gilpin, "Peloponnesian War and Cold War," 38.
40. Gilpin, "Peloponnesian War and Cold War," 38.
41. Gilpin, "Peloponnesian War and Cold War," 39.
42. Gilpin, "Peloponnesian War and Cold War," 39.
43. Gilpin, "Peloponnesian War and Cold War," 40.
44. Gilpin, "Peloponnesian War and Cold War," 40.
45. Gilpin, "Peloponnesian War and Cold War," 41.
46. Gilpin, "Peloponnesian War and Cold War," 41.

47. Gilpin, "Peloponnesian War and Cold War," 42.
48. *New York Times*, March 18, 1976, 14.
49. Gilpin, "Peloponnesian War and Cold War," 45.
50. Gilpin, "Peloponnesian War and Cold War," 47.
51. Gilpin, "Peloponnesian War and Cold War," 48.
52. On the role played by eminent personalities in the formation of foreign policy and politics in the *History of the Peloponnesian War* by Thucydides see chapter below.
53. On the contrary, according to Gilpin, international disequilibrium is due to an "increasing disjuncture between the existing governance of the system and the redistribution of power in the system. Although the hierarchy of prestige, the distribution of territory, the rules of the system, and the international distribution of labor continue to favor the traditional dominant power or powers, the power base on which the governance of the system ultimately rests has eroded because of differential growth and development among States. The disjuncture among the components of the international system creates challenges for the dominant States and opportunities for the rising States in the system" (Gilpin, *War and Change in World Politics*, 186).
54. Thucydides, 1.18. It must be noted, though, that the conservative foreign policy of Sparta, as it shall be shown below, was the main factor which much constrained and prevented her from intervening in favor of the Melians, when the latter desperately called her for help. Actually, the Spartan fleet did set sail towards the island of Melos, but was forced to return to Lacedaemon fearing an eruption of a revolt of the Helot population.
55. Thucydides, *The War of the Peloponnesians and the Athenians*, 130.
56. See chapter below on the analysis of personalities in policy making.
57. See Laurie Johnson, *Thucydides, Hobbes, and the Interpretation of Realism* (Ithaca, NY: Cornell University Press, 1993).
58. Thucydides, 6.89.
59. Thucydides, 5.103.
60. Thucydides, 5.105.1–3.
61. Orwin, *The Humanity of Thucydides*, 104. See also M. Walzer's *Just and Unjust Wars: A Moral Argument with Historical Illustrations* (New York: Basic Books, 2015), where he observes that "it is not only the Melians here who bear the burdens of necessity" (5).
62. Thucydides, 5.111.3–4.
63. Lowell Gustafson (ed.), *Thucydides' Theory of International Relations* (Baton Rouge: Louisiana State University Press, 2000), 35. Steven Forde, "Varieties of Realism: Thucydides and Machiavelli," *The Journal of Politics* vol. 54, no. 2 (May 1992) is then quoted by Laurie M. Johnson Bagby: "The primacy of self-interest over justice, proclaimed for a generation or more as the basis of the city's policy came eventually to infect the city's domestic life. When the community declares itself free from moral restraints in international politics, individuals conclude eventually that those restraints have no claim on them either" ("Fathers of International Relations? Thucydides as a Model for the Twenty-First Century" in Gustafson, *Thucydides' Theory of International Relations*).
64. Thucydides, 5.87: "And the powerful exact what they can, while the weak yield what they must."
65. See the very good position taken by Bagby: "The Athenians at Melos express what has come to be known as the 'Athenian thesis,' that they and all other human beings are *compelled* by fear, honor, and interest to rule wherever they can. This is the justification for either subduing or destroying the rather harmless island city Melos. If through this thesis the Athenians at Melos express the essential elements of realism in its boldest and most extreme form and yet the Melian Dialogue is not saying to be taken as Thucydides' preference, then what is Thucydides saying about the realism used by the Athenians in the Melian Dialogue? Is the dialogue representative of Thucydides' thought? . . . The dialogue may be representative of Thucydides' thought if by this we mean his analysis of the impact of a particularly harsh realism when it is used in practice" ("Fathers of International Relations?," 34).
66. It should be noted that the policy of the Athenians is obviously influenced by the teaching of the sophists. Politics constituted the central issue of the sophists' teaching. The sophists powerfully influenced the political affairs, the people of Athens, and the Greeks at

large in their time. Here one may detect the sophistic origins which are sometimes mistakenly ascribed to political realism. Instead, Thucydides is the scientific source of political realism in the Greek world.

67. Thucydides, 5.88: "As we think at any rate, it is expedient (for we are constrained to speak of expediency, since of justice, suggested that we speak of what is advantageous) that you should not rule out the principle of the common good, but that for him who is at the time in peril what is equitable should also be just . . ."

68. Thucydides's teaching is not morally neutral, but neither do we get the sense that he is passing summary moral judgment for us. How does Thucydides manage to traverse this sensitive area and still leave us with the impression that he has indeed not followed in the footsteps of the poets? Perhaps it is because Thucydides knew that ignoring moral issues in the name of objectivity was really not dealing with the totality of the relevant evidence. In other words, dismissing the impact of values on societies is neither scientific nor objective. A look at the Melians will give us a sense of how Thucydides dealt with moral issues within the overall analysis of the war. As regards the Melians of Thucydides Viotti and Kauppi (quoted in Bagby "Fathers of International Relations?") have stated: "This classic contains the essential ingredients of the realist perspective as stated in perhaps the boldest and most extreme form. Thucydides is sometimes unfairly criticized as an advocate of harsh and brutal wartime policies, one who rationalized such events as he described in the famous Melian dialogue. Thucydides, however, favored the democracy of the Golden Age of Pericles. In fact, the second half of *The Peloponnesian War* is a description of the degeneration of Athenian democracy and the resulting fanaticism that turned the war from a defensive effort to a war of conquest. The Melian dialogue reflects the latter phase of the war and should not be viewed as a personal preference on the part of Thucydides" (See Bagby, "Fathers of International Relations?," 33).

69. Thucydides, 1.22: "But it has served its purpose well enough if it is judged useful by those who want to have a clear view of what happened in the past and what—the human condition being what it is—can be expected to happen again some time in the future in similar or much the same ways. It is composed to be a possession for all time and not just a performance-piece for the moment" (Thucydides, *The War of the Peloponnesians and the Athenians*, 16).

70. See Hans Morgenthau, *Politics among Nations* (New York: Knopf, 1967).

71. See Michael Doyle, "Thucydides: A Realist?" in *Hegemonic Rivalry from Thucydides to the Nuclear Age*, ed. Richard Ned Lebow and Barry S. Strauss (Boulder: Westview Press, 1991), 170.

72. Doyle, "Thucydides: A Realist?," 171.

73. Kenneth Waltz, *Theory of International Politics* (Reading: Addison-Wesley, 1979), 96–97.

74. David Cohen, "Justice, Interest, and Political Deliberation in Thucydides," *Quaderini Urbinati* 16, no. 1 (1984), 37. But see the differing and valuable discussions of this matter in M. I. Finley, "Introduction" in *History of the Peloponnesian War*, ed. M.I. Finley, trans. Rex Warner (London: Penguin Classics, 1954) ("a moralist's work"), 32; G. E. M. de Ste. Croix, *The Origins of the Peloponnesian War* (Ithaca: Cornell University Press, 1972), 11.

75. Francis Cornford, *Thucydides Mythhistoricus* (Philadelphia: University of Pennsylvania Press, 1965).

76. See Richard Schlatter (ed.), *Hobbes' Thucydides* (New Brunswick: Rutgers University Press, 1975), 18.

77. The best account of the speech of Hermocrates, in my view, remains that of R. Connor, *Thucydides* (Princeton: Princeton University Press, 1934), 119–126.

78. Thucydides, 6.76–87.

79. Orwin, *The Humanity of Thucydides*, 164.

80. Thucydides, 4.60.

81. Thucydides, 4.59.3.

82. Thucydides, 4.61.1.

83. Thucydides, 4.59.1, 4.61.3: εν τη Σικελία ἀγαθὸν . . . α κοινεί κεκτήμεθα.

84. So Athenagoras closed his eyes to the menace of an Athenian attack which, according to Thucydides, had originally every chance of success because of the lack of preparation at

Syracuse (VII 42.3). There were of course still other reasons for Athens' failure; nevertheless one reason for it was that Athenagoras' views were not accepted but that the farsighted Hermocrates carried the day. In other words, Thucydides is illustrating in the policies of both Cleon and Athenagoras the possibility, ever present under a democratic government, that politicians for their own partisan ends may jeopardize a people's military effectiveness. Now he himself says that war automatically increases the people's sufferings and thus sows the seeds of partisanship (III 82.2), but on the other hand, there is no reason to suppose that he thought that process of degeneration irresistible. On the contrary, it was to his mind Athens' essential misfortune that she lacked a second Pericles to lead the people sanely and to check the demos, whereas by contrast it was the salvation of Syracuse to have possessed such a man in Hermocrates. Thucydides stresses his understanding in very much the words which Pericles uses of himself (VI 72.2, II 60.5); represents him as, like Pericles, able to rally the people when they were despondent (VI 72.2); and above all, shows him as possessed of the supreme Periclean gift of foresight" (J. Finley Jr., *Three Essays on Thucydides*, Cambridge: Harvard University Press, 1967).

85. Truly, even after having argued forcefully for the blessedness of peace and the riskiness of war, he considers it necessary to emphasize that should they make peace now the cities will certainly war among themselves in the future (Thucydides, 4.63.1–2).

86. Thucydides, 4.64.1.

87. Thucydides, 4.64.3.

88. Thucydides, 4.60.2.

89. See chapter on the causes of war in order to ascertain the connection and parallel of this argument with the protection of nationals abroad, a facet of self-defense in contemporary public international law.

90. Also, as Orwin put it, should Athens come to grief, the defeat of her empire will pave the way for the rise of a Syracusan one—out of that very coalition (6.33.5). Hermocrates casts Athens as the new Mede, Syracuse as the new Athens—and himself as the new Themistocles (*The Humanity of Thucydides*, 167).

91. Thucydides, 4.62.4.

92. Thucydides, 4.63.1.

93. Connor, *Thucydides*, 124. As Hobbes later put it, the passion to be reckoned on. As our most powerful incentive to act with foresight (Thucydides, προμηθία 4.62.4).

94. Bagby, "Freedom and Empire" in Gustafson, *Thucydides' Theory of International Relations*, 147–148: "Hermocrates succeeds, in the only example of its kind in the book, to end a stasis by appeals to the common good (4.61, 4.65) and moderation (4.60, 4.61, 4.64). To be sure, Hermocrates appeals to the common threat presented by the Athenians, who were present on the island with a small force. But the Athenian threat is still far off: up to the instant that the Athenians sailed into the harbor of Syracuse, important elements in the city doubted the threat from Athens (6.32, 6.35, 6.36–40). In addition to this, Hermocrates ends factional strife within the city of Syracuse by making appeals to moderation and the common good (6.33, 6.34). Hermocrates also sets the Syracusans in motion from their habitual rest by an appeal to "daring" to counter Athenian power and daring. Hermocrates is one of the two figures in the whole work who makes a successful appeal to both daring and moderation, and who manages to combine them in his character." For a remarkable treatment of Hermocrates's speech see N. G. L. Hammond, "The Particular and the Universal in the Speeches of Thucydides: With Special Reference to That of Hermocrates at Gela" in *The Speeches in Thucydides*, ed. Philip A. Stadter (Chapel Hill: University of North Carolina Press, 1973), 49–59. For a truly excellent portrait of Hermocrates see H. D. Westlake, *Individuals in Thucydides* (Cambridge: Cambridge University Press, 1968).

95. Thucydides, 4.61.4.

Chapter Two

Grounds of Lawful War in Classical Greek International Law and Causes of War in Thucydides

The aim of the present chapter is, firstly, to unearth the philosophical grounds of just war in classical Greece. Secondly, this chapter aims to indicate specifically that neither the causes nor the theoretical grounds of the Peloponnesian War in the history by Thucydides are in conformity with previously established grounds of warfare. Thirdly, it shall be proved that the philosophical underpinnings of war in Thucydides have formed the theoretical and legal basis of contemporary kinds of military intervention in international law. In this context, the contribution of Thucydides in the theory of the international law of war will be duly emphasized.

An in-depth study of Greek law and civilization in general makes manifest the existence of a concept of international law in the ancient Greek world. It is necessary to clarify at the outset that Greek authors distinguished between unwritten (ἄγραφος) and written law. Unwritten law is defined by Aristotle as the universal law, that is universally recognized principles of morality, whereas written law as the statutes of any given state.[1] Unwritten law is otherwise called natural law or divine law. This distinction is drawn in the *Nicomachaean Ethics*, where Aristotle suggests that civil justice is partly natural and partly conventional: that is, natural in that it possesses the same validity everywhere and does not depend on being deliberately adopted or not, while conventional in that in the first instance it does not matter whether it assumes one form or another, only that it has been laid down.[2] A certain application of these conceptions and distinctions is seen in the sphere of the Greek Law of Nations. Writers frequently refer to "the laws of the Hellenes," "the common laws of Hellas," "the laws of mankind," "the laws common to men." Therefore, expressions such as the following are constantly used: τά τῶν Ἑλλήνων νόμιμα,[3] τά πάντων ἀνθρώπων νόμιμα, τά κοινά τῶν Ἑλλήνων νόμιμα.[4] A large number of important rules and practices of international law are implied in these expressions. The underlying principles belong predominantly to the category of unwritten laws, deriving their juridical force from tradition and custom, and having as their sanction the will of the gods.

The most common grounds considered sufficient for the commencement of operations of war in classical Greece were violation of a treaty, desertion from an alliance or confederation, offenses committed against allies, refusal to receive ambassadors on invalid grounds, breach of neutrality, violation of territorial integrity, and, highly importantly, desecration of sacred places.[5] History offers examples.

A serious injury intentionally committed against an ally was usually considered as an offense against that ally's confederates, and so a ground for just war on part of the latter. Penelope, rebuking Antinous for compassing the death of Telemachus, says: "Do you not remember how your father fled to this house in fear of the people, who were incensed against him for having joined some Taphian pirates, and plundered the Thesprotians, who were at peace with us?"

> Ἡοὐκοῖσθ,' ὅτε δεῦρο πατήρ τεός ἵκετο φεύγων
> δῆμον ὑποδδείσας; δή γάρ κεχολώατο λίην,
> οὕνεκα ληϊστηρσιν ἐπισπόμενος Ταφίοισιν
> ἤκαχε Θεσπρωτούς. Οἱ δ' ἡμιν ἄρθμιοι ἦσαν.[6]

When the province of Macedonia fell by lot to Publius Sulpicius (202 B.C.), he proposed to the people that on account of the injuries and hostilities committed against the Athenians, who were allies of Rome, they should proclaim war against Philip. In the following year the Athenians, having put to death two Acarnanians for straying into their mysteries, the countrymen of the victims appealed for help to Philip who, as they were his lawful allies, permitted them to levy troops in Macedonia. With these reinforcements, they invaded Attica without a formal declaration of war. Accordingly, envoys were sent to Rome to report the attack made by an old ally of the Romans. Therefore, the Senate of Rome, in the following year, proposed to the comitia a declaration of war in consequence of this attack on a state in alliance with Rome.[7]

Supplying assistance to the belligerent enemy, or any other flagrant act of violation of neutrality, was certainly a cause of war. So Demetrius, during his war against the Athenians, captured a ship which was loaded with wheat bound for Athens, and hanged the captain and pilot, a measure, says Plutarch, which terrified other merchants so much that they avoided Athens, and a terrible famine resulted there.[8]

The desecration of sacred places was especially, amongst the Hellenes, considered a cause for embarking upon just war against the offenders. Thus, the reason of the Greek offensive war against the Persians was to exact just retribution for their profanation of sacred places. The Athenians declined to come to terms with Xerxes, and expressed their determination to avenge the destruction by him of their temples and images of gods and heroes.

Πρῶτα μέν καί μέγιστα, τῶν θεῶν τά ἀγάλματα καί τά οἰκήματα ἐμπεπρησμένα τέ καί συγκεχωσμένα, τοῖς ἡμέας ἀναγκαίως ἔχει τιμωρέειν ἐς τά μέγιστα μᾶλλον, ἤπερ ὁμολογέειν τῷ ταῦτα ἐργασαμένω. [9]

The devastation of Persia by Alexander the Great provides further proof of the vengeance exacted by the Greeks upon their enemies, primarily, if not solely, because the latter did not treat with respect the sacred locations of Hellas. [10]

Even more emphatic was the defensive war of the Greeks when they took up arms to defend their homeland in the course of the Persian Wars. Particularly, their valor, as shown in the navy battle of Salamis in 480 B.C., marvelously reported by Aeschylus, needs to be cited:

Ὦ παῖδες Ἑλλήνων, ἴτε, Ἐλευθεροῦτε πατρίδα, ἐλευθερουτε δέ παῖδας, γυναίκας, θεῶν τέ πατρώων ἔδη, θήκας τέ προγόνων, νῦν ὑπέρ πάντων ἀγών. [11]

O ye sons of Hellas, go forth, free your homeland, free your women and children, the temples of your ancestral gods, the tombs of your forefathers. Now, you are fighting for them all.

In this context, it is of crucial significance to mention the role of amphictyonies in classical Greece. Amphictyonies were alliances or confederations in ancient Greece. Amphictyonies denoted the establishment of very strong political and religious ties among city-states, which shared religious ceremonies and temples. [12] Many amphictyonies existed in ancient Greece, notably that of Thermopylae, Delos, and Delphi. Delos the Delphic amphictyony was by far the most eminent and powerful. It was an international association as it was composed of twelve tribes or nations, linked with close ties of kinship. It is often referred to as the Congregation of the Greeks or, in fact, the Council of the Hellenes—*τό κοινόν τῶν Ἑλλήνων Συνέδριον*. There existed two categories of representatives, namely the *ἱερομνήμονες*, otherwise called *Ἀμφικτιόνων οἱ Σύνεδροι*, councilors, and the *πυλαγόραι*. The former, who made up the formal congregation, had the privilege to demarcate the territorial boundaries of the sacred places and sacred lands. [13] As a rule, the fundamental principles that the congregation was called to implement were decided upon and ratified through formal oath. In the case of the Delphic amphictyony, the practice of the councilors and, in essence, of allies who pursued identical policies has been preserved up to nowadays and is no doubt one of the most ancient texts of treaties, providing for the formation of an alliance, in the Western world. The members or councilors took an oath that they would in no event destroy any member city-state of the amphictyony, nor would they cut it off from the supply of drinking water in the course of either war or peace, that they would declare war against anyone who would violate this law and should destroy their cities, and that they would punish in every manner anyone that would plunder the property of the gods and his accomplices in such an act.[14]

Generally speaking, the real objective of war was to effect a reparation, previously denied, of some serious act that had without reason been inflicted, or, more importantly, to exact due revenge of a wrong in conformity and compliance with divine injunctions. Thus, Xenophon exhorted his men to have regard for moderation and honor, and not to plunder any city that was not in any way guilty of offenses against them.[15] The purpose, declares Polybius, for which good men make war is not to destroy and annihilate the wrongdoers, but to alter the wrongful acts. Nor is it their object to involve the innocent in the destruction of the guilty—οὐ γάρ ἐπ᾽ ἀπωλεία δεῖ καί ἀφανισμῷ τοῖς ἀγνοήσασι πολεμεῖν τούς ἀγαθούς ἄνδρας, ἀλλ᾽ ἐπί μεταθέσει τῶν ἡμαρτημένων, οὐδέ συναιρεῖν τά μηδέν ἀδικοῦντα τοῖς ἠδικηκόσιν. This, however, has not always been the sole, let alone the most significant and justifiable, aim of war among the Greeks. The same aforementioned doctrine had long before been affirmed by Plato. In the *Republic*, where Socrates and Glaucon discuss what acts ought to be forbidden in warfare, but distinguish between war against Greeks and that against barbarians, Socrates suggests that the armed conflict with the Greeks must be conducted entirely with a view to conciliation. The rule ought to be not enslavement or destruction of the enemy.

> And as they are Hellenes themselves they will not devastate Hellas, nor will they burn houses, nor even suppose that the whole population of a city—men, women, and children—are equally their enemies, for they know that the guilt of war is always confined to a few persons and that the many are their friends. And for all these reasons they will be unwilling to devastate their lands and raze their houses; their enmity to them will only last until the many innocent sufferers have compelled the guilty few to give satisfaction.[16]

Contrast, though, the firm view of Aristotle, as expressed in the *Rhetoric,* that punishment and just retribution ought to be in every case the predominant object—διά θυμόν καί ὀργήν τά τιμωρητικά.

If we now turn to the causes of the Peloponnesian War, one cannot but see that these very causes have little resemblance with the grounds of war as above elaborated. As a preliminary comment, it should be stressed that this was a civil war amongst the Greeks, not an international armed conflict as the notion is nowadays comprehended. However, the war erupted between city-states of the classical Greek world, so from this perspective it may too be termed as an inter-state war. What is more, Thucydides invented the distinction between the remote and deeper causes of the war and the immediate causes of it. The immediate causes of the Peloponnesian War are well known and there is no need to refer to them extensively: the events at Epidamnus, the political situation in Corcyra, the Megarian Decree, and the incidents at Potidaea. In the *History of the Peloponnesian War*, Thucydides considered the immediate causes, which in fact went back almost five years before the commencement of hostilities, to be less important than the remote causes, which arose from the growth of the Athenian empire during the fifty years before the outbreak of the war. The standpoint of Thucydides that the war was the eventual and inevitable sequence of that empire's growth has been widely accepted among scholars and is hereby too endorsed. Thucydides's main statement of the causes of the war runs as follows:

> Διότι δ'έλυσαν τάς αίτίας προύγραψα πρῶτον καί τάς διαφορᾶς του μή τινά ζητησαι ποτέ ἐξ ὅτου τοσοῦτος πόλεμος τοῖς Ἕλλησι κατέστη. Τήν μέν γάρ ἀληθεστάτην πρόφασιν, ἀφανεστάτην δέ λόγω, τούς Ἀθηναίους ήγοῦμαι μεγάλους γιγνομένους, καί φόβον παρέχοντας τοῖς Λακεδαιμονίοις ἀναγκᾶσαι ἐς τό πολεμοιν. Αἵ δ'ἐς τό φανερόν λεγόμεναι αἰτίαι αἰδ'ἦσαν ἐκατέρων, ἀφ'ὧν λύσαντες τάς σπονδᾶς ἐς τοόν πόλεμον κατέστησαν.

> The reasons why they broke it [the peace] and the grounds of their quarrel I have first set forth, that no one may ever have to inquire for what cause the Hellenes became involved in so great a war. The truest explanation, although it has been the least often advanced, I believe to have been the growth of Athens to greatness, which brought fear to the Lacedaemonians and forced them to war. But the reasons publicly alleged on either side which led them to break the truce and involved them in the war were as follows.[17]

The imperial policy of Athens and ambitions of its ruling elite, which became manifest particularly in the eve of the Sicilian expedition, readily justified or at least explained a policy of counterimperialism on the part of Sparta that eventually led to war. These causes are far more similar to causes of contemporary wars that are characterized by an imperial spirit, that is, wars that are usually the consequence of imperialistic ambitions.

I cannot be in agreement with Kagan, who attempts to disprove the statement of Thucydides and allege that the immediate causes of the war were far more important than the remote ones.[18] Also, economic causes of various forms have been suggested as the real cause of the armed conflict. The proposition of Cornford that there was a party of merchants from Peiraeus who hoped to make gains by seizing control of the routes to the west through Megara, Acarnania, and Corcyra and forced Pericles to lead Athens to war is

Chapter 2

mostly an imaginary proposition.[19] Clearly, the interest of Athens in Corcyra was strategic and not economic. Although there were aggressively imperialistic Athenians who hoped to gain economically from the extension of their empire, the mere fact is that they did not formulate Athenian policy.[20] That policy was made by Pericles, who had previously fought them successfully and was not influenced by them at the stage of the final crisis. The interests of the merchants may only have had some part in the decision made by the Athenian people to embark upon an expedition in Sicily.

Noteworthy is a version of the Thucydidean thesis that the war was the inevitable outcome of the division of the Greek world into two power blocs.[21] This Thucydidean view is reinforced by the weapons of contemporary political science, notably international relation theory. The condition that troubled the Greek world and brought about the war is to be found in the expression "bipolarity." Bipolarity is used to describe a condition in which exclusive control of international politics is concentrated in two great powers solely responsible for the preservation of peace or the making of war expeditions. Such a thesis seems to be convincing, but not distinct from the remote and real causes of the war, as the influence and policies exerted by the two great states of the Greek world were actually the product of their respective inclinations, ambitions, ideologies, and immanent idiosyncracies.

The more important contribution of Thucydides, however, in my view, is to be traced in the grounds of war as described in his history. In this third part of the chapter, an analysis will ensue indicating that the grounds, more properly the justifications, for war as elaborated by this great author have provided the legal basis of some fundamental forms of armed intervention in the modern world, in the sphere of international law science in particular.

The Thucydidean historical work sets an authoritative example of the use of force in the sense of armed intervention in international relations. The affairs which follow should be seen in the light of the fact that the Greek cities in ancient times were states themselves.[22] First, Book IV of the *History of the Peloponnesian War* may at first sight be said to pose an example of self-defense in international law, particularly of protection of nationals abroad, this being a facet or category of self-defense of states. On its way to Sicily, the Athenian fleet was met with a sea storm, which forced the ships to seek refuge in the Peloponnese (Pylos). Since the war between Athens and Sparta was at its height, the Athenian navy members were arrested by the Lacedaemonians. Cleon, the Athenian demagogue, forcefully urged the Athenian assembly for a military campaign to prevent their fellow citizens from being massacred. The incident may be described as an operation to save nationals abroad (since the Athenian prisoners of war were not subjects of the Spartans).

In modern international law, serious efforts have been made to limit the use of force by states. One of the cornerstones of international law is the general prohibition of the use of force as enshrined in the Charter of the United Nations.[23] UN Charter Article 2(4) provides that: "All members shall refrain in their international relations from the threat or use of force against the territorial integrity or political independence of any State, or in any manner inconsistent with the purposes of the United Nations." However, self-defense of states is a commonly accepted exception to the general prohibition of the use of force as embodied in the UN Charter. Article 51 of the charter stipulates that

> nothing in the present Charter shall impair the inherent right of individual or collective self-defence if an armed attack occurs against a member of the United Nations, until the Security Council has taken the measures necessary to maintain international peace and security. Measures taken by Members in the exercise of this right of self-defence shall be immediately reported to the Security Council and shall not in any way affect the authority and responsibility of the Security Council under the present Charter to take at any time such action as it deems necessary in order to maintain international peace and security.[24]

The protection of nationals abroad forms one of the four facets of the right to self-defense. An attack against nationals of a state who happen to be abroad or failure for them to be succored in accordance with international law stipulations, gives the right to this state to use armed force in order to protect its nationals without securing the consent of the foreign government. The right of a state to take military action to protect its nationals in mortal danger is recognized by all legal authorities in international law. In *Self Defence in International Law*, Professor Brierly states, on page 87, that the right of the state to intervene by the use or threat of force for the protection of its nationals suffering injuries within the territory of another state is generally admitted, both in the writings of jurists and in the practice of states.[25]

On June 27, 1976, an Air France airliner bound for Paris from Tel Aviv was hijacked over Greece after leaving Athens airport. Two of the hijackers appear to have been West German nationals; the other two held Arab passports. The airliner was diverted to Entebbe airport in Uganda where the Jewish passengers (about one hundred) were separated from the others and the latter released. The hijackers demanded the release of about fifty Palestinian terrorists imprisoned in various countries. The evidence seems to suggest that Uganda did not take such steps as it might have done against the hijackers and, indeed, helped them, although Uganda denied this. On July 3, 1976, Israel flew transport aircraft and soldiers to Entebbe and rescued the hostages by force. The hijackers were killed during the operation, as were some Ugandan and Israeli soldiers. There was also extensive damage to the Ugandan aircraft and the airport.[26]

The military operation at Pylos has in a magnificent manner also generated the criteria for a legitimate use of force applicable in all cases of military intervention, including self-defense. These were formulated in the speech of the Athenian general Demosthenes only a while before the commencement of the military rescue operation: "Men who have gathered in this venture, let no one of you wish to be esteemed a man of rationality; but, instead, with plain courage, which *leaves no moment for deliberation*, let him attack the opponents and even be optimistic that he will eventually be victorious. When matters reach a point of *overwhelming necessity*, as the present case is, crude reflection is least needed in view of the *instant* danger."[27] Note the striking similarity between the terminology used in this text, and the one employed in the *Caroline* case in 1840,[28] which traditionally, and in a universally acceptable proposition, sets limits to the use of armed force in contemporary international law: "It will be for Her Majesty's Government to show a necessity of self-defence, instant, overwhelming, leaving no moment for deliberation."[29] These were the words of Mr. Webster, US secretary of state, to British minister Mr. Fox (April 24, 1841). It makes one wonder whether Mr. Webster was a fervent reader of Thucydides. In fact, research I have conducted into his biography has revealed that, indeed, he studied Thucydides to a significant extent. This may only be coincidental. But it remains a true fact that the terminology used in both the Pylos incident and the *Caroline* affair is identical. And it remains an undisputable fact that the international law principles laid down in the *Caroline* case, known as the *Caroline* test, were put forward some 2,400 years ago in Pylos, as reported by Thucydides in the *History of the Peloponnesian War*. State practice in the field of the law of war in the twentieth century that has developed in the same pattern as the rescue operation of Pylos (and Sphacteria) affirms the principles born out of the Peloponnesian War. A criterion is that the use of force must correspond to the dictates of the proportionality principle. The *Caroline* case principle may be seen as one that sets limits to the use of force in general and calls for adherence to proportionality. The classic formulation of Mr. Webster in this context may also be quoted: "Did nothing unreasonable or excessive; since the act is justified by the necessity of self-defence, must be limited by that necessity, and kept clearly within it."[30]

Turning back to Thucydides, and examining for a moment the war incident of Pylos from a purely philological (and political) perspective, one cannot fail to see stressed the rather unfair treatment of Cleon on the part of Thucydides. In paragraph 28.5 of Book IV, where Cleon is described as struggling to persuade the Athenian assembly to undertake a military operation in Pylos to rescue the Athenian hostages, Thucydides verbatim says: "ἐνέπεσε μέν τί καί γέλωτος τῇ κουφολογίᾳ αὐτοῦ. Ἀσμένοις δ' ὅμως ἐγίγνετο τοῖς σώφροσι τῶν ἀνθρώπων, λογιζομένοις δυοῖν ἀγαθοῖν τοῦ ἑτέρου τεύξεσθαι. Ἤ Κλέωνος ἀπαλλαγήσεσθαι, ὃ μᾶλλον ἤλπιζον, ἤ σφαλεῖσι γνώμης Λακεδαιμονίους σφίσι χειρώσασθαι."[31] The prejudice against Cleon is evident, though Thucydides, to his credit, seems to take a measured stance when he subsequently (toward the end of the Athenian military campaign) does not hesitate to emphasize the success of Cleon: Καί τοῦ Κλέωνος, καῖπερ μανιώδης οὖσα, ἡ ὑπόσχεσις ἀπέβη (and the promise of Cleon, mad though it was, proved to be successful, paragraph 40). The proverbial objectivity of Thucydides is further confirmed at paragraph 21.3, where it is stated that Cleon was a prominent and most influential demagogue. That statement, of course, carries some irony, but still accurately depicts Cleon himself, who, indeed, exerted influence among the populace.[32]

Cornford's view is that Thucydides emphasized and exaggerated the element of chance in the Athenian victory, in order, according to him, to minimize Cleon's success. In reality, it would serve rather to minimize that of Demosthenes, with whom Thucydides is generally supposed to have been on friendly terms.[33] The war incident at Pylos and Sphacteria was certainly affected by the fortune of war, not chance in the strict sense of the word. The navy battle which took place in the harbor of Pylos remains one of the most impressive ones in the history of naval warfare, and it is worth quoting the historian at this point.[34]

The military operation at Pylos can also be viewed as a paradigm example of unilateral humanitarian intervention, if by extension of the doctrine of self-defense one accepts the existence of a similar right of intervention for humanitarian purposes. The speech of General Demosthenes again lays down the premises of humanitarian intervention. A state can lawfully use armed force to prevent humanitarian catastrophe of its nationals, especially if such a danger is imminent. Such was the action of the Athenian state in Pylos. And, certainly, in modern international law this form of the use of force should conform to the requirements of the principle of proportionality as this was developed in the *Caroline* case, cited above. A UK Foreign Office Policy Document gives an accurate definition of humanitarian intervention: "A substantial body of opinion and of practice has supported the view that when a State commits cruelties against and persecution of its nationals in such a way as to deny their fundamental human rights and to shock the conscience of mankind, intervention in the interests of humanity is legally permissible." [35]

To put this issue into a contemporary context and to address the fundamental issue of the moral justification of humanitarian intervention would require a whole inquiry into the ethical foundations of the international legal system. The tension focuses between sovereignty and human rights.

At first sight, there is a legal duty to refrain from interfering in the internal affairs of other states. Each state is bound to respect the sovereignty of its neighbor states. This view has its roots in legal positivism. The German philosopher Wolff was the first to separate the international law principles from the ethics of the individual. Great academic debate has erupted over the general prohibition of the use of force as stipulated in Article 2(4) of the UN Charter,[36] especially the wording "against the territorial integrity or political independence of any State."[37]

It is necessary to show that a right of unilateral humanitarian intervention is compatible with Article 2(4) of the UN Charter.[38] The only exceptions to the general prohibition of the threat or use of force are the "inherent right of individual or collective self-defence in the face of an armed attack against a State in Article 51 of the UN Charter, and enforcement actions by the Security Council or by a regional organization or group of States authorized to use force by the Security Council under Chapter VII of the Charter." Neither of these provisions is applicable to unilateral humanitarian intervention. Two arguments may be employed: that a genuine humanitarian intervention would not be a use of force against the "territorial integrity or political independence" of another state, or that it would not be "inconsistent with the Purposes of the United Nations." It is noteworthy that in their commentary on the charter, Goodrich and Hambro observed that it is possible to construe the language as allowing certain limited uses of force, such as a temporary intervention for protective purposes.[39] Tesón, noting that the promotion of human rights is as important a purpose in the charter as the control of international conflict, concludes that to argue that humanitarian intervention is prohibited by Article 2(4) is a distortion.[40]

Article 2(4) must be read and interpreted in conjunction with the purposes of the United Nations, one of which is the promotion of human rights. The preamble to the charter reads as follows: "We the peoples of the United Nations determined . . . to reaffirm faith in fundamental human rights, in the dignity and worth of the human person, in the equal rights . . . of nations large and small." Article 1(3) states: "To achieve international co-operation in solving international problems of an economic, social, cultural, or humanitarian character, and in promoting and encouraging respect for human rights and for fundamental freedoms for all."[41] Further, Article 55(c) of the charter declares that the United Nations shall promote "universal respect for, and observance of human rights and fundamental freedoms for all without distinction as to race, sex, language, or religion." More importantly, by Article 56 "all members pledge themselves to take joint and separate action in co-operation with the Organization for the achievement of the purposes set forth in Article 55."[42]

The deduction from the above should be that the right of unilateral humanitarian intervention is clearly not incompatible with Article 2(4) of the UN Charter.

Apart from the legal debate, however, I would suggest, from the moral standpoint, that the rights of states under international law derive from individual rights. The proper role of the state is to ensure protection of the rights of the individuals. As Hersch Lauterpacht very well put it, "states are like individuals; it is due to the fact that states are composed of individual human beings. . . . The dignity of the individual human being is a matter of direct concern to international law."[43] Lauterpacht's rationale for humanitarian intervention is that "ultimately, peace is much more endangered by tyrannical contempt for human rights than by attempts to assert, through intervention, the sanctity of human personality."[44] Therefore, in my opinion, state sovereignty must give way to the protection of human rights whenever these are flagrantly violated.[45] In view of the preceding theoretical discussion in this section, I strongly submit that states have a moral right, to say the least, to unilaterally intervene in cases of overwhelming humanitarian necessity. The writings of learned jurists should, in my submission, be taken much more seriously into account, and perhaps cease to be seen merely as subsidiary sources of public international law (despite Article 38(1)(d) of the ICJ Statute).

A further instance, which could have crystallized into a clear example of humanitarian intervention in the history by Thucydides, and eventually did not materialize as such, is provided in Book III. The Island of Lesbos (member of the Athenian empire-commonwealth or confederation of city-states) revolted from Athens. The Athenians set sail against the Mytilenians (inhabitants of Lesbos) and warned them that if they were to refuse an order to surrender, they would demolish their fortifications. An embassy of Mytilenians sought the help of Sparta thus: "Come to the help of Mytilene. It is our lives that we are risking; an even more general calamity will follow if you will not listen to us."[46] The very basic criteria for humanitarian intervention were in this case fulfilled: (1) the Mytilenians were subjects of a state (Athens), (2) they consented to the military intervention undertaken for their own sake, and (3) they faced imminent danger of humanitarian catastrophe.[47] The Spartans, indeed, dispatched a fleet, which reached the coast of Lesbos but never engaged in fighting. The conservative foreign policy of Sparta dictated that the military forces of the state were to keep an eye on a possible revolt of the Helot population in the Peloponnese.[48] This affair serves, if not else, as an instance clearly showing that humanitarian disaster may, indeed, be the outcome of nonintervention, as it eventually was with the Mytilenians. Therefore, it may be inferred that humanitarian intervention in cases of instant necessity is a must.

The history by Thucydides has undoubtedly laid down the foundations of modern international law of war. State practice of ancient times, indeed the custom of the states of ancient Greece, cannot be neglected.[49] The adoption of the UN Charter is not meant to suggest that precharter international customary law has automatically been abrogated. Instead, customary law can, indeed, be considered as part and parcel of a unified international law tradition, as living international custom, living law, which may still find appeal in the modern world.

Notes

1. Aristotle, *Rhetoric, Ars Rhetorica, Oxford Classical Texts* (Oxford: Oxford University Press, 1959), i. 10: *νόμος δ' ἐστίν ὁ μέν ἴδιος, ὁ δέ κοινός. Λέγω δέ ἴδιον μέν καθ'ὅν γεγραμμένον πολιτεύονται. Κοινόν δέ ὅσα ἄγραφα παρά πᾶσιν ὁμολογεῖσθαι δοκεῖ.*
2. *Τοῦ δέ πολιτικοῦ δικαίου τό μέν φυσικόν ἐστι τό δέ νομικόν, φυσικόν μέν τό πανταχοῦ τήν αὐτήν ἔχον δύναμιν, καί οὐ τω δοκεῖν ἤ μή, νομικόν δέ ὁ ἐξ ἀρχῆς μέν οὐθεν διαφέρει οὕτως ἤ ἄλλως, ὅταν δέ θῶνται* (Aristotle, *Nicomachaean Ethics, Loeb Classical Library* 73, Cambridge: Harvard University Press, 1926, v. 10).
3. Thucydides, *History of the Peloponnesian War*, 4 vols., *Loeb Classical Library* 108, 109, 110, and 169, trans. C. Forster Smith (Cambridge: Harvard University Press, 1919–1923)(hereafter cited as Thucydides), 4.97.
4. Thucydides, 1.3, 1.118; Plutarch, *Pericles, Lives* Volume III, *Loeb Classical Library* 65, (Cambridge: Harvard University Press, 1916), 17.
5. A formal declaration of war was not a necessary prerequisite for commencing military operations, though in the Peloponnesian War the instance of envoy Melisippus sent to the camp of the Lacedaemonians by General Pericles on part of the Athenians, only before the commencement of armed conflict, goes to the contrary. On his way back he notoriously exclaimed μεγάλα κακά ἄρξονται τοῖς Ἕλλησι. Interestingly, in the Roman Law of Nations (*Ius Gentium*) a demand for satisfaction was laid down before declaring war. The Romans, before declaring war, dispatched ambassadors to foreign countries, against which they had a grievance, with a formal demand in the name of the Roman government and people to make reparations for any injury suffered. In case of refusal a declaration of war was pronounced. This criterion of legitimacy of war is echoed in the words of Cicero, who says that "the laws and customs of war are religiously recorded in the code of the Roman people, in pursuance of which no war is deemed to be just or legitimate, unless it is duly declared after a formal demand for satisfaction has been made" (Cicero, *On Duties* (*De Officiis*), *Loeb Classical Library* 30, Cambridge: Harvard University Press, 1931, i. II. 36: "*Ac belli quidem aequitas sanctissime fetiali populi Romani iure perscripta est. Ex quo intelligi potest nullum bellum esse iustum nisi quod aut rebus repetitis geratur aut denunciatum ante sit et indictum*").
6. *The Odyssey of Homer* (New York: HarperCollins Publishers, 2007), xvi. 425–428.
7. Livy, *History of Rome* Volume VIII, *Loeb Classical Library* (Cambridge: Harvard University Press, 1936), XXX. 42.
8. Plutarch, *Demetrius, Lives* Volume IX, *Demetrius and Anthony, Loeb Classical Library* 101 (Cambridge: Harvard University Press, 1920), 33.
9. Herodotus, *The Persian Wars*, 4 vols, *Loeb Classical Library* 117–120, trans. A. D. Godley (Cambridge: Harvard University Press, 1921), viii.
10. Arrian in his *Anabasis of Alexander* ably presents the patriotic, warlike, and justly vengeful temper of Alexander the Great as expressed in his speech before the army at Opis: ἄπιτε πάντες καί ἀπελθόντες οἴκοι ἀπαγγείλατε ὅτι τόν βασιλέα ὑμῶν Ἀλέξανδρον, τόν νικήσαντα Μήδους τέ καί Πέρσας . . . καί τόν Ἰνδόν ποταμόν διαβάντα, καί τόν Ὕφασιν διαπεράσαντα ἄν εἰ μή ὑμεις ἀποκνήσατε, οἴχεσθε καταλοιπόμενοι, παραδιδόμενοι φυλάττειν τοῖς νενικημένοις βαρβάροις. Ταῦτα ἴσως εὐκλεά ἔστε ἀπαγγελθέντα. Ἄπιτε. "Go then! And when you reach home, tell them that Alexander your King, who vanquished Persians and Medes, . . . who crossed the Indus . . . and Hyphasis too, had you not feared to follow . . . tell them, I say, that you deserted him and left him to the mercy of barbarian men, whom you yourselves had conquered. Such news will indeed assure you praise upon earth and reward in heaven. Out of my sight!" (Arrian, *Anabasis of Alexander, Books I–IV, Loeb Classical Library* 236, Cambridge: Harvard University Press, 1976, p. 234, VII, 6).
11. Aeschylus, *Persians, Loeb Classical Library* (Cambridge: Harvard University Press, 1926), 402.
12. The term αμφικτιονία originates in the term αμφικτίονες, practically a synonym of περικτίονες, commonly called περίοικοι, which means "neighbors."
13. Ιερά χώρα (A. Bockh, *Corpus Inscriptionum Graecarum*, Berlin: Officina Academica, 1828, 1171).

14. See I. Kareklas, *Διεθνεσ Δικαιον Και Ελληνικοσ Πολιτισμοσ* [*International Law and Greek Civilization* (Athens: Sideris Publications, 2012), 19 for the text: *Μηδεμίαν πόλιν τῶν Ἀμφικτυονίδων ἀνάστατον ποιήσειν μηδ' ὑδάτων ναματιαίων εἴρξειν μητ' ἐν πολέμῳ μήτ' ἐν εἰρήνῃ, ἐάν δέ τίς ταῦτα παραβῇ, στρατεύσειν ἐπί τοῦτον καί τάς πόλεις ἀναστήσειν, καί ἐάν τίς εἰ συλα τά τοῦ θεοῦ εἰ συνείδῃ τί ἡ βουλεύσῃ τί κατά τῶν ἱερῶν τιμωρήσειν καί χειρί καί ποδί καί φωνή καί πάσει δυνάμει.* See also extensively on the issue of amphictyonies Idem, 15–22.

15. Xenophon, *Anabasis, Loeb Classical Library* 90 (Cambridge: Harvard University Press, 1998), vii. I. 29.

16. Plato, *Republic, Loeb Classical Library* 276 (Cambridge: Harvard University Press, 2013), v. 471A: *Οὐδ' ἄρα τήν Ἑλλάδα Ἕλληνες ὄντες κερούσιν, οὐδέ οἰκήσεις ἐμπρήσουσιν, οὐδέ ὁμολογήσουσιν ἐν ἑκάστῃ πόλει πάντας ἐχθρούς αὐτοῖς εἶναι, καί ἄνδρας καί γυναίκας καί παιδας, ἀλλ' ὀλίγους ἀεί ἐχθρούς τους αἰτίους τῆς διαφορᾶς. Καί διά ταῦτα πάντα οὔτε τήν γῆν ἐθελήσουσι κείρειν αὐτῶν, ὡς φίλων των πολλῶν, οὔτε οἰκίας ἀνατρέπειν. Ἀλλά μέχρι τούτου ποιήσονται τήν διαφοράν, μέχρι οὐ ἄν οἱ αἴτιοι ἀναγκασθῶσιν ὑπό τῶν ἀναιτίων ἀλγούντων δοῦναι δίκην.* "It follows that they will not, as Greeks, devastate Greek lands or burn Greek dwellings; nor will they admit that the whole people of a state—men, women, and children—are their enemies, but only the hostile minority who are responsible for the quarrel. They will not therefore devastate the land or destroy the houses of the friendly majority, but press their quarrel only until the quilty minority are brought to justice by the innocent victims" (Plato, *The Republic*, trans. Sir Desmond Lee, London: Penguin Classics, 1987, 2007, 187–188).

17. Thucydides, 1.23.

18. See D. Kagan, *The Outbreak of the Peloponnesian War* (Ithaca: Cornell University Press, 1989), 345–346: "Our investigation has led to conclude that his judgment is mistaken. We have argued that Athenian power did not grow between 445 and 435, that the imperial appetite of Athens was not insatiable and gave good evidence of being satisfied, that the Spartans as a state seem not to have been unduly afraid of the Athenians, at least until the crisis had developed very far, that there was good reason to think that the two great powers and their allies could live side by side in peace indefinitely, and thus that it was not the underlying causes but the immediate crisis that produced the war."

19. C. F. Cornford, *Thucydides Mythistoricus* (London: Edward Arnold, 1907), 1–51.

20. On this I agree with Kagan. See *The Outbreak of the Peloponnesian War*, 345–356.

21. P. J. Fliess, *Thucydides and the Politics of Bipolarity* (Baton Rouge: Louisiana State University Press, 1966). See also the fundamental work of Polly Low, *Interstate Relations in Classical Greece. Morality and Power, Cambridge Classical Studies* (Cambridge: Cambridge University Press, 2007) for an international or inter-state relations perspective in Thucydides.

22. It is precisely because of the fact that the Greek cities were themselves recognized as states—albeit with common origins of blood, language, and religion—that the Peloponnesian War, though often described as the greatest "Civil War" in antiquity, was in fact an international conflict.

23. Previous efforts had been made to the same effect including primarily the Covenant of the League of Nations 1919, of which Article 12(1) provided the following: "The members of the League agree that, if there should arise between them any dispute likely to lead to a rupture, they will submit the matter either to arbitration or judicial settlement or to inquiry by the Council, and they agree in no case to resort to war until three months have passed after the award by the arbitrators or the judicial decision or the report by the Council." Secondly, and more persistently, the Kellogg-Briand Pact 1928 declared: "The High Contracting Parties solemnly declare that they condemn recourse to war for the solution of international controversies, and renounce it as an instrument of national policy in their relations with one another. "The High Contracting Parties agree that the settlement or solution of all disputes or conflicts of whatever nature or whatever origin they may be, which may arise among them, shall never be sought except by pacific means."

24. The international law of war and its first and foremost category, *jus ad bellum*, which provides for the legal justifications of war, recognizes four instances of lawful war: (1) individual and collective self-defense, (2) humanitarian intervention, though there exist views as to the opposite, (3) collective military action under Chapter VII of the UN Charter after a decision of

the Security Council has been made, when regional or international security is at stake, and (4) war in aid of self-determination. (UN Charter 2[4]).

25. In the *Law of Nations* (6th edition, Oxford: Oxford University Press, 2012), 27, J. L. Brierly states the following: "Every effort must be made to get the United Nations to act. But, if the United Nations is not in a position to move in time and the need for instant action is manifest, it would be difficult to deny the legitimacy of action in defence of nationals which every responsible Government would feel bound to take if it had the means to do so; this is, of course, on the basis that the action was strictly limited on securing the safe removal of the threatened nationals."

26. 15 *International Legal Materials* 1224 (1976). A similar case is one involving the US diplomatic and consular staff in Tehran. On November 4, 1979, several hundred Iranian students and other demonstrators took possession of the US Embassy in Tehran by force. They did so in protest at the admission of the deposed Shah of Iran into the United States for medical treatment. The demonstrators were not opposed by the Iranian security forces who "simply disappeared from the scene." US consulates elsewhere in Iran were similarly occupied. The demonstrators were still in occupation when the International Court of Justice was called to give a judgment. They had seized archives and documents and continued to hold fifty-two US nationals (women had been released). Fifty were diplomatic or consular staff; two were private citizens. In an earlier judgment, the court had indicated interim measures at the request of the United States. In the present judgment, the court ruled on the US request for a declaration that Iran had infringed a number of treaties, including the 1961 and 1963 Vienna Conventions on Diplomatic and Consular Relations. It also asked for a declaration calling for the release of the hostages, the evacuation of the embassy and consulates, the punishment of the persons responsible, and the payment of reparation. In April 1980, while the case was pending, US military forces entered Iran by air and landed in a remote desert area in the course of an attempt to rescue the hostages. The United States justified its action, in a report to the Security Council pursuant to Article 51 of the UN Charter, as being in "exercise of its inherent right of self-defense with the aim of extricating American nationals who are and remain the victims of the Iranian armed attack on our Embassy." The attempt was abandoned because of equipment failure. US military personnel were killed in an air collision as the units withdrew. No injury was done to Iranian nationals or property (*International Court of Justice Reports* 1980, 3). The court by thirteen votes to two, decided that the Islamic Republic of Iran had violated obligations owed by it to the United States of America under international conventions in force between the two countries, as well as under long-established rules of general international law. The court also decided that Iran must immediately take all steps to redress the situation resulting from the events of November 4, 1979, including the release of the hostages and the return of the premises and documents to the United States, and that Iran was under an obligation to make reparation to the United States. Iran, which declined to participate in the proceedings, did not comply with the judgment of the court in any respect. The hostages were ultimately released in January 1981 as a result of a negotiated settlement with the United States.

27. Thucydides, *History of the Peloponnesian War, Loeb Classical Library* (Cambridge: Harvard University Press, 1972), Book IV, para. XXXVIII. (emphasis added).

28. The case arose out of the Canadian Rebellion of 1837. The rebel leaders, despite steps taken by US authorities to prevent assistance being given to them, managed on December 13, 1837, to enlist from Buffalo in the United States the support of a large number of American nationals. The resulting force established itself in Navy Island in Canadian waters from which it raided the Canadian shore and attacked passing British ships. The force was supplied from the US shore by an American ship, the *Caroline*. On the night of December 29–30, the British seized the *Caroline*, which was then in the American port of Schlosser, fired her, and sent her over Niagara Falls. Two US nationals were killed. The legality of the British act was discussed in detail in correspondence in 1841–1842 when Great Britain sought the release of a British subject, McLeod, who had been arrested in the United States on charges of murder and arson out of the incident (David Harris, *Cases and Materials on International Law*, London: Sweet and Maxwell, 1991, 848). See Robert Jennings, "The Caroline and MacLeod Cases," *American Journal of International Law* 32 (1938): 82.

29. Harris, *Cases and Materials in International Law*.

30. Harris, *Cases and Materials in International Law*.

31. This prompted the Athenians to burst out laughing at his empty talk, while the wise heads among them reflected with satisfaction that they would get one or other of two benefits: either they would be rid of Cleon—the result they expected—or if they were wrong about this, they would have the Spartans as their prisoners (Thucydides, *The War of the Peloponnesians and the Athenians, Cambridge Texts in the History of Political Thought*, ed. Jeremy Mynott, Cambridge: Cambridge University Press, 2013).

32. Gomme, in my view, rightly observes that this is "certainly an unexpected description of Kleon after the very similar one in iii. 36. 6, and the prominent and characteristic part there played by him, and not to be justified by Stahl's argument that Kleon's influence was not constant and probably weakened after the second debate over Mytilene" (A. Gomme, *A Historical Commentary on Thucydides*, Volume III, Oxford: Oxford University Press, 1956).

33. I agree with Gomme: "Certainly the word τυγχάνειν occurs frequently: 5.1 (the Spartan festival), 9.1 (the arrival of the Messenian vessels), 13.4 (the omission to block the entrances), and 18.3 (τύχη); also 30.2 (the fire on Sphakteria). But as pointed out in the nn. on i. 57. 6, and iv. 9. 1, τυγχάνειν does not necessarily mean that an event was accidental, but that it was contemporaneous. 'The Spartans were at that time holding a festival': the most that is meant is that Demosthenes had not timed the arrival at Pylos in order to coincide with it. 'The Messenian vessels had just arrived': that the Messenians had arrived by arrangement with Demosthenes is obvious and is implied by 3.3; but to arrive at exactly the expected time was to some extent fortuitous and fortunate. It was similarly fortunate for the Athenians, and again not planned by them, that the Spartans had not blocked the entrances, but it was not chance. The only events that were really accidental were the storm (3.1, κατά τύχην) and the fire on the island; and in the latter case Thucydides makes this clear by ἄκοντος and ἔλαθε—he does not mean 'the fortune of war,' which may be no more due to accident than τό ευτυχησαι, 17.4 or τη παρούση τύχη, 14.3" (*A Historical Commentary on Thucydides*, 488–489).

34. Ἔς τουτό τέ περιέστη ἡ τύχη, ὥστε Ἀθηναίους μέν ἐκ γῆς τέ καί ταύτης Λακωνικῆς ἀμύνεσθαι ἐκείνους ἐπιπλέοντας, Λακεδαιμονίους δέ ἐς τήν ἑαυτῶν τέ καί πολεμίαν οὖσαν ἐπ᾽ Ἀθηναίους ἀποβαίνειν. Ἐπεῖ πολύ γάρ ἐποίει τῆς δόξης ἐν τῷ τότε τοῖς μέν ἠπειρώταις μάλιστα εἶναι καί τά πεζά κρατίστοις, τοῖς δέ θαλασσίοις τέ καί ταῖς ναυσίν πλεῖστον προέχειν (Thucydides, 4.12.3). "So in a chance turn—around of events, the Athenians found themselves repelling the Spartans from the land—and Laconian territory at that—which the Spartans were attacking by sea; while the Spartans were fighting from ships and invading the Athenians on their own land, which had become enemy territory. For at that time the Spartans were renowned as a mainland power excelling in their land forces, while the Athenians were a sea power with a pre-eminent navy" (Thucydides, *The War of the Peloponnesians and the Athenians*, 242–243).

35. UK Foreign Office Policy Document no. 148 reprinted in United Kingdom Materials in International Law 1986, 57 *British Yearbook of International Law* 614 (1986).

36. See, generally, I. Brownlie, *International Law and the Use of Force by States* (Oxford: Oxford University Press, 1963).

37. Walzer proposed that "any use of force by one state against the political independence of another constitutes aggression and is a criminal act" (*Just and Unjust Wars*, Basic Books, 2006, 61).

38. UN Charter Article 2(4): "All Members shall refrain in their international relations from the threat or use of force against the territorial integrity or political independence of any state, or in any other manner inconsistent with the Purposes of the United Nations."

39. Leland M. Goodrich and Edvard Hambro, *Charter of the United Nations: Commentary and Documents* (Boston: World Peace Foundation, 1946), 68–69.

40. Fernando R. Tesón, *Humanitarian Intervention* (New York: Transnational Publishers, 1988), 151.

41. UN Charter, Article 1(3).

42. UN Charter, Article 56.

43. H. Lauterpacht, *International Law and Human Rights* (London: Praeger, 1950), 32 (emphasis original). H. Lauterpacht is late Whewell Professor of International Law in the University of Cambridge.

44. Lauterpacht, *International Law and Human Rights*, 32.

45. Most legal scholars who are opposed to humanitarian intervention emphasizing the danger of abuse, are putting forward a policy objection rather than a principled argument. However, all rights are capable of being abused. The right of self-defense has undoubtedly been the subject of abuse, but it is never seriously suggested that international law should not include the right of a state to defend itself.

46. Thucydides, 2.14.

47. The basic criteria for humanitarian intervention were fulfilled, but the Mytilenaians' constitution was an oligarchy; the majority of the citizens of Mytilene may well have seen things very differently (on this point see G. de Ste. Croix, *The Origins of the Peloponnesian War* (Ithaca: Cornell University Press, 1972).

48. See, however, Simon Hornblower, *A Commentary on Thucydides Volume I* (Oxford: Oxford University Press, 1997), where he argues that the standards of the ancient Greeks were not ours, and by our standards the Spartans were probably among the least "humane" of all ancient Greeks.

49. Thucydides, having detected the unchangeable character of human nature, ably predicted: "My work is not a piece of writing designed to meet the taste of an immediate public, but was done to last for ever" (Thucydides, 1.22).

Chapter Three

Origins of Humanitarian Law of Armed Conflict in Thucydides

The warfare practices which were developed in the time of Thucydides prove that there existed in a systematic form a corpus of law with regard to armed conflict. Legal rules governing the conduct of opponents in the battlefield, were not of a rudimentary form, but, in fact, were sufficiently developed. If it cannot be said that these rules have influenced the formation of rules of equivalent value in modern international law, it could certainly be deduced that they stood firmly in their own right as an aspect of classical Greek international law.

In the first place, the oracle of Delphi usually exerted a powerful influence. Thus, it refused to listen to the Milesians, as they had not duly expiated the excesses committed in their civil wars, though it responded to all others, even to the barbarians, who consulted it.[1] After the defeat of the Cyprians by the Persians, Onesilus, who had led the revolt of the former, was killed, his head cut off and hung over the gates of Amathus, a city he had besieged. The Amathusians, however, were commanded by the oracle to take down the head and bury it, and, as an atonement for their offense, to sacrifice annually to Onesilus, as to a hero—τὴν μὲν κεφαλήν κατελόντας θάψαι, Ὀνησίλῳ δὲ θύειν ὡς ἥρωϊ ἀνὰ πᾶν ἔτος.[2]

In open conflicts between Greek communities and city-states reported by Thucydides, the intervention of the Delphian god had invariably salutary results. In 435 B.C. the Epidamnians, in conformity with the answer of the Delphian god, delivered up their city to Corinth and placed themselves under her protection, when their immediate mother city, Corcyra (itself a Corinthian colony), rejected their appeal for aid.[3]

When the Epidamnians learned that no help would be forthcoming from Corcyra they were at a loss how to deal with the crisis and sent to Delphi to ask the god whether they should make the city over to the Corinthians as their original founders and try to obtain some assistance from them. The god responded that they should do so and should make the Corinthians their leaders. So the Epidamnians went to Corinth in accordance with the oracle and committed the city to them, pointing out that their founder was from Corinth and revealing the terms of the oracle. They petitioned them not to look on while they were being destroyed but to come to their defense. The Corinthians undertook to give assistance, both as a matter of right, since they regarded the colony to be at least as much as theirs as the Corcyraeans', and also out of hatred for the Corcyraeans, since although they were colonists of theirs they were failing to show them respect. They did not present the traditional gifts of honor at their common festivals, nor did they bestow the first portion of the sacrifices on a Corinthian as the other colonists did.

The same year, the Corcyraeans offered to refer a territorial dispute with Corinth to the oracle at Delphi. This fact proves beyond doubt that the oracle at Delphi served also as an organization for the settlement of inter-state or international disputes in ancient Greece, much like modern international organizations purport to resolve international conflicts through the process of mediation, arbitration, negotiation, and conciliation.[4]

When the Corcyraeans learned of these preparations they went to Corinth, taking with them Spartan and Sicyonian envoys, and told the Corinthians to withdraw the troops and settlers they had in Epidamnus since they had no part in the place. If the Corinthians had any counterclaims, they would be willing to submit to arbitration in the Peloponnese by any states both of them agreed upon, and whichever party it was adjudged the colony belonged to should prevail. They were also willing to submit the matter to the oracle at Delphi. War, however, they advise against; otherwise, they said, they in turn would be compelled, if the Corinthians forced them into it, to make new friends not of their choosing and different in kind from their current ones in order to get help.[5]

The Athenians, having expelled the Delians from the latter's country, in 422 B.C., on account of an alleged ancient offense against the sacred character of Delos, restored them the following year, by the command of the oracle.[6]

About the same time during this summer, the Athenians reduced the Scionaeans by siege, slew the adult males, made slaves of the women and children, and gave the land to the Plataeans to occupy, and they brought back the Delians to Delos, taking to heart their mishaps in the battles and obeying an oracle of the god at Delphi.[7]

It seems from the above that a beneficial influence was exerted by the oracle on politics, international law, the comity of nations, and respect for judicial decisions.

With regard to prisoners of war, from a legal point of view, there was but little difference, for practical purposes, between a slave, δοῦλος, and a prisoner of war, αἰχμάλωτος. In 476 B.C. the Athenians under Cimon besieged Eion, took it from the Persians, and sold the inhabitants into slavery.[8]

First, under the command of Cimon, son of Miltiades, they took by siege Eion, a city on the Strymon in the hands of the Persians, and enslaved its inhabitants.[9]

A similar fate befell the people of Melos when their town was captured by Athens.[10]

At about the same time, the Melians seized another part of the Athenians' encircling wall, which was only lightly guarded. However, as a result of this passage of events another force was subsequently dispatched from Athens, under the command of Philocrates, son of Demeas. The Melians were now under heavy siege and there was also some treachery from within, so they surrendered to the Athenians, to be dealt with as they wished. The Athenians killed all the adult males they had taken and enslaved the women and children. The place itself they occupied with their own people, sending out five hundred colonists at some later time.[11]

In 427 B.C. Alcidas, on his return to Peloponnesus, passed through Myonnesus in the territory of Teos, and there slew most of the captives taken on his voyage. But the Samian exiles remonstrated with him for putting to death prisoners who had not been in open hostilities against him, but were allies of Athens from necessity.[12] Paches, after taking the citadel of Notium, slaughtered all the Arcadians and barbarians he found there (427 B.C.) and colonized the place under leaders sent from Athens.[13]

On his way back along the coast, one of the places Paches put in to was Notium, part of Colophon where the Colophonians had settled when the upper city was captured by Itames and his Persians, who had been called in as a result of some internal dispute. The refugees who had settled in Notium were now again split into factions: one group called in Arcadian and Persian mercenaries from Pissouthnes and established them behind a separate wall (where the Persian sympathizers from the Colophonians in the upper town joined them and formed a community), and the other group had seceded from these and it was these exiles who called in Paches. He invited in for a discussion Hippias, the leader of the Arcadians behind the wall, on the understanding that Paches would restore him safe and sound to his enclave if Hippias was not satisfied with what was said. So Hippias came out to join him, but Paches then placed him under guard (though not actually bound) while he himself carried out a sudden and surprise attack on the fortified area, captured it, and put to death all the Arcadians and Persians who were inside.[14]

In 428 B.C., the Mytileneans of Lesbos revolted against Athens, partly through their fear of being reduced to the condition of the other subject-allies, and partly through their repugnance to assist her in her ambitious designs. However, in the following year, they were obliged to capitulate to Paches. The latter dispatched to Athens over a thousand prisoners. Of these Salaethus, a Lacedaemonian envoy, who had encouraged the others to hold out, was at once put to death. The disposal of the other prisoners caused some discussion in the Athenian assembly. At the instigation of the demagogue Cleon, the former opponent of Pericles, an order was first made to slaughter not only the men who had arrived at Athens, but the entire male population of Mytilene that was of military age, and to enslave the women and children. [15]

They debated what to do about the other men and in their anger decided to kill not only the ones there in Athens but also the whole adult male population of Mytilene, and to enslave the women and children. They particularly condemned the revolt because the Mytilenaeans had staged it despite not being subjects like the others, and what made the Athenians really furious was the fact that Peloponnesian ships had dared to venture into Ionia to support them; that, in their view, made it look as though the revolt was not just the result of a sudden decision. They therefore sent a trireme to convey the news of this decision to Paches, with orders to finish off the Mytilenaeans without delay. [16]

At the instigation of Mytilenean envoys, the execution of the order was delayed, for the purpose of calling another assembly. There, Cleon reproached the Athenians for being too foolishly kind to their allies; he pointed out that impolitic indulgence would only make the other allies revolt, and clamored for justice: [17]

> Time and again in the past have I realized that a democracy is incapable of exercising rule over others, but never more so than now in this matter of your change of heart about the Mytilenaeans. Just because you enjoy an absence of fear and intrigue in your everyday relations with each other you assume the same applies to your relations with your allies. You do not realise that with every mistake they talk you into and every concession you make out of compassion your weakness does more to expose you to danger than to win the gratitude of your allies. You do not see that the empire you hold is a tyranny, and one imposed on unwilling subjects who for their part plot against you. They accept your rule not because of any sacrifices you may make to please them but because of the superiority that derives from your strength rather than from their goodwill. [18]

However, an amendment of Diodotus was carried, and the previous order countermanded. [19] As for the prisoners in Athens, they were, on the motion of Cleon, slain to a man. Similarly, the Lacedaemonians put to death all the prisoners taken after the surrender of Plataea. There were two hundred Plataeans and twenty-five Athenians who had assisted them during the siege. All the women were reduced to slavery.

As regards the right of asylum, the common laws of the Greeks, κοινά τῶν Ἑλλήνων νόμιμα, demanded that reverence should be paid to sanctuaries and temples, and that no violation should be inflicted upon those who sought shelter therein.[20] This immunity was bestowed on fugitives from the enemy, on criminals, and even on such as were condemned to death. To take their lives under these circumstances would be universally considered a gross act of sacrilege, ιεροσυλία,[21] and persons guilty of such desecration rendered themselves liable to the most severe of penalties, as well as to divine imprecations against themselves and their descendants.[22]

> Cylon and his besieged companions were meanwhile suffering badly through lack of food and water. Cylon and his brother managed to escape, but the others, since they were in great distress and some were even dying, sat down as suppliants at the altar on the acropolis. The Athenians who had been entrusted with the guard, when they saw them dying in the temple, made them get up on the understanding that they would do them no harm, but then led them away and killed them, and some others, who had taken refuge on the altars of the "Dread Goddesses" as they were passing, they dispatched even there. For this action they were pronounced accursed and offenders against the goddess, they and their descendants with them. The Athenians accordingly banished those under the curse.[23]

Thus a terrible earthquake visited Sparta because, it was thought, the Lacedaemonians had put to death certain Helots who had taken refuge in the temple of Poseidon at Taenarus,[24] and the curse of Athene of the Brazen House was likewise attributed to the murder of Pausanias in the precincts of the temple,[25]

> The Athenians made a counterdemand that the Spartans should drive out the curse of Taenarum. For the Spartans had once made some Helots who were suppliants in the sanctuary of Poseidon at Taenarum get up and leave and had then led them off and done away with them. And they think it was as a direct result of this that they suffered a mighty earthquake in Sparta itself.[26]

Apart from fugitives who claimed the protection of the presiding deities of the temples, it was also forbidden to slay suppliants who, in the course of an engagement in the battlefield, laid down their arms and threw themselves on the mercy of the enemy. In accordance with an ancient oracle of Delphi current among the Lacedaemonians, suppliants of the Ithomaean Zeus were to be spared, and so when Ithome capitulated to Sparta in 455 B.C. the Messenians, along with their wives and children, were allowed to go free and received from Athens a home at Naupactus.[27]

There was also an earlier oracle that the Spartans had from Delphi telling them "to release the suppliant of Zeus at Ithome." So the rebels left with their women and children, and the Athenians accepted them because of the hostility they now felt towards the Spartans and settled them at Naupactus.

The Plataeans, in their speech to the Lacedaemonian judges in 427 B.C., exhorted them not to bring infamy upon themselves by putting suppliants to death, and, apart from the demands of piety, they urged that they had surrendered themselves and stretched out their hands to the captors, and that Hellenic law forbids the slaying of suppliants.

> It is a short matter to take our lives but hard to erase the infamy of the deed. For we are not enemies you have the right to punish but well-wishers, forced into war. Your pious duty as judges, therefore, is to protect our lives, bearing in mind that you took us in involuntary surrender and with the outstretched arms of suppliants (whom Greek law forbids one to slay).[28]

The Athenians invaded Boeotia in the eighth year of the war. Having occupied, fortified, and desecrated the shrine of Apollo at Delium, they suffered decisive defeat in battle, without yet being expelled from the sanctuary. They sought to recover under an armistice the dead bodies of their comrades, but were met by the reaction and advice of the Boeotians that they would not be granted the bodies until they had evacuated the sanctuary. Subsequently, the Boeotians sieged the Athenian garrison and succeeded in forcing it out of the temple. Seventeen days after the initial battle the Boeotians allowed the Athenians to recover the dead bodies.[29]

The two opposing sides to this inter-state dispute address fundamental questions of Thucydidean scholarship: the relation of justice to piety and of both to force. The complaint of the Boeotians runs as follows.

> The Athenians had not acted fairly in transgressing the usages of the Greeks, for it was established practice for them all, when invading each other's territories, to refrain from occupying the sanctuaries therein. The Athenians, however, had fortified Delium and were now making themselves at home there, acting in every respect as men do on unconsecrated ground, even drawing for ordinary use the water they themselves never touched except for use in the sacred rites. Wherefore the Boeotians, on behalf of the god and themselves, invoking the local divinities and Apollo, served them notice to take up their dead upon evacuating the temple.[30]

Before making reference to the Athenian response, it must be said that this incident and the passage itself denote that in ancient Greece, as described in the book of Thucydides, one may trace further elements of international humanitarian law of armed conflict.

In modern international law, the Latin term for this body of law is *ius in bello,* otherwise called the law of armed conflict or humanitarian law of armed conflict. The rationale for this corpus of law is that, if it is really not completely possible to deter war (and, history, indeed, shows that this is not possible), armed conflict ought to be subject to certain humanitarian rules and constraints, so that civilian populations, for instance, along with prisoners of war and wounded soldiers, may be protected, as well as the use of certain weapons may be forbidden.

During the second half of the nineteenth century, states issued manuals of military law (such as the Lieber Code),[31] and in the course of the twentieth century as well as the latter they agreed to abide by certain international conventions that have been incorporated in modern international law. Such conventions are, for example, the Hague Convention of 1954 for the protection of cultural property, sporadically referred to above, and the Geneva Conventions of 1949 for the protection of civilian populations and many others.

Notes

1. Athenaeus, *The Learned Banqueters, Volume V: Books 10.420e-11*, ed. and trans. S. Douglas Olson, *Loeb Classical Library* 274 (Cambridge: Harvard University Press, 2009), 26: διόπερ ὁ θεὸς ἐπὶ πολὺν χρόνον ἀπήλαυνεν αὐτοὺς τοῦ μαντείου καὶ ἐπερωτώντων διὰ τίνα αἰτίαν ἀπελαύνονται εἶπεν.

2. Herodotus, *The Persian Wars*, 4 vols., *Loeb Classical Library* 117–120, trans. A. D. Godley, Cambridge: Harvard University Press, 1920–1925), v. 114.

3. Thucydides, *History of the Peloponnesian War*, 4 vols., *Loeb Classical Library* 108, 109, 110, and 169, trans. C. Forster Smith (Cambridge: Harvard University Press, 1919–1923) (hereafter cited as Thucydides), 1.25.

4. Thucydides, 1.28.

5. Thucydides, *The War of the Peloponnesians and the Athenians, Cambridge Texts in the History of Political Thought*, ed. Jeremy Mynott (Cambridge: Cambridge University Press, 2013), 19.

6. Thucydides, 5.32.1.

7. Thucydides, *History of the Peloponnesian War Books V-VI, Loeb Classical Library*, 63.

8. Thucydides, 1.98.

9. Thucydides, *History of the Peloponnesian War Books V-VI, Loeb Classical Library*, 59.

10. Thucydides, 5.116.

11. Thucydides, *History of the Peloponnesian War Books V-VI, Loeb Classical Library*, 385–386.

12. See the provisions of the Geneva Conventions of 1949.

13. Thucydides, 3.34.

14. Thucydides, *History of the Peloponnesian War Books V-VI, Loeb Classical Library*, 181.

15. Thucydides, 3.36.

16. Thucydides, *History of the Peloponnesian War Books V-VI, Loeb Classical Library*, 182.

17. Thucydides, 3.37–40.

18. Thucydides, *History of the Peloponnesian War Books V-VI, Loeb Classical Library*, 183.

19. Thucydides, 3.49.

20. See correspondingly the Hague Convention for the Protection of Cultural Property of 1954: "Definition of Cultural Property: Article: For the purposes of the present Convention, the term 'cultural property' shall cover, irrespective of origin or ownership: (a) movable or immovable property of great importance to the cultural heritage of every people, such as monuments of architecture, art or history, whether religious or secular; archaeological sites; groups of buildings which, as a whole, are of historical or artistic interest; works of art; . . . objects of artistic or archaeological interest; as well as collections . . . (b) buildings whose main and effective purpose is to preserve or exhibit the movable cultural property defined in subparagraph (a) such as museums, depositories of archives, and refuges intended to shelter, in the event of armed conflict, the movable cultural property defined in subparagraph (a). Protection of Cultural Property: Article 2: For the purposes of the present Convention, the protection of cultural property shall comprise the safeguarding of and respect for such property. Article: The High Contracting Parties undertake to prepare in time of peace for the safeguarding of cultural property situated in their own territory against the foreseeable effects of an armed conflict, by taking such measures as they consider appropriate.

"Respect for Cultural Property: The High Contracting Parties undertake to respect cultural property situated within their own territory as well as within the territory of other High Contracting Parties by refraining from any use of the property and its immediate surroundings or of the appliances in use of its protection for purposes which are likely to expose it to destruction or damage in the event of armed conflict; and by refraining from any act of hostility directed against any such property.

"Article 4.2.: The obligations mentioned in paragraph 1 of the present Article may be waived only in cases where military necessity imperatively requires such a waiver.

"Article 4.3.: The High Contracting Parties further undertake to prohibit, prevent, and if necessary to put a stop to any form of theft or misappropriation of, and of any acts of vandalism directed against, cultural property.

"Article 4.4.: They shall refrain from any act directed by way of reprisals against cultural property.

"Article 4.5.: No High Contracting Party may evade the obligations incumbent upon it under the present Article, in respect of another High Contracting Party, by reason of the fact that the latter has not applied the measures of safeguard referred to in Article.

"Article 5.1.: Any High Contracting Party in occupation of the whole or part of the territory of another High Contracting Party shall as far as possible support the competent national authorities of the occupied country in safeguarding and preserving its cultural property.

"Should it prove necessary to take measures to preserve cultural property situated in occupied territory and damaged by military operations, and should the competent national authorities be unable to take such measures, the Occupying Power shall, as far as possible, and in close co-operation with such authorities, take the most necessary measures of preservation."

21. Plato, *The Republic*, 443A, *Loeb Classical Library* 276 (Cambridge: Harvard University Press, 2013).

22. Thucydides, 1.126, 1.134.

23. Thucydides, *History of the Peloponnesian War Books V-VI, Loeb Classical Library*, 74–75.

24. Thucydides, 1.128.

25. Thucydides, 1.128.

26. Thucydides, *The War of the Peloponnesians and the Athenians*, 75.

27. Thucydides, 1.103: Ἦν δέ τι καὶ χρηστήριον τοῖς Λακεδαιμονίοις Πυθικὸν πρὸ τοῦ, τὸν ἱκέτην τοῦ Διὸς Ἰθωμήτα ἀφιέναι. ἐξῆλθον δὲ αὐτοὶ καὶ παῖδες καὶ γυναῖκες.

28. Thucydides, 3.58: ὥστε καὶ τῶν σωμάτων ἄδειαν ποιοῦντες ὅσια ἂν δικάζοιτε, καὶ προνοοῦντες ὅτι ἑκόντας ἐλάβετε καὶ χεῖρας προϊσχομένους (ὁ δὲ νόμος τοῖς Ἕλλησι μὴ κτείνειν τούτους).

29. Seventeen days is a long time in the sun of the summer, and most critics who have commented upon this passage have taken the side of the Athenians in blaming the Boeotians for violating sacred law in the hope of extorting an unearned victory. See, for example, Gomme, for whom "Thucydides' insertion of this long dispute, his insistence on this argument of words, was due to his feeling that the Boeotian refusal to allow the Athenians to collect their dead was another evil resulting from the war . . . and abandonment of one of the recognized, and humane usages of Greece" (A. Gomme, *A Historical Commentary on Thucydides*, Volume III, Oxford: Oxford University Press, 1956, 571) But, as Orwin ably observes, "what Thucydides' characters dispute, however, is not the 'inhumanity' of the refusal, but whether it and the behavior of the Athenians that provoked it are offences against the law of man that forbids dishonoring he gods" (C. Orwin, *The Humanity of Thucydides*, Princeton: Princeton University Press, 1997, 91 n. 6)

30. Thucydides, 4.97.2–4.

31. In his lecture, in the course of the commencement of the seventh annual meeting of the American Society of International Law, dedicated to the Lieber Code, the president, Elihu Root, emphasized the humanitarian content of the code: "While the instrument was a practical presentation of what the laws and usages of war were, and not a technical discussion of what the writer thought they ought to be, in all its parts may be discerned an instinctive selection of the best and most humane practice and an assertion of the control of morals to the limit permitted by the dreadful business in which the rules were to be applied" (Opening Address by Elihu Root at the Seventh Annual Meeting of the American Society of International Law April 24, 1913, reprinted in *American Journal of International Law* 7, 453 [1913]). Assessing the work of Lieber, Johann Caspar Bluntschli, professor in Heidelberg, said this: "His legal injunctions rest upon the foundation of moral precepts. The former are not always sharply distinguished from moral injunctions, but nevertheless, through a union with the same, are ennobled and exalted. Everywhere reigns in this body of law the spirit of humanity, which spirit recognizes as fellow-beings, with lawful rights, our very enemies, and which forbids our visiting upon them unnecessary injury, cruelty, or destruction. But at the same time, our legislator

remains fully aware that, in time of war, it is absolutely necessary to provide for the safety of armies and for the successful conduct of a campaign; that, to those engaged in it, the harshest measures and most reckless exactions cannot be denied; and that tender-hearted sentimentality is here all the more out of place, because the greater the energy employed in carrying on the war, the sooner will it be brought to an end, and the normal condition of peace restored" (Johann Caspar Bluntschli, "Introduction: Lieber's Service to Political Science and International-al Law," in Francis Leiber, *The Miscellaneous Writings of Francis Lieber: Contributions to Political Science*, 12–13 [1881]). In some respects, including the absolute prohibition of rape and the protection of territories under belligerent occupation, the code was much more advanced than the Hague regulations: "All wanton violence committed against persons in the invaded country, all destruction of property not commanded by the authorized officer, all robbery, all pillage or sacking, even after taking a place by main force, all rape, wounding, maiming, or killing of such inhabitants, are prohibited under the penalty of death, or such other severe punishment as may seem adequate for the gravity of the offense" (Lieber Code, 44). It is noteworthy that the crimes mentioned are punishable by the death penalty.

Chapter Four

Law of Treaties

In this chapter, my aim is to examine some representative and important treaties referred to by Thucydides. In this way, documentation shall be provided for the fact that the historian is a pioneer in preserving with accuracy the diplomatic practices of ancient Greece. Also, the conventions to be surveyed testify to the great diplomatic activity of the Greek people and their tendency to bring about, as far as possible, regularization of international or inter-state relations. The conclusion of treaties was particularly significant in the course of the Peloponnesian War. It must be emphasized that both the ancient Greek text and the English translation from the Harvard edition of Thucydides (Loeb) are hereby laid down. For the sake of absolute accuracy, the English text from the *Cambridge Texts in the History of Political Thought* is also quoted in full in the footnotes. In the case of the Peace of Nicias, first to be reported, the Cambridge version is quoted in the main text of the monograph, because the treaty is extensive and important enough to be accommodated there.

So, in 421 B.C., the Peace of Nicias was concluded between the Athenians and the Lacedaemonians.

Σπονδὰς ἐποιήσαντο Ἀθηναῖοι καί Λακεδαιμόνιοι καί οἱ ξύμμαχοι κατά τάδε, καί ὤμοσαν κατά πόλεις.

Περί μέν τῶν ἱερῶν των κοινῶν, θύειν ἐξεῖναι καί μαντεύεσθαι καί θεωρεῖν κατά τά πάτρια τόν βουλόμενον καί κατά γῆν καί κατά θάλασσαν ἀδεῶς.

Τό δ'ἱερόν καί τόν νεῶν τόν ἐν Δελφοῖς τοῦ Ἀπόλλωνος καί Δελφούς αὐτονόμους εἶναι καί αὐτοτελεῖς καί αὐτοδίκους καί αὐτῶν καί τῆς γῆς τῆς ἑαυτῶν κατά τά πάτρια.

Ἔτη δέ εἶναι τάς σπονδάς πεντήκοντα Ἀθηναίοις καί τοῖς ξυμμάχοις τοῖς Ἀθηναίων καί Λακεδαιμονίοις καί τοῖς ξυμμάχοις τοῖς Λακεδαιμονίων ἀδόλους καί ἀβλαβεῖς καί κατά γῆν καί κατά θάλασσαν.

55

Ὅπλα δὲ μή ἐξέστω ἐπιφέρειν ἐπί πημονή μήτε Λακεδαιμονίους καί τούς ξυμμάχους ἐπ' Ἀθηναίους μήτε Ἀθηναίους καί τούς ξυμμάχους ἐπί Λακεδαιμονίους καί τούς ξυμμάχους, μήτε τέχνη μήτε μηχανῇ μηδεμιᾷ. ἥν δέ τί διάφορον ἤ πρός ἀλλήλους, δίκαις χρήσθων καί ὅρκοις, καθ'ότι ἄν ξύνθωνται.

Ἀποδόντων δὲ Ἀθηναίοις Λακεδαιμόνιοι καὶ οἱ ξύμμαχοι Ἀμφίπολιν. ὅσας δὲ πόλεις παρέδοσαν Λακεδαιμόνιοι Ἀθηναίοις ἐξέστω ἀπιέναι ὅποι ἄν βούλωνται αὐτοὺς καὶ τὰ ἑαυτῶν ἔχοντας. τὰς δὲ πόλεις φερούσας τὸν φόρον τὸν ἐπ'Ἀριστείδου αὐτονόμους εἶναι. ὅπλα δὲ μὴ ἐξέστω ἐπιφέρειν Ἀθηναίους μηδὲ τοὺς ξυμμάχους ἐπὶ κακῷ, ἀποδιδόντων τὸν φόρον. ἐπειδὴ αἱ σπονδαὶ ἐγένοντο. εἰσὶ δὲ Ἄργιλος, Στάγιρος, Ἄκανθος, Στῶλος, Ὄλυνθος, Σπάρτωλος. ξυμμάχους δ'εἶναι μηδετέρων, μήτε Λακεδαιμονίων μήτε Ἀθηναίων. ἥν δὲ Ἀθηναῖοι πείθωσι τὰς πόλεις, βουλομένας ταύτας ἐξέστω ξυμμάχους ποείσθαι αὐτοὺς Ἀθηναίους.

Μηκυβερναίους δὲ καὶ Σαναίους καὶ Σιγγίους οἰκεῖν τὰς πόλεις τὰς ἑαυτῶν, καθάπερ Ὀλύνθιοι καὶ Ἀκάνθιοι.

Ἀποδόντων δὲ Ἀθηναίοις Λακεδαιμόνιοι καὶ οἱ ξύμμαχοι Πάνακτον. ἀποδόντων δὲ καὶ Ἀθηναῖοι Λακεδαιμονίοις Κορυφάσιον καὶ Κύθηρα καὶ Μέθανα καὶ Πτελεὸν καὶ Ἀταλάντην, καὶ τοὺς ἄνδρας ὅσοι εἰσὶ Λακεδαιμονίων ἐν τῷ δημοσίῳ τῷ Ἀθηναίων ἢ ἄλλοθί που ὅσης Ἀθηναῖοι ἄρχουσιν ἐν δημοσίῳ καὶ τοὺς ἐν Σκιώνῃ πολιορκουμένους Πελοποννησίων ἀφεῖναι, καὶ τοὺς ἄλλους ὅσοι Λακεδαιμονίων ξύμμαχοι ἐν Σκιώνῃ εἰσὶ καὶ ὅσους Βρασίδας ἐσέπεμψε, καὶ εἰ τις τῶν ξυμμάχων τῶν Λακεδαιμονίων ἐν Ἀθήναις ἐστὶν ἐν τῷ δημοσίῳ ἤ ἄλλοθί που ἧς Ἀθηναῖοι ἄρχουσιν ἐν δημοσίῳ. ἀποδόντων δὲ καὶ Λακεδαιμόνιοι καὶ οἱ ξύμμαχοι οὕστινας ἔχουσιν Ἀθηναίων καὶ τῶν ξυμμάχων κατὰ ταῦτα.

Σκιωναίων δὲ καὶ Τορωναίων καὶ Σερμυλιῶν καὶ εἰ τινα ἄλλην πόλιν ἔχουσιν Ἀθηναῖοι, Ἀθηναίους βουλεύεσθαι περὶ αὐτῶν καὶ τῶν ἄλλων πόλεων ὅ,τι ἄν δοκῇ αὐτοῖς.

Ὅρκους δὲ ποιήσασθαι Ἀθηναίους πρὸς Λακεδαιμονίους καὶ τοὺς ξυμμάχους κατὰ πόλεις. ὀμνύντων δὲ τὸν ἐπιχώριον ὅρκον ἑκάτεροι τὸν μέγιστον, ἑπτὰ καὶ δέκα ἑκάστης πόλεως. ὁ ὅρκος ἔστω ὅδε. Ἐμμενῶ ταῖς ξυνθήκαις καὶ ταῖς σπονδαῖς ταῖσδε δικαίως καὶ ἀδόλως. ἔστω δὲ Λακεδαιμονίοις καὶ τοῖς ξυμμάχοις κατὰ ταῦτα ὅρκος πρὸς Ἀθηναίους. τὸν δὲ ὅρκον ἀνανεοῦσθαι κατ'ἐνιαυτὸν ἀμφοτέρους.

Στήλας δὲ στῆσαι Ὀλυμπιάσι καὶ Πυθοῖ καὶ Ἰσθμοῖ καὶ Ἀθήνησιν ἐν πόλει καὶ ἐν Λακεδαίμονι ἐν Ἀμυκλαίῳ.

Εἰ δέ τι ἀμνημονοῦσιν ὁποτεροιοὺν καὶ ὅτου περί, λόγοις δικαίοις χρωμένοις εὔορκον εἶναι ἀμφοτέροις ταύτη μεταθεῖναι ὅπη ἄν δοκῇ ἀμφοτέροις, Ἀθηναίοις καὶ Λακεδαιμονίοις.

Ἄρχει δὲ τῶν σπονδῶν ἔφορος Πλειστόλας, Ἀρτεμισίου μηνὸς Τετάρτη φθίνοντος, ἐν δὲ Ἀθήναις ἄρχων Ἀλκαῖος, Ἐλαφηβολιῶνος μηνός.

The Athenians and the Lacedaemonians and their respective allies have concluded a treaty and sworn to it state by state upon the following terms: [1]

1. With regard to the common sanctuaries whomever wishes may offer sacrifices and consult the oracles and attend as a deputy according to the customs of the fathers, both by land and sea, without fear.

2. The precinct and the temple of Apollo at Delphi and the people of Delphi shall be independent, having their own system of taxation and their own courts of justice, both as regards themselves and their own territory, according to the customs of the fathers.[2]

3. The truce shall be in force for fifty years between the Athenians and their allies and the Lacedaemonians and their allies, without fraud or hurt, both by land and sea.

4. It shall not be lawful to bear arms with harmful intent, either for the Lacedaemonians and their allies against the Athenians and their allies, or for Athenians and their allies against the Lacedaemonians and their allies, by any art or device. And if there be any dispute with one another, they shall have recourse to courts and oaths, according as they shall agree.

5. The Lacedaemonians and their allies shall restore Amphipolis[3] to the Athenians. But in the case of cities delivered by the Lacedaemonians to the Athenians, their inhabitants shall be allowed to go away wherever they wish, having their own possessions; and these cities, so long as they pay the tribute that was fixed in the time of Aristeides, shall be independent. And it shall not be lawful for the Athenians and their allies,[4] after the ratification of the treaty, to bear arms against the cities to their hurt, so long as they pay the tribute. These cities are Argilus, Stagirus, Acanthus, Stolus, Olynthus, Spartolus. These shall be allies[5] neither of the Lacedaemonians nor of the Athenians; but if the Athenians can persuade these cities it shall be lawful for the Athenians to make them, with their own free will and consent, allies to themselves.

6. The Mecybernaeans and Sanaeans and Singians shall dwell in their own towns on the same terms as the Olynthians and Acanthians.

7. The Lacedaemonians and their allies shall restore Panactum to the Athenians. The Athenians shall restore to the Lacedaemonians Coryphasium, Cythera, Methana, Pteleum, and Atalante; also they shall set at liberty the Lacedaemonian captives who are in the public prison at Athens or in public prison anywhere else that the Athenians hold sway, and the men of the Peloponnesus who are being besieged in Scione, and all besides who are allies of the Lacedaemonians in Scione, and those whom Brasidas sent into the place,[6] as likewise any of the allies of the Lacedaemonians who are in the public prison in Athens, or in public prison anywhere else that the Athenians have sway. In like manner the Lacedaemonians and their allies shall restore whomsoever they have of the Athenians and their allies.

8. As to Scione, Torone, Sermyle, or any other city which the Athenians hold, the Athenians shall determine about these and the other cities as they may think best.

9. The Athenians shall bind themselves by oaths with the Lacedaemonians and their allies, city by city;[7] and either party shall swear its customary oath in the form that is most binding, seventeen men representing each city. The oath shall be as follows: "I will abide by this agreement and this treaty, justly and without deceit." For the Lacedaemonians and their allies there shall be an oath, in the same terms, with the Athenians. And both parties shall renew the oath year by year.

10. They shall erect pillars at Olympia,[8] Delphi, the Isthmus, and on the Acropolis at Athens, and at Lacedaemon in the temple of Apollo of Amyclae.

11. If either party forgets anything about any matter whatsoever, it shall be consistent with their oath for both,[9] by means of fair discussion, to make a change at any point where it may seem good to both parties, the Athenians and the Lacedaemonians.

12. The treaty begins at Lacedaemon in the ephorate of Pleistolas, on the fourth day from the end of the month Artemisium, and at Athens in the archonship of Alcaeus, on the sixth day from the end of the month Elaphebolion.[10]

Here is the Cambridge version. These were the terms:[11]

Παρόντων οὖν πρέσβεων ἀπὸ τῶν Ἀθηναίων καὶ γενομένων λόγων ξυνέβησαν, καὶ ἐγένοντο ὅρκοι καὶ ξυμμαχία ἥδε.

Κατὰ τάδε ξύμμαχοι ἔσονται Ἀθηναῖοι καὶ Λακεδαιμόνιοι πεντήκοντα ἔτη.

Ἤν τινες ἴωσιν ἐς τὴν γῆν πολέμιοι τὴν Λακεδαιμονίων καὶ κακῶς ποιῶσι Λακεδαιμονίους, ὠφελεῖν Ἀθηναίους Λακεδαιμονίους τρόπῳ ὁποίῳ ἂν δύνωνται ἰσχυροτάτῳ κατὰ τὸ δυνατόν. ἢν δὲ δηώσαντες οἴχωνται, πολεμίαν εἶναι ταύτην τὴν πόλιν Λακεδαιμονίοις καὶ Ἀθηναίοις καὶ κακῶς πάσχειν ὑπὸ ἀμφοτέρων, καταλύειν δὲ ἅμα ἄμφω τῷ πόλει. ταῦτα δ'εἶναι δικαίως καὶ προθύμως καὶ ἀδόλως.

Καὶ ἤν τινες ἐς τὴν Ἀθηναίων γῆν ἴωσιν πολέμιοι καὶ κακῶς ποιῶσιν Ἀθηναίους, ὠφελεῖν Λακεδαιμονίους Ἀθηναίους τρόπῳ ὅτῳ ἂν δύνωνται ἰσχυροτάτῳ κατὰ τὸ δυνατόν. ἢν δὲ δηώσαντες οἴχωνται, πολεμίαν εἶναι ταύτην τὴν πόλιν Λακεδαιμονίοις καὶ Ἀθηναίοις καὶ κακῶς πάσχειν ὑπ'ἀμφοτέρων, καταλύειν δὲ ἅμα ἄμφω τῷ πόλει. ταῦτα δ'εἶναι δικαίως καὶ προθύμως καὶ ἀδόλως.

Ἤν δὲ ἡ δουλεία ἐπανίστηνται, ἐπικουρεῖν Ἀθηναίους Λακεδαιμονίοις παντὶ σθένει κατὰ τὸ δυνατόν.

Ὀμοῦνται δὲ ταῦτα οἵπερ καὶ τὰς ἄλλας σπονδὰς ὤμνυον ἑκατέρων. ἀνανεοῦσθαι δὲ κατ'ἐνιαυτὸν Λακεδαιμονίους μὲν ἰόντας ἐς Ἀθήνας πρὸς τὰ Διονύσια, Ἀθηναίους δὲ ἰόντας ἐς Λακεδαίμονα πρὸς τὰ Ὑακίνθια.

Στήλην δὲ ἑκατέρους στῆσαι, τὴν μὲν ἐν Λακεδαίμονι παρ'Ἀπόλλωνι ἐν Ἀμυκλαίῳ, τὴν δὲ ἐν Ἀθήναις ἐν πόλει παρ'Ἀθηναίᾳ.[12]

The Athenians and the Spartans and their allies made a treaty on the following terms and swore it city by city:

Concerning the common sanctuaries, anyone who wishes can sacrifice, visit, consult the oracles and attend festivals according to their established practices with safe passage by land and sea. The sanctuary and temple of Apollo at Delphi shall be self-governing in their laws, taxes and courts in respect of themselves and their territory according to custom and practice.

The treaty shall be in force for fifty years between the Athenians and their allies and the Spartans and their allies without deceit or intent to harm and shall have effect by land and sea.

It will not be permitted to bear arms with hostile intent either for the Spartans and their allies against the Athenians and their allies or for the Athenians and their allies against the Spartans and their allies by any means or contrivance. And if there is any dispute between them they should have recourse to such legal procedures of justice and oath as they may jointly agree.

The Spartans and their allies are to give back Amphipolis to the Athenians.

In the case of those cities the Spartans have handed over to the Athenians people who so wish are to be allowed to leave taking their belongings with them.

The following cities are to be independent provided that they continue to pay tribute at the level assessed at the time of Aristeides; and the Athenians and their allies are not allowed to bear arms against them to do them harm, provided that they pay the tribute, now that the treaty has been concluded. These cities are: Argilus, Stagirus, Acanthus, Scolus, Olynthus and Spartolus. They are to be allies of neither side, neither of the Spartans nor of the Athenians; but if the Athenians so persuade them and have their consent the Athenians are allowed to make them their allies.

The people of Mecyberna, Sane and Singus shall have their own towns to live in, just like the people of Olynthus and Acanthus.

The Spartans and their allies are to give Panactum back to the Athenians. The Athenians are to give back to the Spartans and their allies Coryphasium, Cythera, Methana, Pteleum and Atalante along with all the Spartan men who are in state prison in Athens or in a state prison in any other place under Athenian control; they should also release the Peloponnesians being besieged as Scione and all the other allies of the Spartans who are in Scione and those whom Brasidas sent in there; and they should release anyone from Sparta's allies who is in the state prison in Athens or anywhere else under Athenian control. The Spartans and their allies are to give back in like manner any Athenians or anyone from the allies of Athens whom they are holding.

In the case of the people of Scione, Torone, Sermyle and any other city the Athenians hold, the Athenians are to make whatever decisions they see fit about these and the other cities.

The Athenians shall swear oaths to the Spartans and their allies, city by city. Each party is to swear the oath in whatever is the most binding local form, seventeen men representing each city. The wording of the oath shall be as follows: "I will abide by this agreement and treaty justly and without deceit." The Spartans and their allies are to swear an oath to the Athenians on just the same terms, this oath to be renewed annually by both sides.

Stelai [13] are to be erected at Olympia, Delphi, the Isthmus, at Athens on the Acropolis and at Sparta on the Amyclaeum.

If they have omitted any point at all on any matter the oath allows for both parties to enter into just and proper discussion to make such changes as they may both agree, Athenians and Spartans.

The treaty begins at Sparta in the ephorship of Pleistolas on the fourth day from the end of the month Artemisium, and in Athens in the archonship of Alcaeus on the sixth day from the end of the month Elaphebolion.

Then an alliance was established between Athens and Sparta. The treaty between Athens and Sparta, entered into in 421 B.C. after the conclusion of the Peace of Nicias, established an alliance for offensive and defensive purposes. In the peace of Nicias, Sparta had sacrificed the interests of her allies in favour of her own; and hence it was regarded by them with jealousy and distrust. Four of the confederates, the Boeotians, the Corinthians, the Eleans, and the Megarians, refused to ratify it. Then Sparta entered into the alliance partly because of this circumstance, and partly because of the expiration of her Thirty Years' Truce with Argos, as she feared a renewal of hostilities by the latter. [14]

Accordingly since envoys were present from the Athenians, a conference was held and they came to an agreement, and oaths were sworn and an alliance made on the following terms:

The Lacedaemonians and Athenians shall be allies for fifty years on the following conditions:

1. If any enemy invade[15] the territory of the Lacedaemonians and be doing them harm, the Athenians shall help the Lacedaemonians in whatever way they can most effectively, with all their might; but if the enemy, after ravaging the country, shall have departed, that city shall be the enemy of the Lacedaemonians and Athenians, and shall suffer at the hands of both, and neither city shall make peace with it without the other. These conditions shall be observed honestly, zealously, and without fraud.
2. If any enemy invade the territory of the Athenians and be doing them harm, the Lacedaemonians shall help the Athenians in whatever way they can most effectively, with all their might; but if the enemy, after ravaging the country, shall have departed, that city shall be the enemy of the Lacedaemonians and Athenians, and shall suffer at the hands of both, and neither city shall make peace with it without the other. These conditions shall be observed honestly, zealously, and without fraud.
3. If there shall be an insurrection of slaves, the Athenians shall aid the Lacedaemonians with all their might, to the utmost of their power.
4. These articles shall be sworn to by the same persons who swore to the other treaty on both sides. They shall be renewed every year, the Lacedaemonians going to Athens at the Dionysia, the Athenians to Lacedaemon at the Hyacinthia.
5. Each party shall erect a pillar, that in Lacedaemon by the temple of Apollo of Amyclae, that at Athens on the Acropolis by the temple of Athena.
6. If it shall seem good to the Lacedaemonians and Athenians to add or take away anything pertaining to the alliance, it shall be consistent with the oaths of both to do whatever may seem good to both.
7. For the Lacedaemonians the following persons took the oath: Pleistoanax, Agis, Pleistolas, Damagetus, Chionis, Metagenes, Acanthus, Daithus, Ischagoras, Philocharidas, Zeuxidas, Antippus, Alcinadas, Tellis, Empedias, Menas, Laphilus; for the Athenians, Lampon, Isthmionicus, Laches, Nicias, Euthydemus, Procles, Pythodorus, Hagnon, Myrtilus, Thrasycles,

Theagenes, Aristocrates, Iolcius, Timocrates, Leon, Lamachus, Demosthenes.[16]

In 420 B.C., some eight years before the dissolution of the first Athenian League, Athens entered into a hundred years' alliance with the Argive confederacy. This is a very interesting example of a convention in respect of the nature of the provisions laid down, and of diplomatic relations in general. The text of the treaty is thus recorded by Thucydides:[17]

Σπονδὰς ἐποιήσαντο ἑκατὸν Ἀθηναῖοι ἔτη καὶ Ἀργεῖοι καὶ Μαντινεῖς καὶ Ἠλεῖοι πρὸς ἀλλήλους, ὑπὲρ σφῶν αὐτῶν καὶ τῶν ξυμμάχων ὧν ἄρχουσιν ἑκάτεροι, ἀδόλους καὶ ἀβλαβεῖς καὶ κατὰ γῆν καὶ κατὰ θάλασσαν.

Ὅπλα δὲ μὴ ἐξέστω ἐπιφέρειν ἐπὶ πημονῇ μήτε Ἀργείους καὶ Ἠλείους καὶ Μαντινέας καὶ τοὺς ξυμμάχους ἐπὶ Ἀθηναίους καὶ τοὺς ξυμμάχους ὧν ἄρχουσιν Ἀθηναῖοι, μήτε Ἀθηναίους καὶ τοὺς ξυμμάχους ὧν ἄρχουσιν Ἀθηναῖοι ἐπὶ Ἀργείους, Ἠλείους καὶ Μαντινέας καὶ τοὺς ξυμμάχους, τέχνῃ μηδὲ μηχανῇ μηδεμιᾷ.

Κατὰ τάδε ξυμμάχους εἶναι Ἀθηναίους καὶ Ἀργείους καὶ Ἠλείους καὶ Μαντινέας ἑκατὸν ἔτη. ἢν πολέμιοι ἴωσιν ἐς τὴν γῆν τῶν Ἀθηναίων, βοηθεῖν Ἀργείους καὶ Ἠλείους καὶ Μαντινέας Ἀθήναζε, καθ'ὅ,τι ἂν ἐπαγγέλλωσιν Ἀθηναῖοι, τρόπῳ ὁποίῳ ἂν δύνωνται ἰσχυροτάτῳ κατὰ τὸ δυνατόν. ἢν δὲ δῃώσαντες οἴχωνται, πολεμίαν εἶναι ταύτην τὴν πόλιν Ἀργείοις καὶ Μαντινεῦσι καὶ Ἠλείοις καὶ Ἀθηναίοις καὶ κακῶς πάσχειν ὑπὸ ἁπασῶν τῶν πόλεων τούτων. καταλύειν δὲ μὴ ἐξεῖναι τὸν πόλεμον πρὸς ταύτην τὴν πόλιν μηδεμιᾷ τῶν πόλεων, ἢν μὴ ἁπάσαις δοκῇ.

Βοηθεῖν δὲ καὶ Ἀθηναίους ἐς Ἄργος καὶ ἐς Μαντίνειαν καὶ ἐς Ἦλιν, ἢν πολέμιοι ἴωσιν ἐπὶ τὴν γῆν τὴν Ἠλείων ἢ τὴν Μαντινέων ἢ τὴν Ἀργείων, καθ'ὅ,τι ἂν ἐπαγέλλωσιν αἱ πόλεις αὗται, τρόπῳ ὁποίῳ ἂν δύνωνται ἰσχυροτάτῳ κατὰ τὸ δυνατόν. ἢν δὲ δῃώσαντες οἴχωνται, πολεμίαν εἶναι ταύτην τὴν πόλιν Ἀθηναίοις καὶ Ἀργείοις καὶ Μνατινεῦσι καὶ Ἠλείοις καὶ κακῶς πάσχειν ὑπὸ ἁπασῶν τούτων τῶν πόλεων. καταλύειν δὲ μὴ ἐξεῖναι τὸν πόλεμον πρὸς ταύτην τὴν πόλιν μηδεμιᾷ τῶν πόλεων, ἢν μὴ ἁπάσαις δοκῇ.

Ὅπλα δὲ μὴ ἐᾶν ἔχοντας διιέναι ἐπὶ πολέμῳ διὰ τῆς γῆς τῆς σφετέρας αὐτῶν καὶ τῶν ξυμμάχων ὧν ἄρχουσιν ἕκαστοι, μηδὲ κατὰ θάλασσαν, ἢν μὴ ψηφισαμένων τῶν πόλεων ἁπασῶν τὴν δίοδον εἶναι, Ἀθηναίων καὶ Ἀργείων καὶ Μαντινέων καὶ Ἠλείων.

Τοῖς δὲ βοηθοῦσιν ἡ πόλις ἡ πέμπουσα παρεχέτω μέχρι μὲν τριάκοντα ἡμερῶν σῖτον ἐπὴν ἔλθωσιν ἐς τὴν πόλιν τὴν ἐπαγγείλασαν βοηθεῖν, καὶ ἀπιοῦσι κατὰ ταῦτα. ἢν δὲ πλέονα βούλωνται χρόνον τῇ στρατιᾷ χρῆσθαι, ἡ πόλις ἡ μεταπεμψαμένη διδότω σῖτον, τῷ μὲν ὁπλίτῃ καὶ ψιλῷ καὶ τοξότῃ τρεῖς ὀβολοὺς Αἰγιναίους τῆς ἡμέρας ἑκάστης τῷ δ'ἱππεῖ δραχμὴν Αἰγιναίαν.

Ἡ δὲ πόλις ἡ μεταπεμψαμένη τὴν στρατιὰν τὴν ἡγεμονίαν ἐχέτω, ὅταν ἐν τῇ αὑτῆς ὁ πόλεμος ᾖ. ἢν δὲ ποῖ δόξῃ ἁπάσαις ταῖς πόλεσι κοινῇ στρατεύεσθαι, τὸ ἴσον τῆς ἡγεμονίας μετεῖναι ἁπάσαις ταῖς πόλεσιν.

Ὀμόσαι δὲ τὰς σπονδὰς Ἀθηναίους μὲν ὑπὲρ τῶν σφῶν αὐτῶν καὶ τῶν ξυμμάχων, Ἀργεῖοι δὲ καὶ Μαντινεῖς καὶ Ἠλεῖοι καὶ οἱ ξύμμαχοι τούτων κατὰ πόλεις ὀμνύντων. ὀμνύντων δὲ τὸν ἐπιχώριον ὅρκον ἕκαστοι τὸν μέγιστον κατὰ ἱερῶν τελείων. ὁ δὲ ὅρκος ἔστω ὅδε. ʽΕμμενῶ τῇ ξυμμαχίᾳ κατὰ τὰ

Chapter 4

ξυγκείμενα δικαίως καὶ ἀβλαβῶς καὶ ἀδόλως, καὶ οὐ παραβήσομαι τέχνῃ οὐδὲ μηχανῇ οὐδεμιᾷ.

Ὀμνύντων δὲ Ἀθήνησι μὲν ἡ βουλὴ καὶ αἱ ἔνδημοι ἀρχαί, ἐξορκούντων δὲ οἱ πρυτάνεις. ἐν Ἄργει δὲ ἡ βουλὴ καὶ οἱ ὀγδοήκοντα καὶ οἱ ἀρτῦναι, ἐξορκούντων δὲ οἱ ὀγδοήκοντα. ἐν δὲ Μαντινείᾳ οἱ δημιουργοὶ καὶ ἡ βουλὴ καὶ αἱ ἄλλαι ἀρχαί, ἐξορκούντων δὲ οἱ θεωροὶ καὶ οἱ πολέμαρχοι. ἐν δὲ Ἤλιδι οἱ δημιουργοὶ καὶ οἱ ἑξακόσιοι, ἐξορκούντων δὲ οἱ δημιουργοὶ καὶ οἱ θεσμοφύλακες.

Ἀνανεοῦσθαι δὲ τοὺς ὅρκους Ἀθηναίους μὲν ἰόντας ἐς Ἤλιν καὶ ἐς Μαντίνειαν καὶ ἐς Ἄργος τριάκοντα ἡμέραις πρὸ Ὀλυμπίων, Ἀργείους δὲ καὶ Ἡλείους καὶ Μαντινέας ἰόντας Ἀθήναζε δέκα ἡμέραις πρὸ Παναθηναίων τῶν μεγάλων.

Τὰς δὲ ξυνθήκας τὰς περὶ τῶν σπονδῶν καὶ τῶν ὅρκων καὶ τῆς ξυμμαχίας ἀναγράψαι ἐν στήλῃ λιθίνῃ Ἀθηναίους μὲν ἐν πόλει, Ἀργείους δὲ ἐν ἀγορᾷ ἐν τοῦ Ἀπόλλωνος τῷ ἱερῷ, Μαντινέας δὲ ἐν τοῦ τῳ ἱερῷ ἐν τῇ ἀγορᾷ. καταθέντων δὲ καὶ Ὀλυμπίασι στήλην χαλκῆν κοινῇ Ὀλυμπίοις τοῖς νυνί.

Ἐὰν δέ τι ἄμεινον εἶναι ταῖς πόλεσι ταύταις προσθεῖναι πρὸς τοῖς ξυγκειμένοις, ὅ,τι ἂν δόξῃ ταῖς πόλεσιν ἁπάσαις κοινῇ βουλευομέναις, τοῦτο κύριον εἶναι.[18]

The Athenians, Argives, Mantineans, and Eleans have made a treaty with one another for a hundred years, on behalf of themselves and the allies over whom they have authority respectively, to be observed without fraud or hurt both by land and sea.

It shall not be allowed to bear arms with harmful intent, either for the Argives, Eleans, Mantineans, and their allies against the Athenians and the allies over whom the Athenians have authority, or for the Athenians and the allies over whom the Athenians have authority against the Argives, Eleans, Mantineans, and their allies, by any art or device.

The Athenians, Argives, Eleans, and Mantineans shall be allies for a hundred years on the following terms: If an enemy invade the territory of the Athenians, the Argives, Eleans, and Mantineans shall bring aid to Athens, according as the Athenians may send them word, in whatever way they can most effectually, to the limit of their power; but if the invaders shall have ravaged the land and gone, that city shall be hostile to the Argives, Mantineans, Eleans, and Athenians, and shall suffer at the hands of all these states; and to discontinue hostilities against that state shall not be allowed to any one of these states, unless all agree.

Likewise the Athenians shall bring aid to Argos and to Mantinea and Elis, if an enemy come against the territory of the Eleans or that of the Mantineans or that of the Argives, according as these states send word, in whatever way they can most effectually; but if the invader shall have ravaged the land and gone, that city shall be hostile to the Athenians, Argives, Mantineans, and Eleans, and shall suffer ill at the hands of all these states; and to discontinue hostilities against that state shall not be allowed to any of these states, unless all agree.

It shall not be permitted to pass under arms with hostile intent through their own territory or that of the allies over whom they severally have authority, nor by sea, unless passage shall have been voted by all of these states, Athenians, Argives, Mantineans, and Eleans.

For the relieving force the state which sends for them shall furnish provisions for thirty days after their arrival in the state which sent for succor, and in like manner on their return; but if they wish to use the army for a longer period, the city which sends for it shall furnish provisions for heavy-armed or light-armed troops or bowmen, three Aeginetan obols per day, and for a cavalryman one Aeginetan drachma. The state which sent for the troops shall have command whenever the war is in its territory. But if it shall seem good to all the states to make a joint expedition anywhere, all the states shall share the command equally.

The Athenians shall swear to the treaty for themselves and their allies, but the Argives, Mantineans, Eleans, and their allies shall swear to it individually by states. And they shall severally swear the oath that is most binding in their own country, over full-grown victims. And the oath shall be as follows: "I will abide by the alliance in accordance with its stipulations, justly and without injury and without guile, and will not transgress it by any art or device."

The oath shall be sworn at Athens by the senate and the home magistrates, the prytanes administering it; at Argos by the senate and the eighty and the artynae, the eighty administering the oath; at Mantinea by the demiurgi and the senate and the other magistrates, the theory and the polemarchs administering the oath; at Elis by the demiurgi and the six hundred, the demiurgi and the thesmophylaces administering the oath.

For renewal of the oath the Athenians shall go to Elis, to Mantinea, and to Argos, thirty days before the Olympic games; and the Argives, Eleans, and Mantineans shall go to Athens ten days before the great Panathenaea.

The stipulations respecting the treaty, the oaths, and the alliance shall be inscribed on a stone column, by the Athenians on the Acropolis, by the Argives in the market-place, in the temple of Apollo, by the Mantineans in the market-place, in the temple of Zeus; and a brazen pillar shall be set up by them jointly at the Olympic games of this year.

It shall seem advisable to these states to add anything further to these agreements, whatever shall seem good to all the states in joint deliberation shall be binding.[19]

After the great battle of Mantineia, 418 B.C., first peace, then a fifty years' alliance were made between Sparta and Argos. A Lacedaemonian envoy, who was the proxenus of the Argives, arrived in Argos, and offered them peace or war. After some discussion the Argives accepted the conditions of peace, as proposed by Lacedaemon.[20]

Κατταδε δοκεῖ τᾷ ἐκκλησίᾳ τῶν Λακεδαιμονίων ξυμβαλέσθαι ποττὼς Ἀργείως.

Ἀποδιδόντας τὼς παῖδας τοῖς Ὀρχομενίοις καὶ τὼς ἄνδρας τοῖς Μαιναλίοις, καὶ τὼς ἄνδρας τὼς ἐν Μαντινείᾳ τοῖς Λακεδαιμονίοις ἀποδιδόντας.

Καὶ ἐξ Ἐπιδαύρω ἐκβῶντας καὶ τὸ τεῖχος ἀναιροῦντας. αἰ δὲ κα μὴ εἴκωντι τοὶ Ἀθηναῖοι ἐξ Ἐπιδαύρω, πολεμίως εἶμεν τοῖς Ἀργείοις καὶ τοῖς

Λακεδαιμονίοις καὶ τοῖς τῶν Λακεδαιμονίων ξυμμάχοις καὶ τοῖς τῶν Ἀργείων ξυμμάχοις.

Καὶ αἴ τινα τοὶ Λακεδαιμόνιοι παῖδα ἔχοντι, ἀποδόμεν ταῖς πολίεσσι πάσαις.

Περὶ δὲ τῷ σιῶ συμᾶτος, αἱ μὲν λήν, τοῖς Ἐπιδαυρίοις ὅρκον δόμεν, αἱ δέ, αὕτως ὀμόσαι.

Τὰς δὲ πόλιας τὰς ἐν Πελοποννάσω, καὶ μικρὰς καὶ μεγάλας, αὐτονόμως εἶμεν πάσας καττὰ πάτρια.

Αἱ δὲ κα τῶν ἐκτὸς Πελοποννάσω τις ἐπὶ τὰν Πελοπόνησον γὰν ἴη ἐπὶ κακῷ, ἀλεξέμεναι ἀμόθι βουλευσαμένως, ὅπα κα δικαιότατα δοκῇ τοῖς Πελοποννησίοις.

Ὅσοι δ'ἐκτὸς Πελοποννάσω τῶν Λακεδαιμονίων ξύμμαχοι ἔντι, ἐν τῷ αὐτῷ ἐσσούνται ἐν τῷπερ καὶ τοὶ τῶν Λακεδαιμονίων καὶ τοὶ τῶν Ἀργείων ξύμμαχοι ἔντι, τὰν αὐτῶν ἔχοντες.

Ἐπιδείξαντας δὲ τοῖς ξυμμάχοις ξυμβαλέσθαι, αἱ κα αὐτοῖς δοκῇ. αἱ δέ τι δοκῇ τοῖς ξυμμάχοις, οἴκαδ'ἀπιάλλην.[21]

It seems good to the assembly of the Lacedaemonians to make an agreement with the Argives on the following terms:

1. The Argives shall restore to the Orchomenians their children and to the Maenalians their men, and to the Lacedaemonians the men they deposited at Mantinea.
2. They shall evacuate Epidaurus and demolish the fortification there. And if the Athenians do not withdraw from Epidaurus, they shall be enemies to the Argives and Lacedaemonians, and to the allies of the Lacedaemonians and to the allies of the Argives.
3. If the Lacedaemonians have in custody any children, they shall restore these in all cases to their cities.
4. As to the offering to the god, if they wish they shall impose an oath upon the Epidaurians; but if not, they shall swear it themselves.
5. The cities in the Peloponnesus, both small and great, shall be independent according to their hereditary usages.
6. If anyone from outside the Peloponnesus comes against Peloponnesian territory with evil intent, they shall repel the invader, taking counsel together, in whatever way shall seem to the Peloponnesians most just.
7. Such states as are allies of the Lacedaemonians outside of the Peloponnesus shall be on the same footing as are the other allies of the Lacedaemonians and of the Argives, all retaining their own territory.
8. They shall communicate this agreement to their allies and make terms with them, if it seem best. But if the allies prefer, they may send the treaty home for consideration.

The Argives having assented to these conditions, the Lacedaemonian army was withdrawn, and negotiations commenced for the establishment of an alliance, offensive and defensive, with the former, who renounced their own former alliance with Athens, Elis, and Mantinea. The second treaty between

Sparta and Argos was of wider scope, providing for the independence of the Peloponnesian cities, and for the submission of international disputes to an arbitral tribunal.[22] It seemed good to the Lacedaemonians and the Argives to conclude a treaty and an alliance for fifty years on the following terms:

Ἐπὶ τοῖς ἴσοις καὶ ὁμοίοις δίκας διδόντας καττὰ πάτρια. Ταὶ δὲ ἄλλαι πόλιες ταὶ ἐν Πελοποννάσω κοινανεόντων τᾶν σπονδᾶν καὶ τὰς ξυμμαχίας αὐτόνομοι καὶ αὐτοπόλιες, τᾶν αὐτῶν ἔχοντες, καττὰ πάτρια δίκας διδόντες τὰς ἴσας καὶ ὁμοίας.

Ὅσσοι δὲ ἔξω Πελοποννάσω Λακεδαιμονίους ξύμμαχοι ἔντι, ἐν τοῖς αὐτοῖς ἐσσούνται τοῖσπερ καὶ τοὶ Λακεδαιμόνιοι. καὶ τοὶ τῶν Ἀργείων ξύμμαχοι ἐν τῷ αὐτῷ ἐσσούνται τῶπερ καὶ τοὶ Ἀργεῖοι, τᾶν αὐτῶν ἔχοντες.

Αἰ δὲ πο στρατείας δέη κοινάς, βουλεύεσθαι Λακεδαιμονίως καὶ Ἀργείως ὅπα κα δικαιότατα κρίναντας τοῖς ξυμμάχοις.

Αἰ δέ τινι τᾶν πολίων ἢ ἀμφίλογα, ἢ τᾶν ἐντὸς ἢ τᾶν ἐκτὸς Πελοποννάσω, αἴτε περὶ ὅρων αἴτε περὶ ἄλλου τινός, διακριθῆμεν. αἰ δέ τις τῶν ξυμμάχων πόλις πόλι ἐρίζοι, ἐς πόλιν ἐλθεῖν, ἄν τινα ἴσαν ἀμφοῖν ταῖς πολίεσσι δοκείοι.

Τὼς δὲ ἔτας καττὰ πάτρια δικάζεσθαι.[23]

1. They shall offer settlements by law under conditions that are fair and impartial, according to hereditary usage. The rest of the cities in the Peloponnesus shall share in the treaty and alliance, being independent and self-governed, retaining their own territory, and offering settlements by law that are fair and impartial according to hereditary usage.
2. Such states as are allies of the Lacedaemonians outside of the Peloponnesus shall stand upon the same footing as the Lacedaemonians; and the allies of the Argives shall be upon the same footing as the Argives, all retaining their own territory.
3. If there be need to send a common expedition to any quarter, the Lacedaemonians and the Argives shall consult and adjudge to the allies their allotments in whatever way is fairest.
4. If there be any dispute on the part of any one of the cities, either of those within the Peloponnesus or without, whether about boundaries or anything else, the matter shall be judicially decided. But if any city of the allies quarrel with another, they shall appeal to some city which both deem to be impartial.
5. Individual citizens shall conduct their suits according to hereditary usage.[24]

A further example may be furnished by the exchange of oaths sworn between Sparta and Argos and the Chalcidians:[25]

Αἱ μὲν σπονδαὶ καὶ ἡ ξυμμαχία αὕτη ἐγεγένητο. καὶ ὁπόσα ἀλλήλων πολέμῳ ἢ εἴ τι ἄλλο εἶχον, διελύσαντο. κοινῇ δὲ ἤδη τὰ πράγματα τιθέμενοι ἐψηφίσαντο κήρυκα καὶ πρεσβείαν παρὰ Ἀθηναίων μὴ προσδέχεσθαι, ἢν μὴ ἐκ Πελοποννήσου ἐξιῶσι τὰ τείχη ἐκλιπόντες, καὶ μὴ ξυμβαίνειν τῷ μηδὲ πολεμεῖν ἀλλ' ἢ ἅμα. καὶ τά τε ἄλλα θυμῷ ἔφερον καὶ ἐς τὰ ἐπὶ Θρᾴκης χωρία καὶ ὡς Περδίκκαν ἔπεμψαν ἀμφότεροι πρέσβεις. καὶ ἀνέπεισαν Περδίκκαν ξυνομόσαι σφίσιν. οὐ μέντοι εὐθύς γε ἀπέστη τῶν Ἀθηναίων, ἀλλὰ διενοεῖτο, ὅτι καὶ τοὺς Ἀργείους ἑώρα. ἦν δὲ καὶ αὐτὸς τὸ ἀρχαῖον ἐξ Ἄργους. καὶ τοῖς Χαλκιδεῦσι τούς τε παλαιοὺς ὅρκους ἀνανεώσαντο καὶ ἄλλους ὤμοσαν.²⁶

Such was the treaty and alliance that was concluded; and all the places which either side had acquired from the other in war they restored, or if there was any other ground of difference between them, they came to an agreement about it. Acting now in concert in their affairs, they voted not to receive herald or embassy from the Athenians, unless they evacuated their forts and withdrew from the Peloponnesus; also not to make peace or carry on war with anyone except together. And not only did they prosecute other matters with energy, but both of them sent envoys to the places in Thrace and to Perdiccas. And they persuaded Perdiccas to swear alliance with them. He, however, did not desert the Athenians at once, but was thinking of it, because he saw the Argives had done so; for he was himself of Argive descent. With the Chalcidians, too, they renewed their ancient oaths, and swore new ones.²⁷

Notes

1. "Σπονδὰς ἐποιήσαντο . . . καὶ ὤμοσαν κατὰ πόλεις: Note that, as usual, Athens speaks for all her allies, who appear to have had no voice in the negotiations, not only the members of the Delian League, whether fully autonomous (now only Chios and Methymna) or not, but also Zakynthos, Kephallenia, and Kerkyra, and probably Akarnania. See iv. 119. 1 n. Sparta, on the other hand, only speaks first among her allies. The allies of Athens only appear in para. 3, 4, and 5. It is indeed possible (in view of 3 and 4) that we should read οἱ ξύμμαχοι (ἑκατέρων) here, in the heading; but this will not affect the truth of the statement that Athens speaks for all her allies" (A. W. Gomme, *A Historical Commentary on Thucydides*, Volume III, Oxford: Oxford University Press, 1956, 667).

2. See Gomme, *A Historical Commentary on Thucydides*, 667: "Τὸ δ'ἱερόν . . . αὐτονόμους εἶναι: the shrine and the community of Delphians are almost one, at least so bound with one another that one could not be free without the other. This clause is primarily directed against the Phokians (though they were allies of the Peloponnesians) and, through them, against Athens (cf. i. 112, 5, iii. 95. 1).

"Αὐτοτελεῖς καὶ αὐτοδίκους: words necessary to define the vague term αὐτόνομοι, which could, for example, be used of the members of the Delian League generally, or of the privileged members, as e.g. iii. 10. 5, or as it is used below, para. 5, of members with a particular privilege. Delphi was not to pay tribute either to a superior power as ὑποτελεῖς, or as a member of a federation as ξυντελεῖς (cf. iv. 76. 3); nor was any other state to interfere with her own administration of her affairs."

3. "ἀποδόντων δὲ: this begins the third part of the treaty—part 1, access to common shrines; 2, duration and general terms; 3, particular claims and concessions; 4, arrangements for the oath, publication, future amendments, and date of coming into force. The arrangement of the treaty is logical and lucid, though this does not mean that one should anticipate a completeness that an international jurist would nowadays acquire."

4. Gomme observes on μηδὲ τούς ξυμμάχους: "another mention of Athenian allies. This must be intended to prevent such an action as that of Dion (if be the right reading) against Thyssos, 35. 1, or Athens encouraging one of her allies to attack one of these six and thus avoiding open aggression herself against the terms of the treaty" (*A Historical Commentary on Thucydides*, 669).

5. See Gomme, *A Historical Commentary on Thucydides*, 670–671: "There remain to be discussed other difficulties in this section; and first the subdivision of the one-time allies of Athens which are mentioned. It is clear that Amphipolis belongs to a different class from those who are to have autonomy on condition of paying their tribute according to Aristeides' assessment; for not only was it not founded till 437, but it did not pay any tribute (at least never appears on our tribute lists; see n. on εξακοσίων ταλάντων ii. 13. 3); but scholars have differed about the other class or classes. Steup, arguing principally that cities which are to be 'handed over' to Athens could not later be given not only autonomy but the right of neutrality between Athens and Sparta (ξυμμάχους εἶναι μεδετέρων), says that ὅσας πόλεις παρέδοσαν Λακ cannot be the six named later, and emends τάς δὲ πόλεις φερούσας to τᾶσδε δὲ πόλεις φερούσας, beginning in a new clause here, with a new class of one-time allies, who have not yet been recovered by Athens but are to be enjoined later by Sparta to accept the peace (21. 1. 35 3); they were never to be 'handed over' or restored to Athens. He assumes as well a lacuna after Ἀμφίπολιν, containing the names of Oisyme and the four cities in Akte which had joined Brasidas (iv. 107. 3, 109. 3–5), about which we have heard nothing since and hearing nothing now in the treaty; Amphipolis will then belong to this class, which is that of the cities to be restored and handed over to Athens, to be as they were before they seceded to Brasidas. The best solution is to suppose that there are mentioned, in this section, not two, but three classes, as Steup suggested: (1) Amphipolis, the colony of Athens and of unique strategic importance, (2) cities which the Peloponnesians have already surrendered, and (3) (since they certainly had not surrendered four of the six named cities and had probably not surrendered any) six cities who are to pay tribute to Athens but with certain privileges and guarantees, and are to be enjoined by Sparta to accept these terms. This means accepting Steup's easy emendation τᾶσδε δὲ πόλεις,

mentioned above, and altering the punctuation (a full stop after ἔχοντας and a colon after αὐτονόμους εἶναι)."

6. "Τοὺς ἐν Σκιώνῃ πολιουρκουμένους Πελοποννησίων ἀφεῖναι: see iv. 121. 2, 131.3. Sparta had given up the cause of Scione as hopeless (cf. the use of ἔχουσιν, para. 8), and had probably abandoned Brasidas' claim that Scione had joined him before the truce of 423 came into force; and the Peloponnesian forces within could do very little to help and were consuming limited supplies of food; but this was a base betrayal of the city which had been welcomed by Brasidas, and had welcomed him, more warmly than any other (iv. 120. 3–121. 1). It is indeed remarkable that Sparta retained the Thracian district and acquired in Ionia any reputation at all for either sincerity or reliability (iv. 81. 3, 108 3–4)" (Gomme, *A Historical Commentary on Thucydides*, 674).

7. Adcock in *Cambridge Ancient History: Volume 5, Athens 478-401 BC* (Cambridge: Cambridge University Press, 1927), 251, well sums up the terms of the treaty: "The attack on the empire had failed, the Long Walls and the Athenian fleet remained intact, the treasury could be replenished; Athens had lost only two strategically important places in the ten years' war, Panakton and Amphipolis, and it was stipulated that they should be returned. Thucydides gives no such summary, not only because he knew that this Athenian victory was dubious. The Athenian defeats in action had occurred towards the end of the war and had not been followed by any success; and the peace was, from the first, obviously unstable." See the comment of Gomme, *A Historical Commentary on Thucydides*, 676 on ὅρκους δὲ ποιήσασθαι—κατὰ πόλεις: "This was done; Athens took the oath first with Sparta, then with each of Sparta's allies in turn. This had not been done for the year's truce, but something very like it was done in the treaty between Athens and Argos, Mantineia and Elis: in each case Athens was on one side, and a number of states on the other, and though these others were of course also at peace and allied with one another, that fact does not form part of the treaty. In the case of this treaty of 421 B.C. Athens had a special reason for asking for a separate oath-taking by each of her former enemies; for during the negotiations it became clear that some of them were reluctant to 'sign,' and four, three of who were her neighbours, finally refused; she had to know where she stood with each state. That is why we have only the Spartan 'signatories' in 19.2: this is a copy of the treaty with Sparta—πρός τούς Λακεδαιμονίους, 17. 2; there were other copies of the treaties with the other states."

8. "Στήλας δὲ στῆσαι Ὀλυμπιάσι: Of the panhellenic shrines two, at Olympia and Isthmos, were controlled by states which refused to take the oath, Elis and Corinth. The stelai may for all that have been set up there, though Kirchhoff thinks not (p. 65); Paionios' Nike at Olympia celebrated a victory of Messenians and Athenians in the Peloponnesian war (above, p. 487: though it may have been set up after 421, and after the Athenian treaty with Elis, Mantineia, and Argos). The Greeks had common customs, a sort of international courtesy, in such matters" (Gomme, *A Historical Commentary on Thucydides*, 677).

9. "Εὔορκον εἶναι ἀμφοτέροις: for the first time in this document Sparta agrees to a clause which altogether ignores her allies, and the latter took umbrage (29. 2); it is indeed a wonder that any of them agreed to it in 421. It savours altogether too much of the attitude expressed by the Spartan ambassadors from Pylos in 425, ἡμῶν γὰρ καὶ ὑμῶν ταὐτὰ λεγόντων τό γε ἄλλο Ἑλληνικὸν ἴστε ὅτι ὑποδεέστερον ὂν τὰ μέγιστα τιμήσει (iv. 20. 4)" (Gomme, *A Historical Commentary on Thucydides*, 677).

10. Thucydides, *History of the Peloponnesian War*, 4 vols., *Loeb Classical Library* 108, 109, 110, and 169, trans. C. Forster Smith (Cambridge: Harvard University Press, 1919–1923) (hereafter cited as Thucydides), 35–39.

11. Thucydides, *The War of the Peloponnesians and the Athenians*, 332.

12. Thucydides, 44–46.

13. Pillars inscribed with public notices.

14. Thucydides, *The War of the Peloponnesians and the Athenians*, 335–336: "The oaths taken and the terms of the alliance were as follows. The Spartans and Athenians shall be allies for fifty years on the following terms:

"If any enemies enter Spartan territory and do harm to the Spartans the Athenians will help the Spartans in whatever way they can with all possible strength at their disposal; and if the invader departs after acts of devastation then that city shall be counted an enemy to the Spartans and Athenians and shall suffer at both their hands, and both cities shall end hostilities at the same time. And these things are to be observed in a spirit of justice and commitment and without deceit.

"And if any enemies enter Athenian territory and do harm to the Athenians the Spartans will help the Athenians in whatever way they can with all possible strength at their disposal; and if the invader departs after acts of devastation then that city shall be counted an enemy to the Spartans and Athenians and shall suffer at both their hands, and both cities shall end hostilities at the same time. And these things are to be observed in a spirit of justice and commitment and without deceit.

"If there is an uprising of slaves the Athenians shall support the Spartans with all their strength to the best of their ability.

"Those who swore to the other treaty on both sides shall also swear to this one. The oath shall be renewed annually, with the Spartans going to Athens at the Dionysia and the Athenians going to Sparta at the Hyacinthia.

"Each side shall erect a stele, the one in Sparta at the temple of Apollo at Amyclae and the one at Athens at the temple of Athene on the Acropolis.

"If the Spartans and the Athenians are minded to add or delete anything to do with this alliance the oath allows them to do whatever they see fit.

"The following swore to the oaths: on behalf of the Spartans, Pleistoanax, Agis, Pleistolas, Damaetus, Chionis, Metagenes, Acanthus, Daithus, Ischagoras, Philocharidas, Zeuxidas, Antippus, Alcinadas, Tellis, Empedias, Menas and Laphilus; and the following on behalf of the Athenians, Lampon, Isthmionicus, Laches, Nicias, Euthydemus, Procles, Pythadorus, Hagnon, Myrtilus, Thrasycles, Theogenes, Aristocrates, Iolcius, Timocrates, Leon, Lamachus and Demosthenes."

15. See Gomme, *A Historical Commentary on Thucydides*, 692–693: "Stahl argued, from the statement in 39. 3, εἰρημένον ἄνευ ἀλλήλων μήτε σπένδεσθαι τῷ μήτε πολεμεῖν, and its repetition in 46. 2, that there must have been such a clause in the treaty (for had it been agreed later, in accord with para. 6, Thucydides must have mentioned it), and proposed to insert here, after καὶ Ἀθηναῖοι, some such words as ἐπὶ τοῖς ἴσοις καὶ ὁμοίοις, μήτε σπένδεσθαι τῷ ἄνευ κοινῆς γνώμης μήτε πολεμεῖν. Εἶναι δὲ τὴν ξυμμαχίαν πεντήκοντα ἔτη. We should thus as well have an explanation of δέ at the beginning of the next sentence, which Kruger (followed by Hude and Stuart Jones) felt obliged to bracket. Kirchhoff and Steup replied that no such comprehensive clause could possibly have been included in a purely defensive treaty of alliance (and neither Athens nor Sparta would have so tied her hands), and anyhow it would not have been the first clause—it might have come after para. 3. The former thought that the words in 39.3 and 46.2 could be confined to the case of the Boeotians and their occupation of Panakton; for Panakton being within Athenian territory, if the ten-day truce between Boeotia and Athens were once not renewed, the Boeotians would be enemies invading Attica, and Sparta would be bound by para. 2 of this ἐπιμαχία. Steup, as his manner was, would bracket the offending words in 39.3 and 46.2. Here I would say that I think δέ should be kept, for it introduces what is in effect a new clause: 'the treaty is to be for fifty years. If,' etc. I should prefer to read καὶ Ἀθηναῖοι. Εἶναι τὴν ξυμμαχίαν πεντήκοντα ἔτη. Ἢν δέ τινες, like 79. 1–2."

16. Thucydides, 45–47.

17. Thucydides, *The War of the Peloponnesians and the Athenians*, 354–356: "The Athenians and the Argives, Mantineans and Eleans shall be allies for one hundred years on the following terms. If enemies invade the territory of the Athenians, the Argives, Mantineans, and Eleans will come to the aid of Athens, in accordance with such requests as the Athenians may make, with all the strength at their disposal; and if the invaders have wasted the land and have departed, the city in question shall be declared an enemy of the Argives, Mantineans, Eleans, and the Athenians and shall suffer harm at the hands of all of them; and it will not be permitted for any of these cities to end the war against the offending city unless this is agreed by them all.

"The Athenians will come to the aid of Argos, Mantineia, and Elis if enemies invade the territories of the Argives, Mantineans, or Eleans, in accordance with such requests as these cities may make, with all the strength at their disposal; and if invaders have wasted the land and departed the land, the offending city shall be declared an enemy of the Athenians, Argives,

Mantineans, and Eleans and shall suffer harm at the hands of all of them; and it will not be permitted for any of them to end the war against that city unless that is agreed by all [the cities].

"No armed force shall be allowed to pass for purposes of war through the land either of their own or of the allies they each rule over, or by sea, unless approval for such passage is voted by all the cities—Athenians, Argives, Mantineans, and Eleans.

"The city that sends troops in support shall provision them for thirty days from the time they come to support the city that requested them, and similarly on their departure. If the city that sent for them wishes to have the use of the forces for any longer period of time it should maintain them, at the rate of three Aiginetan obols a day for each hoplite, light-armed soldier and archer, and one Aeginetan drachma a day for each cavalryman.

"The city summoning help shall have command of the forces when the war is in its territory; but if all the cities agree on a joint campaign elsewhere then all the cities shall participate equally in the command.

"The Athenians shall swear to the treaty on their own behalf and that of their allies; the Argives, Mantineans, and Eleans shall swear to it individually by city. And each city shall swear the oath over full-grown sacrificial victims in whatever local form is most binding. The wording of the oath shall be as follows: 'I shall abide by the alliance in accordance with the terms agreed, justly and without harmful intent or deceit, and I shall not transgress it by any means or contrivance.'

"The oaths shall be sworn at Athens by the council and the city magistrates, and they shall be administered by the prytanes. In Argos these shall be sworn by a council and the Eighty and the administrators, and administered by the Eighty. In Mantinea sworn by the representatives, the council and other officials, administered by the inspectors and the polemarchs. At Elis sworn by the representatives and the principal office holders and the Six Hundred, administered by the representatives and the trustees.

"To renew the oaths, the Athenians shall go to Elis, Mantinea, and Argos thirty years before the Olympic Games; the Argives, Eleans, and Mantineians shall go to Athens ten days before the Great Panathenaea."

18. Thucydides, 92–96.

19. Thucydides, 93–97.

20. Thucydides, *The War of the Peloponnesians and the Athenians*, 373–374: "It is resolved by the Spartan assembly to make an agreement with the Argives on the following terms.

"The Argives shall restore to the Orchomenians their children and to the Maenalians their men; and they shall restore to the Spartans the men they deposited in Mantinea.

"They shall also evacuate Epidaurus and demolish the fortifications there. And if the Athenians do not withdraw from Epidaurus they shall be enemies of the Argives and the Spartans and of the allies of the Spartans and of the allies of the Argives.

"And if the Spartans are holding any children they shall restore them in all cases to the cities they came from.

"Concerning the sacrifice to the god, the Argives shall if they wish get the Epidaurians to swear the oath; if not, they shall swear it themselves.

"The cities in the Peloponnese, whether large or small, shall all be independent in accordance with custom and practice.

"If anyone from outside the Peloponnese invades Peloponnesian territory with hostile intent they shall repel the invader after consulting each other about the most equitable arrangements for involving the other Peloponnesians.

"Those allies of the Spartans who are from outside the Peloponnese shall have the same status as the allies of the Spartans and Argives within it, and shall remain in possession of their territories.

"The two parties are to present these terms to their allies and make an agreement with them, if they so decide; but if the allies have any points to raise they should refer them back."

21. Thucydides, 142–144.

22. Thucydides, *The War of the Peloponnesians and the Athenians*, 374: "The Spartans and the Argives have resolved to make a treaty and an alliance for fifty years on the following terms.

"They shall settle legal disputes on fair and equal terms according to custom and practice. The other cities in the Peloponnese shall be parties to the treaty and the alliance as independent states in their own right, each retaining possession of their own territory, and shall settle legal disputes on a fair and equal basis in accordance with custom and practice.

"Those allies of the Spartans outside the Peloponnese shall have the same status as the Spartans in these matters; and the allies of the Argives shall have the same status as the Argives, and they shall retain possession of their own territory.

"If it is necessary to make a joint military expedition anywhere the Spartans and the Argives will consult about the fairest division of responsibilities between the allies.

"If any of the states, either within the Peloponnese or outside it, has a dispute either about boundaries or anything else, the matter shall be settled as follows: if any of the allied cities has a dispute with another one they shall appeal to some other state agreed by both sides to be impartial.

"Private citizens shall pursue their legal rights according to custom and practice."

23. Thucydides, 146.

24. Thucydides, 143–147.

25. See Thucydides, *The War of the Peloponnesians and the Athenians*, 374–375: "That was the treaty and the alliance they concluded; and they dealt with all the places either side had acquired from the other in the war and any other issues they had. Acting together now in the conduct of their affairs, the Spartans and the Argives voted not to offer access to herald or envoy from the Athenians unless they abandoned their efforts and withdrew from the Peloponnese; they also voted to make neither peace nor war with anyone unless they did so jointly. They then set to with a will and among other activities both of them sent envoys to places in Thrace and to Perdiccas, whom they succeeded in persuading to pledge allegiance to them. He did not immediately make a break with the Athenians, however, though he did contemplate it because he saw the Argives doing so and he was himself of Argive descent. With the Chalcidians too they renewed their ancient oaths of allegiance and swore new ones."

26. Thucydides, 146–148.

27. Thucydides, 147–149.

Chapter Five Point One

Personalities in Thucydides

ALCIBIADES

In this subchapter, it is my purpose to briefly present the personality of Alcibiades.[1] I share the opinion of MacGregor, "that at all stages of his career Alcibiades knew exactly what he was doing and did it with deliberation, and that he possessed an uncanny, as well as lucky, ability to forecast what would happen under given circumstances,"[2] and that he was not a mere opportunist. I should, therefore, relate and rely upon the events of Alcibiades's life. Alcibiades, son of Kleinias, was born in 450 B.C., an Alcmaeonid on the side of his mother. Plutarch[3] reports that he was μειράκιον when he served at Potidaea. He employs the same characterization when Alcibiades entered public life in about 420 B.C. At the time of the Peace of Nicias (421 B.C.), he was obviously mature enough to be considered as a forceful political personage, though Thucydides seems to take a rather critical view of his youth: "A man who would have been considered still young in another city, but who enjoyed prestige because of the reputation of his forbears." "Youth" used by way of criticism pursued him for a few more years. For example, in 415 B.C., Nicias said of him that he was too young to command: "The enterprise is a great one and not such as can be entrusted to a young man for planning and quick execution."[4] Alcibiades became a general in 420 B.C. and it may be supposed that thirty was the minimum age for one to hold this office.[5] It must have been a source of annoyance for Alcibiades to be charged of youth by Nicias some five years later, only before the expedition to Sicily. Indeed, Plutarch mentions some anecdotes about the youth of Alcibiades, and it may be noticed that the freedom from inhibition which marked his early years continued through his maturity. This is confirmed by Thucydides, certainly in the words of Nicias. It would only be a matter of speculation to say that he was affected by the education provided by sophists of his day, but he was surely influenced by the sophists.

In his twenties, Alcibiades fought at Potidaea and Delion, and was a witness at the political debate between the conservative Nicias and the nationalist demagogue Cleon. It ought to have been particularly instructive for a man of his intellect to watch Cleon, most influential among the people as Thucydides is willing to confess (τῷ πλήθει πιθανώτατος), persuading the Athenian demos with his powerful arguments. Alcibiades was to take advantage of this feature of the Athenian democratic constitution.

In 421 B.C., the Peace of Nicias was concluded between Athens and Sparta. Alcibiades did not approve of this treaty of alliance, and took advantage of the deterioration of the relation between the two city-states. He practically deceived the Lacedaemonian delegation and his opponents in Athens in 420 B.C. At the time, Argos was in alliance with Mantineia, Corinth, Elis, and the Chalcidice. Lacedaemon was forced into a treaty of alliance with the Boeotians, previously her allies, and therefore, could be accused of bad faith by the Athenians. Alcibiades called in representatives from Argos, Mantineia, and Elis to discuss the prospects of a treaty of alliance in Athens. Thereupon, Lacedaemon dispatched her own political representatives, much pro-Athenian, in order to reach a peaceful settlement to the dispute. Initially, the Lacedaemonians spoke before the council. Alcibiades, fearing a consequent loss of an alliance with Argos, persuaded them, by promising firm support to the materialization of their goals, to deny in the *ekklesia* their authority to settle the issue. The Lacedaemonian envoys were convinced and, in their address to the *ekklesia*, contradicted their statements which had already been made before the council. From then on Alcibiades assailed them for duplicity and untrustworthiness. The Lacedaemonians remained idle, providing no reply. The outcome was that, according to Alcibiades's plan, Athens concluded an alliance with Argos, Mantineia, and Elis.[6] Alcibiades's master plan indicates that he had a very strong perception of the character of Athenians and Lacedaemonians.

One question remained, why did he really ruin the perspective of reconciliation with Lacedaemon? On the one hand, Nicias argued that it was in the interest of Athens to postpone hostilities with Lacedaemon. This eventuality would be also in the interest of Lacedaemon. The report of Thucydides that Alcibiades was somewhat jealous of Nicias and his colleagues may be rejected as a little prejudicial, and I say prejudicial (if not malicious), because clearly Thucydides favored Pericles, whose policy was diametrically opposed to the one subsequently pursued by Alcibiades. However, Thucydides himself, in the same passage, states that Alcibiades could plan as a statesman and strategist: "It really seemed to him that it was much preferable to effect alliance with the Argives."[7] As MacGregor pointedly observes, Alcibiades regarded the Peace of Nicias as no peace at all, a transition to a period of what we call "cold war," a mere prelude to a resumption of hostilities.[8] He considered that an effective way of diminishing the power of Sparta was to destroy her hegemony in the Peloponnesus. Alliance between Athens on the one hand and Argos, Mantineia, and Elis on the other resulted in having Lacedaemon encircled. Having at our disposal, even ex post facto, the sequence of events up to the battle of Mantineia, it is difficult not to admit that the assessment of Alcibiades was accurate.

Despite the outcome of the battle of Mantineia, Alcibiades regarded that the issue was merely bad luck, but worth the risk. In 415 B.C., during an address to the *ekklesia*, speaking forcefully against Nicias, he stressed: "Consider whether I manage public affairs worse than anyone else. For it was I who united the greatest powers of the Peloponnese without your incurring considerable danger and expense, and I forced the Lacedaemonians to risk all they had on a single day at Mantineia. And, although they survived the battle, they do not even yet display firm confidence."[9] Plutarch also accurately presents this fact: "His accomplishment was a great one, to divide and confuse nearly the whole of the Peloponnese, to pit so many shields against the Lacedaemonians on a single day at Mantineia and to organize the battle and the danger very far from Athens; in that battle victory brought no significant gain to the victorious Lacedaemonians, whereas, if they had lost, it would have been a struggle for Lacedaemon to survive."[10]

Therefore, in 420 B.C., Athenian troops were deployed in the Peloponnese. The outcome of the blockade of Epidauros (winter of 419 B.C.) was that Alcibiades had to once again put in practice his diplomatic talents so as to maintain harmonious relation with the Argives. In the battle of Mantineia, Alcibiades does not appear to have been a general, though Athenian detachments did participate. He served as ambassador (πρεσβευτής) at Argos prior to the battle. The battle of Mantineia did not really help his political perspectives, but he was nevertheless elected *strategos* in 417 B.C., that is, a year after the battle. His policy and predictions had not, in fact, proved wrong. The Lacedaemonians had staked everything on a single battle.

The ostracism of Hyberbolos, deemed as the immediate outcome of the political crisis that erupted in Athens after the battle of Mantineia, though not of particular interest, unveils once again a plan most likely made by Alcibiades and executed with accuracy. Plutarch's account sheds light on the facts and indicates that Alcibiades was the one who took the initiative for the ostracism of Hyberbolos: συνήγαγε τάς στάσεις εἰς ταὐτὸν ὁ Ἀλκιβιάδης, καὶ διαλεχθεὶς πρὸς Νικίαν κατὰ τοῦ Ὑπερβόλου τὴν ὀστρακοφορίαν ἔτρεψεν.[11] It need be mentioned here, frankly by way of criticism, that Alcibiades was really destroying an institution that had stood as a safety mechanism for the city-state of Athens. For Alcibiades success was the primary aim. He was elected in the *strategia* in 417 B.C. He was reelected in 416 B.C., after the *ostrakophoria*. He survived the disaster at Mantineia, which proved to be at best a doubtful victory for the Lacedaemonians. In 416 B.C., having returned from Argos, Alcibiades fully justified his policy in the making of a treaty of alliance for fifty years between Athens and Argos. The Lacedaemonian power was in this way surely diminished, given that the Argives later took part in the Sicilian expedition on the side of the Athenians.

Further, it looks as though Alcibiades was especially involved in the assault on the island of Melos, though it is not to be found in the *History of the Peloponnesian War* that this was the policy of Alcibiades specifically. Alcibiades was a general in that year and he had commanded a naval attack in the Argolid against pro-Lacedaemonian Argives.[12] What one can infer from Thucydides, though, is that Andokides charged that Alcibiades favored the enslavement of the Melians.[13] Plutarch seems to be making the same point when he reports that Alcibiades supported the execution of the male population of Melos.[14] If these versions are to be believed, and I cannot see why not, then this act of Alcibiades can be interpreted in view of his policy to weaken Lacedaemon's allies. The island of Melos was one such ally.

The crucial affair, from which one may reach various inferences about the personality of Alcibiades, is the Sicilian expedition. Thucydides reports: "Alcibiades, son of Kleinias, was most zealous in advocating the expedition. He had two motives: his desire to oppose Nicias, for they were political rivals and Nicias had referred to him slightingly; and, especially, his eagerness to command and his expectation that his efforts would acquire Sicily and Carthage and his success would win him wealth and fame."[15] The Sicilian expedition is commonly regarded as the cause of the disaster of the city of Athens. Simultaneously, Alcibiades is regarded as the individual responsible for this disaster, mainly because he allegedly chose to pursue his ambitions instead of safeguarding the well-being of his city. It shall be proved later in this chapter, however, that this is not the position taken by the author of the present monograph. It was precisely the absence of Alcibiades from the command of the expedition, suffice it here to say, which ruined Athens, as Thucydides reports much to his credit. And this was the mere outcome of plots of ambitious politicians that along with the Athenian people must be held responsible for the outcome of the Sicilian disaster and its calamitous consequences on the city-state of Athens.

These were the arguments of Alcibiades before the Athenian assembly, as recorded by Thucydides:

1. The population of the cities of Sicily is a motley one, ill prepared for defense and without patriotism.
2. We shall be joined by the non-Hellenic peoples of Sicily.
3. The enemies we shall leave behind will be powerless to do us more harm than they could now, thanks to our navy.

4. We have a duty to our allies in Sicily, and it is fulfillment of such obligations that wins empires.
5. The expedition will have a depressing effect upon our enemies at home.
6. Because of the navy, we shall be able to withdraw at will.
7. In increasing lies security for the imperial power.
8. Ultimately, with overwhelming resources, we shall strike at the Peloponnese.

The outcome of the Sicilian expedition was of course disastrous, but the incident which mostly contributed to it was the recall of Alcibiades. What actually happened prior to the expedition? Alcibiades had planned the actions of the Athenian fleet. Before the departure of the fleet, the mutilation of the Herms, Thucydides reports, brought him his first reverse at the hands of Fortune.[16] The outcry, for which Alcibiades was certainly not responsible, gave his many political enemies the opportunity to act against him. The Thucydidean history is clear on this. In 6.29.3 it is mentioned: "βουλόμενοι ἐκ μείζονος διαβολῆς . . . μετάπεμπτον κομισθέντα αὐτὸν ἀγωνίσασθαι," which is to say that "they wished him to face trial on a graver accusation." The noun διαβολή and the verb διαβάλλω in Thucydides imply that the charge is false, based on prejudice. The parodying of the mysteries, though, of which Alcibiades had almost surely been guilty,[17] was not helpful to him. However, the history by Thucydides vividly describes and reveals the motives of his opponents: "They took the crime quite seriously; for it seemed to be an omen for the expedition and to have been committed as a plot both to bring about revolution and to destroy the democracy."[18] Alcibiades was accused of this parody: "The case was welcomed by Alcibiades' most bitter opponents—bitter because he prevented them from securing firm control of the demos; they thought that if they got rid of him they would be supreme and so they exaggerated and cried out that the mysteries had been violated and the Herms mutilated as a contribution to the destruction of the demos."[19] Thucydides also reports that the fear of tyranny aggravated Athenian suspicions: "At that time the people were angry and suspicious towards those who had been blamed in connection with the mysteries; and the whole business seemed to them to have been perpetrated as part of an oligarchic and tyrannical plot."[20] To the same effect, Thucydides writes about Alcibiades, introducing him in the debate on the expedition to Sicily: "Most people were afraid of him, because of the extent of his personal licentiousness and the motives by which he acted on every occasion; so they became his enemies on the grounds that he was aspiring to tyranny."[21]

Consequently, it must be stressed, the people have to be held responsible for the fact that Alcibiades was then recalled and lost command of the fleet at the Sicilian expedition. The Athenian people were those that were willing to accept that he was allegedly guilty. Thucydides presents oligarchy and tyranny as the feared aims of Alcibiades.[22] Simultaneously, it needs to be emphasized that those who first incited the people (in fact, the *ekklesia*) against Alcibiades were the political enemies of Alcibiades, that is, the demagogues. Particularly, Androkles, later assassinated, is named by Plutarch as Alcibiades's mortal enemy.[23]

Lacedaemon is the place where Alcibiades next stops, having evaded imprisonment. He has been occasionally accused of treason, but it is my purpose here to show that he was far from a traitor. He had always remained a fervent Athenian. His actions at and for Lacedaemon were done merely because he was unfairly treated by his political opponents at Athens and by the Athenian people. In a persuasive address, he urged the Lacedaemonians to dispatch a commander and troops to Syracuse in Sicily and to fortify Deceleia. The Lacedaemonians were, indeed, convinced. Gylippos was sent to Syracuse and arrived there in 414 B.C.[24] Also, Deceleia was fortified by Agis. The effect of the latter was that the morale in the city of Athens went through a phase of decline and, correspondingly, the effect of the former was that Gylippos strengthened Syracusan resistance against Athenian expansionist policy. It is worth noting in this context the precise phrases used by Alcibiades in his speech toward the Lacedaemonians: Οὐδὲ ὑποπτεύεσθέ μοι ἐς τὴν φυγαδικὴν προθυμίαν τὸν λόγον. Φυγαδικὴ προθυμία, according to the Liddell and Scott Greek-English Lexicon is the wish of someone to commit treason against his own city-state. Alcibiades, here, quite on the contrary confirms that his actions have nothing to do with willingness to betray his city. He explains exactly the grounds upon which his actions are founded, that is the reason he really provides succor to the Lacedaemonians. He says: "φυγάς εἰμὶ τῆς τῶν ἐξελασάντων πονηρίας καὶ οὐ τῆς ὑμετέρας ὠφελείας, ἣν πείθησθέ μοι." Lucidly, this genitive of cause reveals that his motives were, far from causing harm as such to his own city, to avenge the malpractices of his political opponents that were actually responsible for his exile and fleeing to Lacedaemon. It will afterwards, in this paper, become evident that he was eager to go back to Athens, his motherland.

For the moment, his hatred against his unjust political enemies directed him towards sailing with a Spartan contingent to Ionian waters (412 B.C.), where he fostered the wide-spread revolt from Athens that was stimulated by the defection of Chios and Erythrai.[25] He supported a military alliance between Lacedaemon and the Persian satrap Tissaphernes, on the basis of the argument that an alliance of this kind along with the revolt in Ionia would bring the Athenian empire to an end. However, in Lacedaemon, his seduction of Timaia, wife of Agis, had led to the passing of a death penalty on him in 412 B.C. He escaped to the court of Tissaphernes, where he advised the Persian satrap on how to keep the Hellenes divided among themselves and, consequently, play a hegemonic role in Greek political matters. His strategy, from the Persian point of view, was effective. Thucydides, however, recognizes that Alcibiades enjoyed no security with Tissaphernes nor was he particularly interested in working for Persian expediency and political interest: "For his relationship with Tissaphernes was not very secure."[26]

In Athens he was under a sentence of death. It was to Athens, though, that he turned his attention: "At the same time he was fostering thoughts of his return to his native land. For he knew that, if he did not destroy it (ει μή διαφθερει), he could one day win restoration by his powers of persuasion. In particular he thought that he could persuade the Athenians on some such grounds as this, that Tissaphernes was obviously his friend. And this is what actually happened."[27]

The policy of Alcibiades of withholding full Persian support from the Peloponnesians marked his wish to work for his recall in Athens. If there was any chance for him to be recalled, this seemed to be most impossible under the democratic constitution of the day, which was responsible for his condemnation and death sentence. The stance taken then in Athens is shown by the violent protests that greeted Peisandros when he reached Athens with the proposals of Alcibiades. The political opponents of Alcibiades cried out against his return immediately, and were joined by the Kerykes on sacred grounds.[28]

As a consequence, Alcibiades took the plunge to take steps so as to ensure that the government was overthrown. The oligarchic conspiracy was initiated on Samos with the assistance of Pisander, democracy was subverted, and the Four Hundred took up the executive power. Alcibiades took part in the plot in its every detail. General Phrynichos, whom Thucydides respected (8.68.3), and whose political sentiments were with the oligarchy, did not exhibit any will to coordinate with Alcibiades in this conspiracy. He considered that Alcibiades did not really care about oligarchy.[29] In this he was certainly right, but the Athenians could not be persuaded by him. While Pisander worked closely with Alcibiades, Phrynichos sent a letter to the Lacedaemonian commander of the army Astyochos and to the Persian satrap Tissaphernes claiming that Alcibiades was not to be trusted. Thucydides writes: "Alcibiades seemed to be untrustworthy; knowing the enemy's plans in advance, he had apparently, in personal enmity, fixed the blame on Phrynichos as a conspirator."[30] There ensues a conference among Pisander, the oligarchs, Alcibiades, and Tissaphernes, at which Pisander (along with his oligarchic faction) concluded that they had been deceived, left the conference steeped in anger, and took the decision not to allow Alcibiades to participate in the new oligarchic constitution on the grounds that he was unreliable and unsuitable.[31]

Alcibiades was well acquainted with this enmity and could not have expected to be recalled by an oligarchy in Athens which was, in fact, his real opponent acting behind scenes. His objective was still his return to Athens and he worked hard towards this direction. A revolution, a change in the constitution, was needed. A democratic government was, indeed, consecrated on Samos by the Athenian crews and its assembly voted for the return of Alcibiades (ἄδεια),[32] who in turn promised the people of Samos that they would receive prompt assistance from Tissaphernes, and hence he was elected general. Alcibiades was now to play the Athenians and Tissaphernes and against one another. According to Thucydides, he rendered great service to his country by dissuading the fleet from sailing to Athens and thus abandoning Asia Minor to the enemy. In the words of Thucydides, "Alcibiades seems then for the first time to have rendered a service inferior to no man's to his city."[33] One should not forget, though, that the strategic plans to conquer Sicily were, in the first place, drafted by Alcibiades, so this was not really the first time that he rendered his beneficial services to his country.

It is interesting to review in this context the events which induced Tissaphernes to stipulate his third treaty with the Lacedaemonians and the role of Alcibiades. Thucydides devoted himself to an exploration of the motives of the Persian satrap and of the choices by which he tries to achieve his goal of reestablishing Persian dominion over the Ionian Greeks. We learn at 8.45 that, by the time he had walked out of the Spartan meeting (8.43.4), he had already received the visit of Alcibiades, now a fugitive from Lacedaemon, who intended to promote and materialize his own interests. Alcibiades becomes Tissaphernes's instructor in every political issue, the designer of his policy, and also arguably his agent. He advises Tissaphernes not to be too much in a hurry to bring the war to an end by helping the Lacedaemonians and their allies, but to let the Hellenes wear each other out.[34] The Athenians, he says, would make better partners of the empire, since unlike the Lacedaemonians they have no commitment to liberate Hellas. Tissaphernes ought to therefore wear out both opponents[35] and, after acquiring as much Athenian territory as possible, expel the Peloponnesians.[36] According to one view, Alcibiades is the typical Greek at an Eastern court (obviously like Themistocles) making trouble for the Greeks.[37] The historiographic purposes of Thucydides here may be to separate Tissaphernes from Alcibiades, deliberation from advocacy, and what is visible and documented from what is not.[38] Thucydides reports Alcibiades's advice and actions at great length, but, in his attempt to determine the real motivations of a Persian grandee in an unfamiliar setting, he appears to find himself with no reliable source. Tissaphernes, writes Thucydides, reasoned for the most part in the same way as Alcibiades (διενοεῖτο τὸ πλέον οὕτως)[39] at least if one were to guess from what he did (ὅσα γε ἀπὸ τῶν ποιουμένων ἦν εἰκάσαι). Tissaphernes pursues closely the advice of Alcibiades firstly by paying the Lacedaemonian sailors badly and irregularly. He had followed this practice on his own in the past, but his purpose on this occasion, suggested by his *didaskalos* Alcibiades, is to ruin their mission, causing their ships to lose their fitness. It is added by Thucydides that "one could not possibly miss the lack of energy he put into the common war."[40]

Even then, Alcibiades did not make for Athens, as the return of the navy might lead to a civil war and put at stake the position of Athens in the whole Peloponnesian War. He demanded the removal of the Four Hundred and he was prepared to accept a government of the Five Thousand. The moderate politicians pursuing Aristokrates's tactic prevailed over the extreme oligarchs and the Five Thousand were established as government. Alcibiades's military operations reached their apex in the victorious battle of Kyzikos in 410 B.C. Eventually, he returned to Athens in 407 B.C., as until then his presence in the east was necessary on military grounds, and he received a welcome reserved for a hero. As Xenophon reports, he was at the time απάντων ηγεμών αυτοκράτωρ.[41]

Notes

1. See the article of Malcolm MacGregor, "The Genius of Alkibiades," *Phoenix* 19, no, 1 (1965), which is the best portrayal of Alcibiades I have come across in the course of my research on Thucydides.

2. MacGregor, "The Genius of Alkibiades," 27.

3. Plutarch, *Alcibiades, Loeb Classical Library* (Cambridge: Harvard University Press), 7.2.

4. Thucydides, *History of the Peloponnesian War*, 4 vols., *Loeb Classical Library* 108, 109, 110, and 169, trans. C. Forster Smith (Cambridge: Harvard University Press, 1919–1923) (hereafter cited as Thucydides), 6.12.2.

5. C. Hignett, *A History of the Athenian Constitution to the End of the Fifth Century B.C.* (Oxford: Oxford University Press, 1952), 224.

6. Thucydides, 5.44–46 (και εγένετο ούτως).

7. Thucydides, 5.43.2.

8. MacGregor, "The Genius of Alkibiades," 30.

9. Thucydides, 6.16.6.

10. Plutarch, *Alcibiades*, 15.1.

11. Plutarch, *Alcibiades*, 13.

12. Thucydides, 5.84.1.

13. Thucydides, 4.22.

14. Plutarch, *Alcibiades*, 16.5.

15. Thucydides, 6.15.2.

16. Thucydides, 6.27.

17. See Thucydides, 6.61.1.

18. Thucydides, 6.27.3.

19. Thucydides, 6.28.2.

20. Thucydides, 6.60.1.

21. Thucydides, 6.15.4.

22. For a good account of the manner in which Thucydides treats the character of Alcibiades in relation to the Sicilian expedition, see J. Finley Jr., *Three Essays on Thucydides* (Cambridge: Harvard University Press, 1967): "To turn now to his judgment of Athens' policies, it is sometimes said on the basis of II 65.11 that he did not think the Syracusan expedition a mistake. But he says rather that it was not so great a mistake as the Athenians' subsequent failure to support it by the right decisions. Thus he saw in the expedition two cardinal errors, of which the latter was the more costly: first, ever to have undertaken a venture so contrary to Pericles' sound plan of war, and second, once it had been decided on, to have exiled the one man [Alcibiades] who might have carried it off successfully. To take up these points in order, that he considered the expedition a mistake is shown by his repeated remarks on the Athenians' ignorance of Sicily (IV 65.4, VI 1.1) and by Alcibiades' quite incorrect estimate of the resistance that would be met there (VI 17). As future events proved, it was Nicias who more correctly forecast the difficulty of the task ahead (VI 20–32). Now Alcibiades carried his proposal by appealing to what he called Athens' very nature as an expanding, dominating state—that is, by the democratic doctrine of πολυπραγμοσύνη (VI 18)—and when Thucydides himself sums up the motives behind the expedition, he says that the ordinary people expected so to extend the empire that they would henceforth enjoy an αΐδιος μισθοφορά (VI 24.3). Accordingly, he describes them as possessed of an άγαν τών πλεόνων έπιθυμία (VI 24.4), and says that entire venture was conceived επί μεγίστη έλπίδι τών μελλόντων πρός τά ύπάρχοντα (VI 24.4). There can be no doubt that he is signalizing in these statements the supreme rejection of Pericles' advice, first given in I 144.1 and repeated in II 65.7, that Athens should attempt no foreign conquests in the course of the war."

23. See also MacGregor: "It is my view that the demagogues and the Assembly were exploited skillfully by the oligarchic faction in the city. After the mutilation, Thucydides describes the city's shock and the revelation of other acts of sacrilege. Then comes the outcry made by Alkibiades' most bitter opponents (οἱ μάλιστα ἀχθόμενοι), who thought that by getting rid of him they might themselves become pre-eminent; the verb used, ἐξελαύνειν,

means "to get rid of him by exile." Shortly thereafter, his enemies, οἱ ἐχθροὶ, fearing his influence with the demos, did all they could to delay immediate investigation and trial; they produced other orators (ἄλλους ῥήτορας ἐνιέντες) to urge that Alkibiades should sail with the fleet at once. Their plan was to assail Alkibiades in his absence. It is generally assumed, I believe, that οἱ μάλιστα ἀχθόμενοι and οἱ ἐχθροὶ, in the words of Thucydides, represent a single group. I suggest to you that οἱ μάλιστα ἀχθόμενοι are the popular leaders, usually called demagogues, who lost no time in accusing Alkibiades and demanding prompt punishment; that οἱ ἐχθροὶ, who persuaded others to speak for them, are the oligarchs, who perforce act more subtly. Thucydides' adverb, μάλιστα, might be better placed with οἱ ἐχθροὶ. The oligarchs, in 415, had to be circumspect. So far their intrigues had been covert and an open attack might make of Alkibiades a democratic champion, as he foresaw in urging an immediate trial. The demos feared oligarchy as much as tyranny and it is significant that Thucydides links the two (ἐπὶ ξυνωμοσίᾳ ὀλιγαρχικῇ καὶ τυραννικῇ—καὶ, not ἤ). The phrase reflects the activities of Alkibiades's friends and the confusion of the demos" ("The Genius of Alkiabedes.") Plutarch's version adds to the facts: "His enemies contrived that some of the orators who did not appear to be hostile to Alcibiades but who in fact hated him no less than did those who admitted it should speak in the Assembly" (Plutarch, *Alcibiades*, 19.3–4).

24. Thucydides, 7.2.3.
25. Thucydides, 8.6.4.
26. Thucydides, 8.56.2.
27. Thucydides, 8.47.1.
28. Thucydides, 8.53.2.
29. Thucydides, 8.48.4.
30. Thucydides, 8.51.3.
31. Thucydides, 8.56.4.
32. Thucydides, 8.81.1.
33. Thucydides 8.86.4 (καὶ δοκεῖ Ἀλκιβιάδης πρῶτον τότε καὶ οὐδενὸς ἔλασσον τὴν πόλιν ὠφελῆσαι).
34. Thucydides, 8.46.2: αὐτοὺς περὶ ἑαυτοὺς τοὺς Ἕλληνας κατατρῖψαι.
35. Thucydides, 8.46.4: τρίβειν ἀμφοτέρους.
36. Thucydides, 8.46.1–4.
37. Rosaria Vignolo Munson, "Persians in Thucydides" in *Thucydides and Herodotus*, ed. Edith Foster and Donald Lateiner (Oxford: Oxford University Press, 2012), 265.
38. Munson, "Persians in Thucydides," 265.
39. Thucydides, 8.46.5.
40. Thucydides, 8.47.5: τά τε ἄλλα καταφανέστερον ἢ ὥστε λανθάνειν οὐ προθύμως. See, however, Munson, "Persians in Thucydides," 266–267: "Thucydides indicates Tissaphernes' independence from his Greek adviser by mentioning nothing in this chapter about his reaction to Alcibiades's suggestion to find an accommodation with the Athenians. Things change somewhat only after the quarrel with the Peloponnesians at Cnidos (8.52; 8.43), when Tissaphernes realizes (ᾔσθετο) the Spartans's conflicted attitude with regard to the treaty. Lichas's complaint in fact verifies Alcibiades's argument that the Spartans were unlikely to set out to liberate the Greeks from Athens only to enslave them to the Persians. It also perhaps implicitly gives some credit to the other side of Alcibiades's argument, namely that the Athenians, accustomed as they are to holding the Greeks under their rule, would be more willing 'to share their enslavement (ξυγκαταδουλοῦν), keeping the sea for themselves and leaving to Tissaphernes the Greeks who inhabit the king's country.' After Cnidos, therefore, although Tissaphernes is afraid of the Peloponnesians' presence in Asia (δεδιότα, with the indicative, παρῆσαν, indicates that the fear is not unjustified) he starts considering Alcibiades's plan, but without great conviction: 'he . . . wanted to be persuaded if he possibly could' (βουλόμενον δέ . . . εἰ δύναιτό πῶς, πεισθῆναι). This is the closest Tissaphernes comes to agreeing with the idea of an Athenian alliance. Alcibiades's elaborate argumentations are designed to manipulate his internal audiences— Tissaphernes, the Athenians and the Spartans (8.83.2, 87.1). But Thucydides's narrative makes clear that from Tissaphernes's perspective a deal between Persia and Athens remains unlikely. Both Tissaphernes's treaties with the Peloponnesians and Alcibiades's negotiations with the Athenians in Tissaphernes's name bargain away the freedom of the Greeks of Asia and cause

84

Chapter 5.1

internal dissent. In Athens the mere prospect of Persian support has disproportionate consequences, persuading the demos to give up its rights (8.53, 65–9). The Athenians continue to hope against all hope (8.76) and Alcibiades encourages them by reporting the satrap's alleged assurances in exaggerated orientalizing terms (8.81.3)."

41. Xenophon, *Hellenica* (Cambridge: Harvard University Press, 1921), 1.1.9–10. See the view of MacGregor, which I fully agree with: "Alkibiades, at least from the moment he realized his insecurity with Tissaphernes, perhaps even before, cold-bloodedly made a plan for the distant future, a plan that did not actually reach consummation, *his* consummation, until his return to Athens in 407 B.C. The oligarchs and the clubs were prepared to risk a coup and this gave him the desperate chance (8.47.2). He plotted the oligarchic revolution that produced the Four Hundred, knowing that he could not live under oligarchy, that the oligarchs would not accept him, and that the demos as a whole detested oligarchy as much as tyranny. His intention was then to proclaim himself the champion of the democracy. He manufactured an oligarchy in order to have a target for destruction. Although he had been condemned by a democratic State, revolution would give him the opportunity of using his powers of oratory before the ousted demos, his best audience. That demos, which loves to change its mind, would surely forgive the man who led them to restoration and Alkibiades would become the democratic hero. . . . So he was quite sincere in persuading Tissaphernes to withhold pay from the Peloponnesian fleet, quite sincere in discouraging the Phoenician fleet (if he did this), quite sincere in opposing the Four Hundred, quite sincere in refusing to lead the Athenian fleet to Athens prematurely. He let it be known also that he had been unwilling rather than unable to establish a satisfactory liaison between the Tissaphernes and the Athenian oligarchs through Peisandros . . . and he had the patience to wait" ("The Genius of Alkibiades," 42–43).

Chapter Five Point Two

The Funeral Oration of Pericles

The personality of Pericles will be examined, not with regard to policy making or strategy, which has been seen before, but through his funeral oration. Any thoroughgoing analysis of Thucydides would be inadequate if it does not include an overview of this famous oration and the corresponding ramifications of the Periclean personality.

Of course, glimpses on the policy of Pericles are inevitably cast.

In fifth-century Athens, the bodies of those who died in wars abroad were burnt, and the remains (called οστά here) were gathered and sent home; there they were interred together in the same way as other dead, following a laying out (πρόθεσις) and funeral procession (ἐκφορὰ). The ceremony was held at public expense, and culminated in a funeral oration delivered by a leading citizen. This practice is first alluded to by Aeschylus,[1] and there survive λόγοι ἐπιτάφιοι (or fragments of them) ascribed to Gorgias, Lysias, Plato (in the dialogue *Menexenus*), Demosthenes, and Hyperides. In the common elements of these we may see the traditional themes of an επιτάφιος: praise of the ancestors, praise of the fallen warriors, exhortation to citizens, and consolation to relatives.[2]

In the Funeral Oration of Pericles, first comes Athens's glorious past. Pericles divides Athenian history into three parts: (1) the ancestors (πρόγονοι), who lived before the Persian War, (2) the preceding generation, who won the Persian Wars and established the Athenian empire, and (3) the present generation (αὐτοὶ ἡμεῖς), who strengthened the empire and made the city-state of Athens self-sufficient. The segments of the glory of the past and the defeat of the Persians are quite lengthy in the oration.

Second comes praise of Athens as it stood in the age of Pericles, at the exact time that the oration was presented. Athens's government is depicted as combining the best features of democracy (equality for all) and aristocracy (preference for merit) in a complex structure of antitheses. The patriotic speech of Theseus parallels a number of those claims, but with none of the balance and complexity of the Thucydidean description, which is recalled in the Menexenus (238c7-d2).[3]

In the Funeral Oration Pericles emphasizes the quality of the Athenian constitution and character, and this means the spirit of the institutions and of the citizens. Truly, though, on the basis of the Funeral Oration it would be impossible to give even a vague description of this constitution. The view expressed by Edmunds, however, that Pericles does not praise the structure of the constitution or the political institutions but rather the spirit of Athenian life[4] is not shared in this treatise. The extract which follows, in which reference to the constitutional laws is constantly made, proves precisely the opposite:

> Χρώμεθα γὰρ πολιτείᾳ οὐ ζηλούσῃ τοὺς τῶν πέλας νόμους,
> παράδειγμα δὲ μᾶλλον αὐτοὶ ὄντες τισὶν ἢ μιμούμενοι ἐτέρους. καὶ
> ὄνομα μὲν διὰ τὸ μὴ ἐς ὀλίγους ἀλλ᾽ ἐς πλείονας οἰκεῖν[5] δημοκρατία
> κέκληται. μέτεστι δὲ κατὰ μὲν τοὺς νόμους πρὸς τὰ ἴδια διάφορα πᾶσι
> τὸ ἴσον,[6] κατὰ δὲ τὴν ἀξίωσιν, ὡς ἕκαστος ἐν τῷ εὐδοκιμεῖ, οὐκ
> ἀπὸ μέρους τὸ πλέον ἐς τὰ κοινὰ[7] ἢ ἀπ᾽ ἀρετῆς προτιμᾶται, οὐδ᾽ αὖ
> κατὰ πενίαν, ἔχων γέ τι ἀγαθὸν δρᾶσαι τὴν πόλιν, ἀξιώματος
> ἀφανείᾳ κεκώλυται.

> We enjoy a constitution that does not copy the laws of our neighbors;
> rather, we ourselves are a model for others, not imitators.
> In name it is called a democracy because it is governed in the interest not of
> the few but of the many.
> By the laws, all have equal justice in private differences;
> by merit, each man, according as his particular ability is recognized, is advanced in public life—not by lot but by virtue. Nor again is a man held back
> by poverty and obscurity of rank, if he is able to benefit the city.

The whole statement is built on a *μέν-δέ* antithesis between what the Athenian constitution is called and what it, in fact, is. It is necessary to consider this main antithesis if one is to comprehend the meaning of democracy in the *μέν* clause. The meaning of democracy is not rule by the whole people but rule by the many as opposed to the few (aristocrats). Thus, in the first of the two main parts of the antithetical *δέ* clause, Pericles says that the laws afford equality to all. It might be alleged that there is an antithesis between democracy in the sense of rule by one party and in the sense of rule by all the citizens. However, equality in classical Athens, much like nowadays, most likely meant equality before the laws or equal protection of the laws, and simultaneously equal opportunities for all, not that all should rule the city or that all are equal in every respect.

Tolerance for divergent lifestyles is also stressed in the Funeral Oration.[8] Pericles boasts that Athenian democracy offers unparalleled freedom for the individual (ἐλευθερία), and Nicias, in a speech to the Athenian army at Syracuse, appeals once more to this toleration.[9] Pericles stresses that the populace is also especially obedient, not only to local magistrates and laws, but to the unwritten laws which governed all human behavior. Again, this contravenes the statement of Lowell Edmunds that "the fact that Pericles says nothing of the gods in the Funeral Oration is an indication of his humanism."[10] Edmunds's statement is refuted the more by the Periclean reference to recreation and religious festivals, which strengthens the opinion that Pericles's religious belief or at least affinity to the traditional Greek religion was actually intense: ἀγῶσι μέν γε καὶ θυσίαις διετησίοις νομίζοντες. It is to be noted that the expensive public buildings on the Acropolis for which Athens was notorious are excluded here—they do not serve recreational purposes.[11]

Pericles's description of Athenian democracy appropriately finds an echo in Thucydides's description of Pericles's relation to that democracy: ἐγίγνετό τε λόγῳ μὲν δημοκρατία, ἔργῳ δὲ ὑπὸ τοῦ πρώτου ἀνδρὸς ἀρχή (in name it was a democracy but in fact it was rule by the first man).[12] The echo cannot be mistaken. As in 2.37.1, it is said that Athens is only nominally a democracy. What this means comes into the open in 2.65.9, though, where Thucydides explains that the true character of the constitution was rule by the first man. If this is the truth about Athens in Pericles's time, then Pericles's praise of Athens is really, at least to some extent, a self-praise,[13] or, to put the matter differently, Pericles's praise of Athens is Thucydides's praise of Pericles. Pericles represents Thucydides's formulation of an ideal which Pericles did in fact realize but which the other Athenians did not approach.

Further, Pericles regards the city from the point of view of the individual, in particular of the individual's subjective conviction concerning the worth of the city and of political life. This concept of the city-state of Athens emerges from the following famous passage of the Funeral Oration:

Ἐλευθέρως δὲ τά πρὸς τὸ κοινὸν πολιτεύομεν καὶ ἐς τὴν πρὸς ἀλλήλους τῶν καθ᾽ἡμέραν ἐπιτηδευμάτων ὑποψίαν, οὐ δι᾽ὀργῆς τὸν πέλας, εἰ καθ᾽ἡδονήν τι δρᾷ, ἔχοντες, οὐδὲ ἀζημίους μέν, λυπηρὰς δὲ τῇ ὄψει ἀχθηδόνας προστιθέμενοι. Ἀνεπαχθῶς δὲ τὰ ἴδια προσομιλοῦντες τὰ δημόσια διὰ δέος μάλιστα οὐ παρανομοῦμεν, τῶν τὲ αἰεὶ ἐν ἀρχῃ ὄντων ἀκροάσει καὶ τῶν νόμων, καὶ μάλιστα αὐτῶν ὅσοι τε ἐπ᾽ὠφελίᾳ τῶν ἀδικουμένων κεῖνται καὶ ὅσοι ἄγραφοι ὄντες αἰσχύνην ὁμολογουμένην φέρουσιν.

We conduct our political life in a spirit of freedom both as regards the public realm and as regards suspicion of one another in daily affairs, without anger against our neighbor if he does as he likes, and without casting glances which, though harmless, are painful annoyances. Associating with one another unvexatiously in private, we do not break the laws, especially because of proper fear, through obedience to those in office at any given time and to the laws, and especially those laws which have been made for the help of the injured and those which, though unwritten, bring an acknowledged shame upon the transgressor. [14]

Commenting upon this passage, Lowell Edmunds puts forward an interesting view. He says that "the subjectivity of Athenian citizenship is what makes it possible for the citizen to be 'released from chance,' that is, freed of the whims of fortune. In choosing to die for the city, the citizen places the continued existence of the city and the values it represents above the continued enjoyment of his own individual existence or whatever hopes for the future he may have. Patriotism of this sort is a release from fortune, because the city is considered itself to embody the values of the individual citizen so that he knows in advance—and all the more so if he risks his life in battle—that the individual mischance of his own death will not have destroyed what was most essential to him, his character as an Athenian citizen." [15] If I may comment on Edmunds's viewpoint, it is surely a most interesting opinion on the character of Athenian citizenship. However, I would suggest that the better term to be used in this context is not "subjectivity of Athenian citizenship" but "independence of the Athenian citizens." Such an independence should not preclude any affiliation of the Athenian citizens to religious beliefs or convictions as to objective moral and ontological standards. In other words, subjectivity should not in this context be seen or interpreted as a form of subjectivism with regard to moral values. In fact, it has already been shown above that the Funeral Oration denotes the deep-rooted religious beliefs of the Athenians in the classical era. [16]

The oration may, of course, be said as being, in the main, an analysis of democracy as a form of government. That analysis is as searching as it is because Pericles pauses only briefly on the historical achievements of Athens or even on the actual democratic practices in force there—majority rule, freedom of speech, equality of opportunity, equality before the law—but passes, almost at once, to the effect of these practices on the public. Thus, he rests his claims for democracy on what has come to be recognized as its principal sanction, its educative value to the human spirit rather than its mere efficiency as a form of government. Or, to put the matter in another way, he presents democracy as a force which sets in motion a multitude of lesser forces, namely the lives of individual citizens, and shows how these in turn endow the democratic state with funds of self-directed energy unknown under other constitutions. [17]

More remarkable is another aspect of the relationship between the citizen and his city: Pericles's emphasis on the relaxed quality of Athenian life. While paying tribute to former generations of Athenians who, among their other accomplishments, turned back the Persian invasion and built the Athenian empire (2.36.2), the oration emphasizes the confident amateurism of Athenian life. This point is developed by a rhetorical strategy unparalleled in other extant funeral orations. Pericles passes over the customary survey of Athenian history, real and mythic, and concentrates instead on those habits, civic arrangements, and dispositions that stand behind Athens's growth to greatness:

> Since you know them so well, I will avoid long-winded reiteration of the accomplishments in war by which our dominance was progressively acquired or of the various successes our fathers and we have had in our determination to ward off Greek and Persian aggression. Instead I will first make clear from what patterns of conduct we attained this level and with what civic structure and from what dispositions such greatness derives. Then I will proceed to the praise of the fallen with the view that these observations would be far from inappropriate in our present situation and that this entire gathering, both citizens and visitors, would benefit from hearing them.[18]

The substitution of a discussion of patterns of Athenian life for the traditional material of funeral oratory opens the way for a discussion of the difference between Athenian ways and those of other Greek cities, as noted above: "We enjoy a style of civic life that does not copy the *nomoi* of our neighbors and is more a model to some than an imitation of others."[19] The contrast between Athens and the unnamed "others" gradually concentrates on her differences from the iron-disciplined life of Lacedaemon,[20] so much admired by other Greeks,[21] yet stressing Athenian military training:

> We also differ in our war preparations from our opponents, in these respects: We allow our city to be accessible to all and there is never an occasion when we use *xenelasiai* (expulsions of foreigners) to keep someone from learning something or seeing something, even though by our failing to preserve secrecy, some enemy might derive some advantage. Our reliance is not so much in preparations and deceptions as in that courageous readiness for action which we derive from our own selves. In their education others from earliest youth chase after manliness by an effortful discipline, but though we live in a relaxed style we march out no less than they to fair and square contests.[22]

It must be said, however, not least because I am, admittedly, also an admirer of Lacedaemon, that Sparta had developed a strongly disciplined state in part due to the constant fear of a Helot revolt, but also in order to retain a hegemony in the Peloponnesian League. It goes without saying that the traditionally rigorous military training of Sparta aimed at repelling external threats and dangers. Also, expulsions of foreigners from the city-state of Sparta were justified by a deep-rooted belief of the Lacedaemonians that their city should retain its own distinctive ethnic character and be kept intact from any unhappy foreign influences. This policy sounds hard, and in reality it was very tough; nevertheless, through such institutions Lacedaemon remained by far the most powerful city-state in ancient Greece for eight centuries.

In the Funeral Oration, an analysis of the Athenian character then follows. The harmony of Athenian life and the excellence of the Athenians in a wide range of activities are emphasized in what has become one of the most notorious passages of the Funeral Oration:

> For in the first place (τε) we seek what is noble with moderation in expense, and seek wisdom without becoming soft; furthermore (τε) wealth is for us an opportunity to act rather than something about which to speak boastfully, and as for poverty, it is not a disgrace for anyone to admit to it, but it is a disgrace not to attempt actively to escape it; finally (τε), those who manage our city do the same for their households as well, and others, even though they pursue their trades, have a thorough knowledge of politics. [23]

The occupational categories—lovers of wisdom (intellectuals), of wealth (businessmen), and of public service (politicians)—are meant as alternatives. It would be preposterous to ascribe to every single Athenian citizen the simultaneous pursuit of philosophy, wealth, and political power, especially since, in the case of wealth and politics, an explicit reference is added to those outside these spheres as well. [24]

The confident belief that privilege evokes a corresponding sense of responsibility is summed up by Pericles in the words φιλοκαλοῦμέν τε γὰρ μετ' εὐτελείας καὶ φιλοσοφοῦμεν ἄνευ μαλακίας ("We love beauty with simplicity; we pursue without softness.") The phrase μετ' εὐτελείας, "with simplicity," means that beauty does not depend on monetary value and can be available to all. The words ἄνευ μαλακίας, "without softness," express his faith that philosophy does not spoil men for action. The restrained grace and measured optimism of the Greek spirit at its best could not be more fitly described. He concludes this part of his speech by saying that not poverty but the failure to struggle against it is considered disgraceful in Athens, and, again, that all are expected to share in the city's administration, those who refuse being considered not gentlemen of leisure (the oligarchic ideal) but useless. Actually, what is here more accurately implied is that those who do not engage in politics and political discourse are or should be seen as useless. [25] Pericles continues his description of the Athenian outlook by mentioning two beliefs which are in effect the principles underlying all that he had said. "All of us," he claims, "can either initiate policy or at least judge it intelligently. Debate in our opinion is not harmful to action. What is harmful, on the contrary, is failure to discuss a matter thoroughly before carrying it out." [26] That all citizens can and should share in the making of policy and that free public debate is essential are, of course, the basic tenets of democracy. Pericles is therefore assumed as expressing not Thucydides's later insight but views known and held at the time.

Having given a traditional definition of friendship, a basic component of male ἀρετή (virtue), which consisted in outdoing one's friends in kindness and one's enemies in harm,[27] Pericles sums up the ideal of full and rounded humanity in a famous sentence: "In a word I say that our city as a whole is the education of Hellas[28] and that Athenians as individuals would seem to me supremely fitted to meet the varied circumstances of life with grace and self-reliance."[29] Again, it is to the individual that he returns, the man liberated by democracy to a fuller consciousness of his own powers and inspired by it to their effective use. He concludes by praising Athens's achievements as beyond those sung by earlier poets, and by urging the relatives of the fallen to find comfort in the greatness of the city. "In the knowledge that your happiness is your freedom and your freedom your courage, do not shrink the dangers of war," καὶ τὸ εὔδαιμον τὸ ἐλεύθερον, τὸ δ' ἐλεύθερον τὸ εὔψυχον κρίναντες, μὴ περιορᾶσθε τοὺς πολεμικοὺς κινδύνους.[30] Formally, the words recall those of Archidamus: "We are courageous because self-control derives from a sense of honor and courage from self-control."[31] But the underlying ideas could hardly be more opposed. The Spartan king had described an essentially negative, limiting discipline; Pericles holds up the positive hope of a fuller and more humane freedom.[32]

It would be interesting to contrast the Funeral Oration with the purely political first oration laid out to support the Periclean policy pursued. The purpose of Pericles in this oration is to dissuade the Athenians from any concession and to convince them that Athens can overcome in a war with the Peloponnesians. This compelling speech is not balanced against the words of a rival politician in a typical Thucydidean antilogy. It is rather an antilogy at a distance, answering point by point the arguments of the Corinthians at the Spartan Congress. The answer is premised to a large extent upon the power analysis in the archaeology of the *History of the Peloponnesian War*, and also reinforces the arguments of King Archidamus regarding the difficulties that confront the Peloponnesians:

> And if they march with their infantry against our territory, we will sail against theirs. It will not be an even trade to ravage part of the Peloponnese and all of Attica, for they will not acquire other territory without a fight, while we have abundant land on the islands and on the mainland. The command of the sea is a great thing.[33] Consider this: if we were islanders, who would be less vulnerable? In our present circumstances we should develop a strategy that approximates this situation, by letting our land and houses go, while guarding our city and the sea. We must never get angry over them and join battle with the Peloponnesians who far outnumber us, for if we win, we will battle again with no fewer opponents, while if we blunder, we lose in addition the source of our

strength—the control of our allies. They will not stay tranquil if we cannot mount an expedition against them. [34]

The Peloponnesians, Pericles shows, will not find it easy to hire away the rowers on the Athenian fleet, since higher pay will not outbalance the greater danger. Nor can they swiftly acquire the naval skill that the Athenians have been developing since the Persian Wars, nor will any enemy fortification in Attic territory prove effective. Whatever damages it inflicts will be outweighed by Athenian naval attacks on their territory. While refuting these arguments, Pericles can drive home the significance of financial resources and of naval strength which emerges from the analysis of the archaeology and has been confirmed by Archidamus.

Pericles's first oration is the culmination of the analysis of the book and carries with it the rigor of its analysis. His strategy originates from the Themistoclean transformation of Athens into a walled naval power ($ξύλινα τείχη$) and from the analysis of power that looks so lucidly affirmed by the analysis of the first book. He spots what must be done and persuades the assembly of the people [35] that his advice is best. [36] Unchallenged, he seems properly described by Thucydides's introduction: "a man who was at that time the first of the Athenians, most powerful in word and action." [37] Nevertheless, the undercurrent of doubt and tension that we have felt in other passages persists even at this stage. The course of the war will not be as simple as Pericles seems to imply. With it will come loss and sufferings of the worst kind, of great intensity. The war as progressed through the orations of the first book is like a chess game, a testing ground of strategies and policies. Pericles initially seems to be a superb player, but what will the outcome be when the game moves to the battlefields? Already one may detect signs of problems in the policy of Pericles. When, for instance, Pericles points out that the war may prove to be a long one, he adds "for them," the enemy. [38] But the reader is aware it is not only "for them" that the war turns out to be longer than anticipated. Its unexpected duration affects all participants, not least the Athenians. Although in the short term the Lacedaemonian arguments are flawed, in the long run they can prove correct. It is not easy for them to hire the crews away from the Athenian navy nor to develop comparable naval skill of their own, but eventually they succeed in accomplishing both. An effective Peloponnesian base of military operations in Attica is not established in the opening years of the war, but ultimately the fortification at Deceleia reduces Athens to a virtual garrison. When Pericles in the terminology current at the moment of the outbreak of the war says, "if we were islanders, who would be less vulnerable?" he makes a telling point about the ability of Athens to resist and potentially repel a Lacedaemonian invasion into its interior. But the reader is again aware of the fact that there is an irony surrounding the present question. Athens is not, in fact, an island and will find it extremely difficult to pretend to be one. A policy, or, more accurately in this case, a strategy of self-confinement behind the walls may not be as easy as it appears. Pericles's comment that he has a greater fear of Athenian errors than of Lacedaemonian planning hints not only at the Athenian mistakes during the war but at the possibility that even Pericles's analysis may yet be flawed.

The effect of this oration then is, as often in Thucydides, complex. We are carried along by its force, but remain aware simultaneously of ironic possibilities. Knowing the effect of the war, we recognize the discrepancy between his confidence and the difficulties that await both opponents. The underpinning tension that has been detected through the first book persists up until the very end.

Notes

1. Aeschylus, Oresteia, *Agamemnon. Libation Bearers. Eumenides, Loeb Classical Library* (Cambridge: Harvard University Press, 2009), 429-48.

2. Thucydides, *The Peloponnesian War Book II, Cambridge Greek and Latin Classics,* ed. J. S. Rusten (Cambridge: Cambridge University Press, 1990), 135.

3. Thucydides, *The Peloponnesian War Book II*, 143.

4. Lowell Edmunds, *Chance and Intelligence in Thucydides* (Cambridge: Harvard University Press, 1975), 47.

5. "Not for the few, but for the many": Thucydides, *The Peloponnesian War Book II*, 145.

6. "Equality is shared by all": Thucydides, *The Peloponnesian War Book II*, 145.

7. As to the Athenian practice of choosing most magistrates in a yearly lottery, which was often considered a major defeat of Athenian democracy, see W. K. C. Guthrie, *The Sophists* (Cambridge: Cambridge University Press, 1971), 319 n. 3. The real power, as noted by Pericles, was wielded by men of distinction, notably the στρατηγοί.

8. Thucydides, *History of the Peloponnesian War*, 4 vols., *Loeb Classical Library* 108, 109, 110, and 169, trans. C. Forster Smith (Cambridge: Harvard University Press, 1919–1923) (hereafter cited as Thucydides), 2.37.2: ἐλευθέρως: "It is with tolerance that we behave."

9. Thucydides, 7.69.2. Even Plato, who was no friend to democracy, nevertheless allowed that because of its tolerance it might well be the most attractive system (certainly not the best however); just like a multicoloured cloak embroidered with every hue, a democracy, adorned with every lifestyle, might appear the fairest (Plato, *Republic, Volume I: Books 1–5, Loeb Classical Library 237* [Cambridge: Harvard University Press, 2013, 557c2]).

10. See Lowell Edmunds, *Chance and Intelligence in Thucydides* (Cambridge: Harvard University Press, 1975), 46.

11. Thucydides, *The Peloponnesian War Book II*, 148.

12. Thucydides, 2.65.9.

13. "The Funeral Oration is almost entirely an address in the first person plural—as we would expect in this genre. Pericles is the spokesman for civic values and attitudes. But in his last speech, the form of address alternates between the first singular and the second plural. 'We' disappears: 'I' and 'you' become the means of discourse: 'I am the same and don't shift; you are the ones who change' (61.2). Pericles speaks of himself more directly and more frequently and with unabashed self-praise. He contrasts himself with his audience, and hence naturally has need of the second plural. The language reflects the tension between Pericles and the Athenians, a tension that becomes fully evident at the end of the debate when Pericles is fined and removed from command. By the end of the sequence, the valedictory on Pericles, the leader appears in a new light. His effectiveness derives not so much from his ability to express the characteristics and attitudes of his people as from his ability to counterbalance some of their tendencies. The structure, in other words, helps lead to a more subtle understanding of the nature of Athenian political leadership" (W. Robert Connor, *Thucydides*, Princeton: Princeton University Press, 1934, 65). It is, in my view, eventually evident that Pericles was not the great political leader that it has been imagined he was, but rather a giant with clay legs.

14. Thucydides, 2.37.2–3. Once again, inter alia, here is evident the deep law-abiding character of the Athenians and Pericles's (or more accurately Thucydides's) emphasis on this issue. The spirit of freedom in the public realm refers to the statement in which Pericles rather obliquely describes the aristocratic element immanent in the democratic constitution. It is noteworthy that Athenian individualism comes up in another passage of the Funeral Oration: "Neither preferring the future enjoyment of wealth did any one of these men play the coward nor in the poor man's hope, that one might yet escape poverty and be rich, did any one of these delay terror. Taking vengeance on the enemy to be more desirable than future prospects, and at the same time believing this to be the fairest of risks, they wanted to run the risk, to punish the one (the enemy) and renounce the other (the future), having committed to hope the obscurity of success, and seeing fit in action to rely on themselves in regard to what presently lay before their eyes. And considering that in resistance itself and suffering they found safety rather than in submission, they escaped a disgraceful account of themselves and in their own person endured the deed. In the briefest moment they were, at the height of their glory, released from

chance rather than from proper fear. Such were these men, as befits the city. Those who survive them should pray to make safer choices but should not at all deem it right to have a less bold spirit in the face of the enemy, considering not only the advantages, on which one could expatiate to you who yourselves know as well as he—he could tell you how many benefits there are in defense against the enemy—but rather in fact looking upon the power of the city day to day and becoming lovers of her, and, when she seems great to you, reflecting that men acquired all this acting boldly, knowing their duty, and acting out of fear of disgrace, thinking it wrong to deprive the city of their bravery if they failed in some attempt and offering it to her as their fairest gift" (Thucydides, 2.37.2–3).

15. Lowell Edmunds, *Chance and Intelligence in Thucydides* (Cambridge: Harvard University Press, 1975), 67.

16. A better, and more accurate view, I propose, is that of Connor, *Thucydides*, 68–69: "In passages such as these the Funeral Oration develops an image of a society that sustains individual freedom and fulfillment and is in turn sustained by its citizens' willingness to fight and die for it. That willingness emerges not from compulsion but from the relationship of the citizen to his city, a bond described by the metaphor of falling in love: 'Beholding day by day the power of the city and becoming her lovers, and when you recognize her greatness, bear in mind that the men who entitled her to that greatness knew and dared what had to be done and in action would not be disgraced. If in some undertaking they met failure, they did not think that they should refuse to offer their valour to their city. They brought their contribution to their fairest of love feasts. Their communal gift of their bodies won for each individual the praise that grows not old' (2.43.1–2)." Also important and lucid is the view expressed by John Finley Jr. in *Thucydides* (Cambridge: Harvard University Press, 1942), 147: "Evidently, in justifying freedom, the advocates of democracy commonly argued, as here, that precisely by stripping men of petty controls, it left them more simply responsive to the great natural sanctions of morality. Certainly, at least, this trust in human nature which Pericles expresses forms the ultimate difference between Athens and Sparta and thus between democracy and oligarchy."

17. Finley, *Thucydides*.

18. Thucydides, 2.36.4.

19. Thucydides, 2.37.1.

20. Μὴ μετὰ νόμων τὸ πλέον ἢ τρόπων ἀνδρείας: "Not with courage from rules (which the Spartans have) rather than from character" (Thucydides, *The Peloponnesian War Book II*, 151).

21. See, for example, Xenophon, "The Constitution of the Lacedaemonians," *Xenophon* Volume VII, *Loeb Classical Library* 183, trans. E. C. Marchant (Cambridge: Harvard University Press, 1925). For an excellent commentary see Vivienne Gray, *Xenophon on Government, Cambridge Greek and Latin Classics* (Cambridge: Cambridge University Press, 2007).

22. Thucydides, 2.39.1.

23. Thucydides, *The Peloponnesian War, Book II*, 152.

24. Plato ridicules the democratic man as unable to concentrate on a single life (*Republic*, 561D): "Therefore he lives for the day, gratifying whatever desire comes over him . . . sometimes doing physical training, sometimes lying idle and caring for nothing, or sometimes pretending to engage in philosophy; often he takes up politics, and jumps up in the assembly to say or do whatever occurs to him; if he is taken with warriors he is drawn in that direction, or if he likes businessmen, to this activity. His life possesses no order or direction whatsoever—and yet he continues to practice it, calling this life pleasant, free and blessed."

25. The balance of debate and action in Athenian life is ably presented in the Cambridge edition of Thucydides, *The Peloponnesian War Book II*, 154: "For those who are ignorant of public policy we have nothing but contempt, while we ourselves always participate, either recognizing good policies (of others) or actually formulating them. Despite Pericles' claim of Athenian uniqueness, the structure of his analysis is at least as old as Hesiod." On abstinence from politics as the proper stance to be taken see W. R. Connor, *The New Politicians of Fifth-Century Athens* (Princeton: Princeton University Press, 1971).

26. Thucydides, 2.40.1.

27. See K. Dover, *Greek Popular Morality* (Berkeley: University of California Press, 1974), 180–184. The Spartans attempted to apply such a generalization to treaty negotiations, an inseparable subfield of international law.

28. Thucydides, 2.41.1: *λέγω τὴν πόλιν ἡμῶν τῆς Ἑλλάδος παίδευσιν εἶναι.*
29. Thucydides, 2.43.4.
30. Thucydides, 2.43.4. The reasoning is "happiness is freedom, and freedom is bravery (so as to be happy, be brave)" (Thucydides, *The Peloponnesian War Book II*, 171). Μὴ περιορᾶσθε τοὺς πολεμικοὺς κινδύνους: περιορᾶσθε means to watch from the sidelines (without participating) (Thucydides, *The Peloponnesian War Book II*, 171).
31. Thucydides, 1.84.3.
32. Finley, *Thucydides*, 149.
33. *Μέγα τὸ τῆς θαλάσσης κράτος*, as the famous phrase from Thucydides's History goes.
34. Thucydides, 1.143.4–5.
35. The assembly of the people (*ἐκκλησία τοῦ δήμου*) in classical Athens was the political body that took decisions about major issues of foreign policy.
36. Thucydides, 1.145.1: *ἄριστα.*
37. Thucydides, 1.139.4: *πρῶτος ἀνήρ . . . ἔργῳ τε καὶ λόγῳ.*
38. Thucydides, 1.141.5.

Chapter Six

Political Intelligence in the War of the Lacedaemonians and the Athenians

The terminology in the context of this chapter is used to imply a fifth column, a modern term. For current purposes, a fifth column is defined as a group in a state which acts subversively or commits treason in cooperation with the enemy.[1] The nature and ultimate effect of the subversive activities depend upon the ingenuity of the fifth columnists in particular. For example, in the Peloponnesian War the Athenian *proxenoi* at Mytilene sent information to Athens concerning the revolt of Mytilene.[2] This constitutes giving information of strategic importance to the opponent. A second example is overthrowing the government in coordination with the enemy. Thucydides describes the activities of a pro-Lacedaemonian group at Argos of which the purpose was to overthrow the democratic government at Argos.[3] This forms what is commonly called subversion and is not exactly the same as opening the gates and admitting enemy forces to capture the city, though this is the standard form of treason. Treason means προδοσία, and as the betrayal of a city or a military operation by a fifth column is a kind of treason, it should not be surprising that the phenomenon is generally termed προδοσία in ancient sources.[4]

It is noteworthy that in the Peloponnesian War, in twelve of the instances of προδοσία Thucydides uses the term to describe fifth-column actions.[5]

The gist of a fifth column is the idea of betrayal from within the city. The fifth columnists are referred to by Thucydides as "some in the city" or "those." For instance, the suggestion to the generals Demosthenes and Hippocrates for the betrayal of Chaeronea comes ἀπό τινων ἀνδρῶν ἐν ταῖς πόλεσιν.[6] The use of the verb ἐπάγειν normally means "bring in to one's country, or introduce as allies," or it may mean to invite foreign intervention. This verb is employed by Thucydides in his reference to the fifth column activities at Torone: καὶ αὐτὸν (Βρασίδαν) ἄνδρες ὀλίγοι ἐπήγοντο ἕτοιμοι ὄντες τὴν πόλιν παραδοῦναι.[7]

It is necessary to take a look at some of the most important and obvious cases of betrayal in the history by Thucydides.[8]

In the spring of 431 B.C. in Plataea a group of oligarchic Plataeans, led by Naucleides, agreed to betray their city to the Thebans, so as to gain political power for themselves. The actual betrayal and entry into Plataea by the Theban troops succeeded, but the Thebans did not succeed in following up and retaining their advantage and the loyal Plataeans overcame them by the next day.[9]

In the summer of 429 B.C., the Athenians militarily proceeded to Spartolus on the expectation that the city would be betrayed by a faction from within. The fifth columnists, however, are not here identified by name or members of a specific political faction. Thucydides merely reports that the city was supposed to be delivered over to the Athenians ὑπό τινων ἔνδοθεν πρασσόντων. Those who did not wish these things sent word to Olynthus for troops to garrison the town. The betrayal never took place.[10]

In the summer of 428 B.C., in the course of the revolt at Mytilene, the Mytileneans marched on Methymna, which was supposed to be betrayed. The Mytileneans did attack the city, but the betrayal did not materialize and they withdrew. The traitors are not personally reported.

In the summer of 427 B.C., after the revolt of Mytilene had been suppressed by the Athenians, Teutiaplos and Elean suggested to Alcidas, the Lacedaemonian admiral, that the Spartan military forces should attempt a sudden assault in the night against Mytilene. Teutiaplos's idea was that with the succor of those within the city who were still amicable to their cause they would recapture the city. The fifth whose support was the primary element in the plan of Teutiaplos were no doubt pro-Lacedaemonian Mytileneans who had taken part in the revolt. The proposal was not eventually accepted by Alcidas.[11]

In 425 B.C., in the summer, Simonides, the Athenian general, captured Eion by betrayal. The traitors are not identified by Thucydides. The betrayal was short lived, though, as Boeotian and Chalcidian military forces drove Simonides out soon afterwards.[12]

In the summer of 425 B.C., the Athenians sailed to Camarina to prevent its betrayal to the Syracusans. The pro-Syracusan fifth columnists are reported to have been Archias and his political faction. The betrayal did not occur.[13]

In the summer of 425 B.C., the Athenians and their allies from Acarnania conquered Anactorium, a Corinthian city on the Ambracian Gulf. The traitors are not identified by the historian, but they were most likely members of a pro-Corcyrean party in Anactorium. Originally, Anactorium was a colony of Corcyra and Corinth, and the animosity which had broken out among the founding cities ended up creating a party division in the colony. In September 433 B.C., the Corinthians had captured Anactorium with help from within and in 425 B.C. the Athenians regained it. [14]

In the summer of 424 B.C., Mytilenean and other exiles from Lesbos launched an assault on Antandrus and captured it προδοσίας γενομένης. Thucydides does not give any further information with regard to the betrayal. [15]

In the summer of 424 B.C., the leaders of the Megarian democratic party under pressure from their oligarchic opponents, in particular because a proposal was under consideration to restore oligarchic exiles, arranged to betray their city to the Athenian general Demosthenes and Hippocrates. The betrayal of the Long Walls was accomplished but the plot to betray the upper part of the city was not successful. The arrival of the Spartan admiral Brasidas had as a result the defeat of the democrats in Megara, and the Athenian troops abandoned the place having left a garrison at Nisaea. [16]

During the summer of 424 B.C. some men in Siphae and Chaeronea planned to betray the cities to Athens in combination with an attack on Delium, so as to cause revolts in various city-states of Boeotia. The fifth columnists had as their leader Ptoeodorus, an exile from Thebes, and their members included parties in Siphae and Chaeronea. The fifth column aimed at establishing democratic constitutions in the city-states. The operation was revealed and therefore the traitorous actions never took place. [17]

In the winter of 423 B.C. a political party in Amphipolis planned to betray the city to Brasidas. The members of the fifth column were natives of Argilus that resided in Amphipolis, and other citizens of Amphipolis. The conquest of territory outside the walls of the city was successfully accomplished by Brasidas, who was aided by the members of the fifth column. However, the betrayal of the city was at some point prevented by the political party that then was in the majority, and which subsequently asked for the dispatch of Athenian support. Eventually Brasidas prevailed, having used diplomatic methods. [18]

In 423 B.C., during the winter, Brasidas captured Torone, which was betrayed by a group from within the town. The members of the fifth column are reported by Thucydides as ἄνδρες ὀλίγοι. [19]

In the summer of 423 B.C., Mende revolted to the benefit of the Lacedaemonians. Before the revolt, Thucydides reports, a fifth column in Mende was working for the betrayal to the Spartan admiral Brasidas. [20] Skione also joined Brasidas. [21]

In the summer of 423 B.C., Brasidas had plans on Potidaea, and the historian says that a fifth column in the city was in touch with him regarding a potential betrayal. The betrayal, though, was never implemented. [22]

In 421 B.C. in the summer, a pro-Lacedaemonian political group in Parrhasia, which was an ally of Mantinea, called in the Lacedaemonians to free the city from the control of Mantinea. Thucydides reports that the pro-Lacedaemonians were acting κατά στάσιν, but nothing is further told about this civil discord and conflict in the area.[23]

In the summer of 418 B.C., before the battle of Mantinea, a few Tegeans were making preparations to betray their city, which was then an ally of Lacedaemon, to the military forces of Athens, Argos, and Mantinea. The allied forces were about to assault Tegea, but the pro-Spartan Tegeans, who had been informed about the betrayal, sent a request to Sparta for help. Military succor was dispatched from Lacedaemon and the betrayal was therefore thwarted.[24]

In 416 B.C., the final surrender of the island of Melos to the Athenians was completed, as Thucydides reports, γενομένης καί προδοσίας τινός ἀφ'ἑαυτῶν (Μηλίων). Thucydides does not put down any other elements regarding the betrayal of Melos.[25]

In the winter of 414 B.C., the Athenian military force, which was based at Catana, set sail to Messina, the city being expected to be betrayed to them. But Alcibiades, having been dismissed from the command of the Athenian fleet and called back to Athens, informed the pro-Syracusan party of the plan. Subsequently, the leaders of the fifth column were executed, and while the campaign of the Athenians was at work, the pro-Syracusans fought against the pro-Athenians that remained and therefore prevented the betrayal from occurring. The vessels of Athens were at a standstill at Messina, and the betrayal not having been materialized, they set sail to Naxos.[26]

In the summer of 413 B.C., throughout the siege of Syracuse by the Athenians, a little while before the actual fall of the city, a fifth column existed within the city, which was in contact with Nicias regarding surrender or betrayal. There is no precise information as to the identity of the fifth columnists, but it is very possible that these have been men of Leontini who resided in the city of Syracuse. A betrayal was not, in fact, attempted.[27]

In the winter of 411 B.C., after the revolt of Chios, a pro-Athenian faction existed in Chios aiming at betraying the city to Athens. The pro-Lacedaemonian oligarchs of Chios found out about it, and with the help of Astyochus the conspiracy was suppressed. Later, Pedaritus put Tydaeus, son of Ion, and his supporters to death, upon the charge of Atticism. Eventually, the betrayal did not occur.[28]

In 411 B.C., during the summer, Thucydides reports that the fortification of the Eetioneia by the oligarchs of the Four Hundred in Athens aimed at leading the opposition whenever the oligarchs so dictated. The efforts of the moderates had, as a result, the dismantling of the fortification and the frustration of the betrayal.

It would be inaccurate, however, to suppose that the motives of fifth columns rested only upon politics. *Stasis* as used by Thucydides means factional strife or civil war within a city-state. The term does not refer only to political opposition between parties, but the condition which results from the fact that the parties no longer operate or feel the legal and moral obligation to operate within the boundaries laid down by the constitution. In *stasis,* the parties resort to illegal means, and violent means too, such as assassination, fighting, and expulsion of their political opponents. Thucydides reports that law breaks down, religious and moral constraints cease to function, the meanings of words and expressions are twisted to suit the needs of the occasion, and party loyalty becomes the strongest loyalty.[29] The term *stasis* was later used by Aristotle in a wider sense to include political and social strife as well as revolution in the city-state (μεταβολή πολιτείας).[30] The case of Corcyra provides a clear case of a planned betrayal which developed out of political and social strife between democrats and oligarchs. This incident, as reported by Diodorus, lays emphasis on the acute animosity between these political parties. In the winter of 411 B.C., the oligarchs planned to hand over the city to the Spartans. No further information is given regarding the plot of the pro-Lacedaemonian oligarchs. Corcyra remained democratic and attached to Athens as the *stasis* of 427 B.C. was resolved to the benefit of the democrats. What is known is that, as soon as the plot was discovered, the Corcyraean democrats sent for help to the city of Athens. The Athenians responded immediately by sending Conon with six hundred Messenian troops, which subsequently put to death the oligarchs, simultaneously driving into exile another thousand.

The report of Diodorus reveals a social distinction among the Corcyraean factions apart from the political one. At the very beginning, while emphasizing that this *stasis* had as its primary cause the deep-rooted hostility between the political parties, he goes on to say that it was due to other factors as well.[31] The pro-Lacedaemonian oligarchs are certainly depicted as προέχοντες τοῖς ἀξιώμασι τῶν Κορκυραίων καὶ τοὺς δυνατωτάτους τῶν πολιτῶν ὄντας. The fact that the fifth columnists numbered one thousand supporters suggests that, though they did not command a majority, many citizens of some social standing adhered to their party. To a certain extent this proposition finds support in the fact that, having expelled the oligarchs and their adherents, the democrats enlisted slaves and foreigners as citizens so as to strengthen the city as against the numbers and power (δύναμιν) of the exiled opponents.[32] The social and economic influence of the oligarchs in this case is confirmed by the sequence of events whereby the supporters of the Spartan faction succeeded in controlling the agora and calling back the exiles. Such political divisions between oligarchs and democrats were surely common in Greek city-states, but on this occasion, as well as others, the grounds for civil strife were not purely political.[33]

Let us examine in this context the fifth columnists, leaders of the Megarian democrats. Thucydides calls them οι τοῦ δήμου προστάται, the protectors of the popular party, not the protectors of the majority of the people, because they did not carry the majority with them. In an examination of this fifth-column activity, Ronald Legon has put forward a view which is important in assessing the motives of the *prostatai*. He asks, "why did the leaders of the Megarian democracy have to resort to treachery to achieve their ends? Why could they not openly propose a change of alliance to the Megarian demos gathered in assembly?" The answer he gives is that they did not suppose that the demos would approve an alliance with Athens under any circumstances, although there is no certain evidence as to why the democratic leaders were of this opinion. To quote the position he takes:

> The ordinary people of Megara seem to have been unable to view this political crisis in the same context as it was viewed by either the democratic leaders or their oligarchic counterparts. To the demos Megara was a sovereign state whose freedom was jeopardized by Athens. Any concession to the Athenians would have diminished Megara and exalted her enemy, and no Megarian patriot could allow this to happen. Even when the issue at stake was the democracy for which it had fought a few years earlier, the demos's attitude toward Athens was unchanged. Thus the common people of Megara adopted an inflexible stance which ultimately resulted in their loss of an effective franchise and any voice in their own government.
>
> This noble, if somewhat unrealistic, attitude on part of the demos was not shared by any other group. The democratic leaders realized that continued association with the Peloponnesian League would destroy democracy in Megara, and they took steps to preserve it, even at the cost of treating with Athens, Megara's old enemy. It is equally clear that the exiles and their friends in Megara relied upon the sympathy and even the intervention of the Peloponnesian states for their ultimate triumph. The responses of the great powers to the designs of the Megarian factions conform to this pattern. The Spartans had already befriended the Megarian oligarchs by allowing them to occupy Plataea, and there is little doubt that Sparta would have continued to use her influence on their behalf. Furthermore, the purpose of the garrison at Nisaea indicates that the Peloponnesians expected, or feared, a move toward Athens on the part of the Megarian democrats, made in the interests of preserving democracy and themselves. No more need be said regarding Athens's readiness to assist the Megarian democrats in their enterprise. In sum, all parties involved, with the sole exception of the Megarian demos, saw an inexorable link between Megara's international alignment and her internal government. Leaving aside the moral aspect of this issue, it is plain from the sequel that the demos was mistaken, and suffered for it.[34]

The view he is putting forward is that the Megarian *prostatai* acted to preserve democracy, and the lack of political awareness of patriotism of the Megarian demos forced them to commit treason and not openly propose alliance with Athens. Thus his conclusion is as follows:

> These observations cast a new light on what might otherwise appear as treasonous or subversive activity on the part of eminent politicians—democrats and oligarchs—in the smaller *poleis*. In reality, in the cases treated above, and

in numerous other instances, such apparent deviousness was the only course of
action open to political factions with even legitimate aspirations. [35]

Nevertheless, this proposition remains problematic. Firstly, the explanation
of why the demos could not have been expected to support a proposal for an
alliance with Athens is questionable. Initially, patriotism of the Megarian
people is offered as an explanatory factor. Later, it is said that the majority of
the people were not aware of the implications of the particular policies of the
day, which may hold some truth, but the report of Thucydides does not
actually support this proposition.

Secondly, irrespective of why the demos would not support the *prostatai*,
the fact remains that they did not, and, on Legon's argument, this in turn
forced the *prostatai* to commit treason. One could agree that the loss of the
support of the demos was the main incident in the political situation which
caused the *prostatai* to turn to committing a treasonous act. Nevertheless, it
also must be noted that the hypothetical explanation of the demos's failure to
support the *prostatai* has an important bearing on ascertaining the motives of
the *prostatai*. On the basis of the argument that he put forward, the *prostatai*,
in betraying the city, were defending the best interests of the demos, which
did not understand that the survival of democracy was at stake. So, in the
conclusion, the argument is "what might otherwise appear as treasonous or
subversive activity on the part of eminent politicians was in reality the only
course of action open to political factions with even legitimate aspirations."
This may be possible. However, the reader of the Thucydides would not fail
to spot the clear report that their action does not just appear as treasonous, but
it is treason. Thucydides does not attribute to them any honorable motives.
The *prostatai* acted to save themselves, no doubt. Thucydides lays emphasis
on such individuals's seeking to preserve themselves, not the democracy. [36]
The democratic leaders were aware of the fact that the *demos* would not hold
out under their (μετά σφων) leadership. [37] Furthermore, it could be argued
that the democratic *prostatai* were not motivated by concern for democracy,
the democratic institutions, or the democratic processes, because democracy
means the rule of the majority of the demos. The majority were no longer in
support of the *prostatai*.

Other instances of fifth columns, especially in the form of subversion in
cooperation with the enemy, include Argos. Argos, a democracy, remained
neutral in the course of the Archidamian War. There were, though, some
Argives who were for the Lacedaemonian cause. In 425 B.C., the Corinthians
received information from Argos of the forthcoming Athenian military intervention. [38] It may be supposed that the pro-Lacedaemonian Argives were
oligarchs that supported the Spartan cause in the hope of gaining control of
the government of the city.

After the conclusion of the alliance between Lacedaemon and Athens in 421 B.C., the democratic government of Argos initiated negotiations with the Corinthians and Boeotians, and eventually created an alliance with the Mantineans, Eleans, and Athenians. The Argives also organized a military force of one thousand young men, being both the strongest and the wealthiest. This force proved to be the force which dismantled the democracy. In the summer of 418 B.C. Agis led an army into the territory of Argos. The campaign ended in a truce, and the events leading to it indicate that the Argive oligarchs were cooperating with the Lacedaemonians. Thrasyllus, an Argive and one of the five generals, concluded a four-month truce with the Spartans. Thucydides reports that they arranged this truce entirely on their own and not by order of the people.[39] Not surprisingly, as soon as the Argive army returned home, the people prosecuted Thrasyllus, and his property was confiscated though he managed to flee. It is evident that the pro-Lacedaemonian oligarchs retained their political influence; hence they asked the Athenian military force to leave the city as Thucydides mentions. The battle of Mantinea followed at which the Spartans proved victorious. They sent political proposals to Argos to make arrangements for peace. The pro-Lacedaemonian oligarchs had as their political objective since the outset the subversion of the democracy. The battle of Mantinea had strengthened their position, because democracy effectively deteriorated and the only significant military force in Argos was the one thousand oligarchs. Thucydides vividly describes the way in which these fifth columnists intended to put their plan in practice. Firstly, they concluded a peace treaty and then they attacked democracy as such. The Thousand brought about the renunciation of the alliance between Athens, Elis, and Mantinea and concluded an alliance with Lacedaemon. In the spring of 417 B.C., the Thousand and the Lacedaemonians overthrew the democracy in Argos and consecrated an oligarchy.

The case of Corcyra is also characteristic of the manner in which fifth columns operated, aiming at subverting the constitution. In 427 B.C., the oligarchs of Corcyra overthrew the democratic government of the city-state by form of a coup, followed by the *stasis*.[40] The coup originated in a plan with the Corinthians. In particular, it encompassed the return of 250 Corcyreans, captives of the Corinthians, since the victory of the latter at Sybota. The prisoners were supposedly ransomed, with the *proxenoi* in Corfu, producing the appropriate amount of money required. The true facts were that they were convinced by the Corinthians to bring Corfu over to Corinth.[41] The captives had remained in Corinth for almost six years. As Gomme points out, these men had fought against Corinth in the 430s. "Perhaps the majority of them were moderately honest and patriotic and there had not always been friendship between Corinth and the first families in Kerkyra."[42] The motives here were political and economic, too. The prisoners and the oligarchs were no doubt men of wealth. The fact that they lived around the agora[43] and the harbor indicates that they were most probably merchants and landowners. It is very likely that they were persuaded by the Corinthians that, despite differences of the past, their political and economic interests would best be served through an alliance with the Peloponnesians. Much like the Argive fifth column, the oligarchs of Corcyra had two separate aims: the change in the foreign alignment of their city-state and the assumption of governmental control. Like the Argive oligarchs, it was their conspiracy that had internal disorder of the state as a result. The fifth column betrayals were sometimes the result of *stasis*. Here the opposite took place. The political and economic divisions were evident in Corcyra before the eruption of *stasis*. The conspiracy of the fifth column traitors in this case was the one which ignited the aggressive civil war.

Having examined the most important and conspicuous cases of betrayal, and, therefore, the corresponding activities of fifth columns, it is at this stage necessary to look at how the fifth columns acted in reality in the course of their subversive actions and what methods they used.

The tactics used involved attacks or betrayals in the course of the night. At night, when most of the citizens would be asleep, a setting of cover was provided. For example, the Plataean fifth columnists admitted the Thebans at night,[44] the betrayal of Amphipolis began at night,[45] and the betrayal of the walls of Megara took place before dawn.[46] The stormy weather was also a factor in the capture of the territory outside the walls of the city. The entrance of Brasidas into Torone took place at night when the Athenian soldiers were sleeping in the agora. Another especially dangerous timing for a city was a celebration or festival. A surprise attack during a festival was a method used on at least three occasions in the *History of the Peloponnesian War*. Plataea, for instance, was betrayed on a night in the course of a festival.[47] The subversion of the constitution by the oligarchs in Argos took place during a celebration. Attacks of this kind aimed at generating panic and confusion. At night or in the course of a celebration, causing confusion was much more attainable. Citizens asleep or in the midst of a festival could hardly be able to resist in an organized way. They would not be in a position to be informed about how many of the opponents had entered their city, or what places of the city the enemy controlled. In the case of the betrayal of Amphipolis, Brasidas was successful in causing confusion among the inhabitants.[48] At Plataea, Thucydides says that the citizens could not see at night.

The third part of this chapter will explore the way in which fifth columns were deployed in the strategy of the Peloponnesian War by the two main opponents, the Spartans and the Athenians, respectively.

In the Ten Years War, even before the war broke out, the Peloponnesians were aware that an effective strategy would be the instigation of revolts among the Athenian allies, depriving Athens of its revenues. Archidamus pointed out that such an enterprise would require naval power and money.[49]

In 428 B.C., the Mytilenaeans revolted from Athens and asked Sparta for succor. One argument they put forward to the Spartans was that support for their revolt would encourage further defections by allies of Athens. The relief force of Sparta under Alcidas arrived too late to save Mytilene. At that point, Teutiaplos suggested to Alcidas that an attempt be made to retake Mytilene with the help of fifth columnists. Alcidas, however, turned down this suggestion. Clearly, the fifth column in this context is connected with the strategy of Lacedaemon of instigating revolts within the Athenian alliance. Some historians have condemned the lack of daring on part of the Spartan admiral. But Alcidas may have been on a fund-raising mission, and this may well have influenced his decision to return to Sparta as quickly as possible. Beyond this, Alcidas may well have had a keener appreciation of the military realities of his time than posterity has attributed to him. His failure to undertake the instigation of revolts, given the fact that he could have had some fifth column support, and his later failure to support the fifth columnists in Corcyra should be understood in the light of Archidamus's statement at 1.80.4–81.4. Even with the aid of fifth columns, the Spartans could not successfully instigate revolts among Athens's maritime allies because Sparta did not control the sea.[50] Alcidas may have appreciated that control of the sea was necessary.

The most successful Spartan offensive of the Ten Years War was Brasidas's campaign in the north. His campaign best illustrates the strategy of wearing down Athens by detaching the allies, and the fifth column clearly played a vital role in his plans.

In the Sicilian expedition, on the other hand, Alcibiades argued that the Sicilian cities would not be capable of unified action due to their mixed populations, especially if they were in a situation of *stasis*, in the form of internal revolt and in the process of constitution changing, as he had heard. Alcibiades proposed that efforts be made so as to bring over the Sicilian cities. He suggested that Messina be approached first because of its strategic position.[51] The proposal of Alcibiades was pursued.[52] Eventually the diplomatic attempts were not successful. Therefore, preparations were made for the betrayal of the city. It is noteworthy that Thucydides, commenting on the Athenian failure at Sicily,[53] reports that the Athenians were not able to bring about a constitutional change by which they were accustomed to bringing over enemies. The recall of Alcibiades ruined the plan to take Messina. As Westlake observed,

> The Athenian failure at Messina, which Thucydides mentions almost casually, is of considerable significance because it suggests that, if Alcibiades had remained in Sicily for even a few more weeks, his plan might well have achieved a greater measure of success. He probably had in hand similar intrigues elsewhere. When after his recall a second attempt was made to win the support of Camarina (7.53; 88.2), public feeling there was well disposed towards Athens (88.1). If Alcibiades instead of the unknown spokesman Euphemus had con-

ducted the negotiations, he might well have devised some means of bringing about a result more favourable to the Athenians."[54]

Thucydides held that the political dissension in Athens, interpreted to mean the political attack on Alcibiades, was responsible for the defeat.[55] The view expressed by Gomme on this occasion does not find me agreed. Gomme put forward that "no one would conclude from Thucydides's narrative that it (the recall of Alicibiades) was decisive."[56]

The strategy of the Athenians up until now was not successful, and the Syracusans were becoming increasing confident. The Athenians made their first attack on Syracuse using the fifth-column stratagem to draw the Syracusans out to Catana, which, indeed, they accomplished. In accordance with the proposal of Alcibiades, the Athenians should have launched a large-scale attack against Syracuse, in case the betrayals failed. When the command was left solely to Nicias, he proved to be reluctant to follow up the first attack of the winter of that year. Nicias was against the Sicilian expedition from the outset, emphasizing the difficulties of supply, money, and lack of cavalry, and feared prosecution should he failed in the campaign. Plutarch mentions that "he impressed his colleagues as lacking in daring, that they talked of his waste of time."[57] Despite the shortcomings of Nicias at Syracuse, a factor in his conduct of the siege is the fifth column in Syracuse. A significant view has been put forward that Nicias was reluctant to raise the siege until his position became wholly untenable because he expected the fifth columnists to bring about either a capitulation or a betrayal.[58] Thucydides clearly mentions that there were fifth columnists that wished to betray the city.

Notes

1. See generally the excellent study of Luis Losada, *The Fifth Column in the Peloponnesian War* (Leiden: Brill, 1972).

2. Thucydides, *History of the Peloponnesian War*, 4 vols., *Loeb Classical Library* 108, 109, 110, and 169, trans. C. Forster Smith (Cambridge: Harvard University Press, 1919–1923) (hereafter cited as Thucydides), 3.2.3

3. Thucydides, 5.76.2: τόν δῆμον ἐν Ἄργει καταλύσαι.

4. Many other acts constituted treason nevertheless. Athenian generals were aware of the fact that they might face a charge of treason because of defeat in the field of battle. Interesting evidence for the application of the charge of προδοσία is provided by an Attic inscription, I. G. I2 105; M. N. Tod, *A Selection of Greek Historical Inscriptions* I (Oxford: Oxford University Press, 1947), 91; R. Meiggs and D. Lewis, *A Selection of Greek Historical Inscriptions* (Oxford: Oxford University Press, 1969), 91.

5. "Προδιδόναι: The verb means to betray, deliver up, give up and naturally, therefore, describes the actions of the fifth columnists. It occurs thirty-one times in Thucydides, of which sixteen instances, or a little more than fifty percent, refer to fifth-column activities. Of course the word is often used where it does not specifically refer to the act of treason. It is possible to "betray" one's friends, expectations. . . . Thucydides explains that the Syracusan soldiers at Syracuse were not inferior to the Athenians in courage but, because of their lack of experience, τήν βούλησιν ἄκοντες προυδίδοσαν. If we look more closely at the fifteen instances of προδιδόναι in Thucydides which do not refer to fifth columns, we find that only two refer to other acts of treason. This confirms our findings with respect to προδοσία: when Thucydides mentions treason, he is almost always talking about fifth columns" (Losada, *The Fifth Column in the Peloponnesian War*, 9).

6. Thucydides, 4.76.2.

7. Thucydides, 4.110.1. "Other expressions describe the negotiations or arrangements between the fifth columnists and the enemy: at 4.54.3 we are told that the capitulation of Cythera was accomplished more speedily and advantageously because during the siege some men of Cythera had been in communication with Nicias, ἦσαν δέ τινες καὶ γενόμενοι τῷ Νικία λόγοι πρότερον πρός τινας τῶν Κυθηρίων" (Losada, *The Fifth Column in the Peloponnesian War*, 13).

8. For a useful list of betrayals see Losada, *The Fifth Column in the Peloponnesian War*, 16–21.

9. Thucydides, 2.2–4, 3.65.2.

10. Thucydides, 2.79.2.

11. Thucydides, 3.30.

12. Thucydides, 4.7.

13. Thucydides, 4.25.7.

14. Thucydides, 4.49.

15. Thucydides, 4.52.1.

16. Thucydides, 4.66–74.

17. Thucydides, 4.76–77.

18. Thucydides, 4.103.2–106.

19. Thucydides, 4.110–112.

20. Thucydides, 4.121.2.

21. Thucydides reports that the natives welcomed Brasidas, ὥσπερ ἀθλητῇ. Gomme, quoting Grote, observes on this: "The sympathy and admiration felt in Greece towards a victorious athlete was not merely an intense sentiment in the Grecian mind, but was perhaps of all others the most widespread and Panhellenic. It was connected with the religion, the taste, and the love of recreation common to the whole nation—while politics tended rather to disunite the separate cities: it was further a sentiment at once familiar and intensely personal. Of its exaggerated intensity throughout Greece the philosophers often complained, not without reason. But Thucydides cannot convey a more lively idea of the enthusiasm and unanimity with which Brasidas was welcomed at Skione . . . than by using this simile" (*A Historical Commentary on Thucydides*, Volume III, Oxford: Oxford University Press, 1956, 610).

22. Thucydides, 4.121.2.
23. Thucydides, 5.33.1–3.
24. Thucydides, 5.62.2.
25. Thucydides, 5.116.3.
26. Thucydides, 6.74.1–2.
27. Thucydides, 6.103.4.
28. Thucydides, 8.24.6, 31.1, 38.3.
29. Thucydides, 3.82.2.8.
30. See *Politics*, Book VIII, *Oxford Classical Texts* (Oxford: Oxford University Press, 1957).
31. Diodorus Siculus, *Library of History, Volume 6, Loeb Classical Library* (Cambridge: Harvard University Press, 1952), 13.38.1.
32. Thucydides uses the word δύναμις to mean power of money in 2.97.3 and 6.46.3.
33. As Gomme pointed out, Thucydides wrote a history of the war, not a political history of Athens or Greece (*A Historical Commentary on Thucydides*, Volume I, Oxford: Oxford University Press, 1956, 25). In fact this is an oversimplification of the matter, because the Thucydidean history is full of valuable reports on political events and factors that shaped life in the Greek world, and even analysis of social conditions that contributed to the eruption of the great civil war that he purports to describe and hand down to subsequent generations.
34. Legon, R., "Megara and Mytilene," *Phoenix* 22 (1968): 221.
35. Legon, "Megara and Mytilene," 223.
36. Thucydides, 4.66.3.
37. According to Gomme, *A Historical Commentary on Thucydides*, Volume III, 528: "μετά σφων καρτερειν: 'to hold out (both against the hardships of the war and the oligarchic pressure) under *their* leadership,' 'with their help alone.' Note that, in effect, τόν δῆμον is something quite different from του δήμου, though these leaders would identify them. Similarly, below σφίσι is themselves (the leaders), but ὑπό σφῶν to be taken with κατελθειν, is 'by their fellow citizens.' (We could take ὑπὸ σφῶν with τούς ἐκπεσόντας, so that it again means 'themselves the leaders'; but this is less effective than the contrast with the Athenians, who would be safer for them than their own countrymen)."
38. Thucydides, 4.42.3.
39. Thucydides, 5.60.1.
40. Thucydides, 3.70.6.
41. Thucydides, 3.70.1.
42. Gomme, *A Historical Commentary on Thucydides*, Volume II (Oxford: Oxford University Press, 1956), 359.
43. Thucydides, 3.72.3.
44. Thucydides, 2.2.1.
45. Thucydides, 4.103. Thucydides says that Brasidas pushed on to Amphipolis on a stormy night (ἐχώρει τήν νύκτα), wishing to escape the notice of those in the city except the traitors (Thucydides, 4.103.1–2).
46. Thucydides, 4.67.2.: ἤσθετο οὐδείς. "Grote, v, p. 288 notes the surprisingly successful secrecy kept in this affair by all concerned, who must have been fairly numerous. At Athens presumably the expedition had been voted as an ordinary invasion of the Megarid; if Demosthenes had simply asked for some light-armed and περίπολοι to accompany the force, it would have been granted him after his success at Sphakteria" (Gomme, *A Historical Commentary on Thucydides*, Volume III, 530). It is noteworthy that light-armed troops were also employed in the course of operations such as this along with περίπολοι. Gomme says that "very little is known of this military force. It is often stated that they were foreign mercenaries; but for this there is little evidence—none here nor at viii. 92. 2, 5 (their only mention in Thucydides), nor for two-thirds at least of the fourth century, Xenophon, Poroi, 4. 47, 52; only towards the end of the century does the evidence of inscriptions show that foreigners were engaged; and Xenophon says that the *peripoloi* would always be there to help the cavalry check raiding of the mines of Laureion by a force from Boeotia. They seem in Thucydides' time and later to be a special mobile force, in peace-time at least probably already formed of epheboi who got their

training partly in this way, partly by garrison—duty in the fortresses" (*A Historical Commentary on Thucydides*, Volume III, 529).

47. Thucydides, 3.56.2.

48. Thucydides, 4.111.2.

49. Thucydides, 1.80.4.

50. Losada, *The Fifth Column in the Peloponnesian War*, 119.

51. Thucydides, 6.48.

52. Thucydides, 6.50.1.

53. Thucydides, 7.55.2.

54. H. D. Westlake, *Individuals in Thucydides* (Cambridge: Cambridge University Press, 1968), 224–225.

55. Thucydides, 2.65.2.

56. A. W. Gomme, *A Historical Commentary on Thucydides*, 196.

57. Plutarch, *Lives Volume III: Nicias, Loeb Classical Library 65* (Cambridge: Harvard University Press, 1916), 21.4.

58. Losada, *The Fifth Column in the Peloponnesian War*, 128–129.

Chapter Seven Point One

Strategy in the Peloponnesian War and Modern International Politics

The contribution of Thucydides in strategic studies is due to the fact that he analyzed, for the first time in history, the two most important forms of strategy: the strategy of exhaustion and the strategy of nullification.

The most widely accepted and pursued kind of strategy is that of nullification. This strategy aims at the destruction of the military forces and equipment of the opponent through decisive battles. The campaigns of Napoleon constitute typical examples of this strategy, whereas the classical theoretical statement of it may be found in the book by Carl von Clausewitz, *On War*.[1]

The grand strategy of Lacedaemon in the course of the Peloponnesian War corresponds fully to the model laid down by Napoleon and Clausewitz, the Prussian general who fought against Napoleon himself. During many years, the Spartans attempted to bring about a decisive land victory. Similarly, they made every effort to achieve the same result at sea, when they acquired sufficient naval power to pursue this goal. In the course of armed conflict, Sparta proved victorious by land and by sea on numerous occasions. As far as land conflicts are concerned, since the Athenians chose not to come out of their walls to fight, the decisive victory was won against the Argives and their allies in Mantinea in 418 B.C., thus securing Spartan sovereignty in the Peloponnese. As far as navy battles are concerned, victory over the Athenians in Aigospotamoi in 405 B.C. was the most decisive one in the great war. So one may trace in the Lacedaemonian strategy the ancient model of the strategy of nullification, which was destined to dominate Western strategic thought for many centuries.

The dominant position of the strategy of nullification reached its apex during the period from the end of the wars of Napoleon to the end of the Second World War (1815–1945). The first instance of its implementation in the course of this period occurred with the general who was in charge of the military forces of the South during American Civil War (1861–1865). His victories in the battles of Bull Run (1862) and Chancellorsville (1863) caused serious damage and brought about crisis to the military administration of the North. In the long run, however, the superiority of the North in terms of military equipment was sufficient to secure its victory in the American Civil War. It is particularly interesting, however, that the strategy pursued by the North, under the command of General Grant, was also a strategy of nullification. The aim was to utterly destroy the military forces of the opponent through the invincible military manpower and surplus of military equipment of the North. It is noteworthy that, ever since, this is precisely the form of strategy which the US armed forces follow in the field of battle. Mostly, they openly face and straightforwardly attack their enemy through causing various attritions and by using huge militia that far supersede those acquired by the majority of their opponent states.

As far as the European continent is concerned, the strategy of nullification reached a point of perfectionism in the Prussian headquarters under the leadership of General von Moltke. Through the political leadership of Bismarck, the decisive victories of the Prussian army in Santova (1866) against the Austrians, and against the French, brought about dramatic changes in the map of Europe, which culminated in the formation and foundation of the German empire. The campaigns of Moltke constitute characteristic examples of an approach which clearly pursues the model laid down by Clausewitz. Firstly, war was used as a tool to achieve the objectives explicitly put down by the political leadership, and secondly the destruction of the military forces of the opponent was the further aim to be pursued and eventually achieved.

The strategy of nullification was employed in particular during the two world wars. However, the large-scale mobilization of the forces of the sides engaged in these wars proved that it was impossible for victory to be achieved only through one decisive battle, no matter how important this might have been. The notion of battle extended itself to cover long and sustained armed confrontations, which lasted over weeks and months, unlike many operations in the Peloponnesian War (though one may therein also trace military campaigns of similar magnitude and duration). The Battle of Britain (1940–1941) is a paradigm example of such significant battles. The world wars were pointedly and characteristically termed as "total wars," because engaged in battles was not only the armed forces of the opponents, but, in the end, major parts of the civilian population and infrastructures, too.

The nullification form of strategy diminished to some extent, because of the creation of nuclear weapons. Since the end of the Second World War (1945), the use of armed force, that is war, as a means to materialize and fulfill political objectives did not altogether disappear, though it has been somewhat restrained, especially among nuclear powers. It is almost certain that in the event of nuclear war, the states involved will not be able to avoid disaster.[2] However, the same conclusion may be said to apply in the case of a conventional war, that is, one launched with use of conventional (nonnuclear) weapons.[3] Nevertheless, this is not to suggest that the phenomenon of war is going to disappear from the international sphere. The post–Cold War era denotes that war plays a significant role in international politics as well as in the domestic affairs of states.

Powerful states have not abandoned their firm political aims, that of world dominance and primacy. Quite the opposite. States have recalled and pretty much implemented the so-called strategy of exhaustion. This form of strategy gives emphasis to a number of means, beyond the military ones, and further causes economic losses and damages to the opponent. This strategy has a glorious past. The strategy of Pericles in the Peloponnesian War was one such form of strategy, which proved effective and victorious, at least in the first phase of the Peloponnesian War.

In accordance with the strategy and policy of Pericles, the Athenians avoided fighting battles on the land, choosing to remain fortified in their walls. By using their naval power, they discouraged or even frustrated disertion by their allies on the one hand, and they unleashed large-scale naval attacks against the Lacedaemonians, on the other. The immediate outcome of this policy was for Sparta to recognize that it was not possible at the time to dissolve the Athenian alliance and empire, and that they had to come to terms with Athens by concluding the Peace of Nicias in 421 B.C.[4]

Many centuries later, since the seventeenth century, another great naval power, namely Great Britain, pursued a grand strategy of exhaustion similar to that of Pericles, termed as "the British way of war." The British strategy emphasized (1) blockades of European harbors, (2) distant naval operations against colonies of her opponent states, (3) economic support to allied states, (4) symbolic presence of marines in European countries, and (5) regional raids in coastal areas of states of Europe through an impressive navy.

The United States of America, in order to face effectively the USSR during the Cold War, drew from past experience and implemented the strategy of exhaustion. The similarity between the strategy of Pericles and the American strategy in the course of the Cold War is striking and really impressive. The American strategy against the Soviet Union, as it then was, included the following measures:

1. Containment of the Soviet power and influence through a network of alliances around the frontiers of the USSR. (This policy is actually still pursued by the United States in the post–Cold War era.)
2. Economic preclusion of the USSR from having access to the economy and technology of the Western world.

3. Undermining of the legitimacy of the Soviet internal political system through providing support to political opposition parties and groups.
4. Strengthening the technological and military capacity of the United States (through "Star Wars," for instance), so that the USSR might reach a point of economic exhaustion.
5. Emphasizing the leadership role of the United States in the West.
6. Keeping large budgets for defense purposes over long periods of time, so that the balance of power might be retained.
7. Supporting enemies of the USSR, for example Afghanistan.
8. Undermining the USSR internationally, by stressing the "illegitimate" character of the Soviet governmental system and model.

As a result, the Soviet Union could not sustain American pressures any longer, and therefore its political system, as it was then structured, collapsed soon afterwards (1989–1990).

The Cold War is not the only modern instance of the use of the strategy of exhaustion. This strategy was also pursued by the United States and allied countries in Bosnia in 1995. The United States employed a variety of measures, so that they might bring about exhaustion of their opponent: economic war, diplomatic isolation of Bosnia, and political pressures, to name a few. The air strikes which ensued were not but a single measure among those implemented by the Americans in that crisis. Prior to those strikes and air raids, the Serbs of Bosnia were already economically weakened and diplomatically isolated. Further, the United States had influenced the local balance of power by providing military equipment to Croatia and Bosnian Muslims, plainly put, the enemies of Bosnian Serbs, and had also encouraged formation of military alliances among Croatians and Muslims of Bosnia. Finally, the United States made sure that public opinion in the United States was firmly for the operations in Bosnia, in an effort to legalize its actions in a way. These strategic elements and methods, when having been used, were sufficient to effectuate acceptance on part of the Serbs of the terms laid down by the United States and NATO in the context of the Dayton Agreement.

In the years to come, the strategy of exhaustion may be further used, in view of the sensitivity shown by Western societies stemming from the vicissitudes of war and its losses, as well as the rising cost of maintaining strong armies and capably using military power in armed operations internationally. Processing information for military purposes and other methods are expected to succor significantly the use of armed force. A parallel, rather distant on this occasion, may be inferred from the strategy of Pericles in the Peloponnesian War. Some Athenian achievements of the day, for example the buildup of powerful and fast triremes, reinforced naval operations, which thus became an indispensable part of the strategy of Pericles.

The world will most likely witness, if this has not already been witnessed, wars which will mainly comprise air strikes and economic embargos (see for example the first Iraq War in 1991). This kind of war may actually find its close parallel in the strategy of Pericles. Naval operations commonly pursued by Pericles are the counterpart of the modern use of submarines and aircraft carriers that primarily bring about heavy destruction of the opponent's military forces and simultaneously lessen the possibility of grave losses to the detriment of states using the above-mentioned methods and strategy.[5]

Despite the above, the primary importance attached by experts in international politics and strategic studies to the strategy of exhaustion and the strategy of nullification, the pioneer of which is the state of Sparta, has not at all been eliminated. It is noteworthy that even the strategy of Pericles was mostly successful only when it pursued the fundamental and powerful strategy of nullification, which involves face-to-face military attack against the enemy. The incident of Pylos and Sphacteria attest to the credibility of this strategy and the truth of these words.[6] In modern international politics, the wars in Iraq in 2001 and 2011 demonstrate the primacy that is still attached to this form of strategy. Iraq had already faced economic and political pressures prior to the air raids, but the latter were mainly the ones that brought about destruction of the Iraqi military forces and equipment. Final and total subjugation of Iraq came with the protracted land campaigns of the United States in the Iraqi mainland, where the Americans proved that they are magnificently well trained to sustain the peculiar morphology and climatic conditions of a desert. Thus, the Thucydidean and Napoleonic model still stands firmly in modern international politics.

Only recently, though, in 2014, the United States was skeptical in launching air and land military operations against Syria, not because the American strategic analysts ceased to be more keen on practicing the strategy of nullification, but because of the danger originating from the neighboring state of Iran unleashing weapons of mass destruction against the Israeli state. This danger was further reinforced by the fact that Russia, with its strong military base in the area, would most likely have been involved in that armed crisis.

In the future, if one might foretell political developments in this regard, the military strategy to be predominantly used will be that of nullification. The objective will be the classic one, that is, total destruction of the enemy's military forces. Both the United States and Russia will most probably attempt to take advantage of their enormous capacity in terms of land, air, and sea power.

Notes

1. Carl von Clausewitz, *On War*, trans. J. J. Graham (London: N. Trübner, 1873).

2. It goes without saying that the threat of use of nuclear weapons is still employed as a means of policy.

3. See John Mearsheimer, *Conventional Deterrence* (Ithaca: Cornell University Press, 1983), 1–66, where it is stated that theoretically it is still possible for states to achieve victory quickly in the course of a conventional war, thus avoiding incurring the severe losses of such a protracted nonnuclear war.

4. In the final sections of his first speech, Pericles must convince the Athenians that Attica, land Athens has held for hundreds of years, should be sacrificed so that Athens can fight a war to protect her claim on an overseas empire. In order to accomplish this, Pericles argues not that Attica has been wasted before by Athens's enemies, and that the Athenians know from experience that Attica can recover, but much more radically that Attica is dispensable: "If they attack our land with their infantry, we will sail against theirs, and it will not be the same thing for some part of the Peloponnesus to be wasted as for all of Attica [to be wasted]. For they will not have any other place they can take as a replacement without a battle, but we have much land both on the islands and the continent. For control of the sea is a great thing (μέγα το της θαλάσσης κράτος). Only consider: if we were islanders, who would be harder to capture?" (Thucydides, *History of the Peloponnesian War*, 4 vols., *Loeb Classifcal Library* 108, 109, 110, and 169, trans. C. Forster Smith [Cambridge: Harvard University Press, 1919–1923] [hereafter cited as Thucydides], 1.143.4–5).

"All of Attica can be wasted without much harm to Athens, Pericles argues since this loss can be compensated with holdings elsewhere. Although the allies' land must be taken and held by force, Pericles does not distinguish Athens's ownership of this land from Athens's ownership of territory in Attica. His rhetorical stance throughout the speeches will be to treat allied land as a unified and subordinated entity, particular problems which he will not address" (Edith Foster, *Thucydides, Pericles, and Periclean Imperialism*, Cambridge: Cambridge University Press, 2010, 147).

5. "For you [Athenians] believe that you rule only the allies. But I argue that of the two visibly useful parts of the world, namely earth and sea, you are the absolute masters of all of the latter, both to the extent that you now possess it and also to whatever extent you wish, since no one, neither the King nor any other people of those presently existing will hinder you from sailing with your present naval resources" (Thucydides, 2.62.2). Athens rules the empire and the Athenian navy is invincible, Pericles argues, by any human force; furthermore, no one can hinder the Athenians from making themselves masters of as much of the sea as they wish: the sea, an element of the world, is a possession of their will. Like gods, the Athenians will decide their wishes (these will include possessing more of the world) and fulfill them, such is the power of Athens's navy to elevate mortal men. But, see Foster, *Thucydides, Pericles, and Periclean Imperialism*, 187: "Pericles's claims are un-Thucydidean, and ought to have been un-Periclean: Thucydides repeatedly shows that Pericles knew both Athens' vulnerabilities, and also the real extent of Athens' resources, down to the last penny."

6. Ἐγένετό τε ὁ θόρυβος μέγας καὶ ἀντηλλαγμένος τοῦ ἑκατέρων τρόπου περὶ τὰς ναῦς. Ὥστε Ἀθηναιους Λακεδαιμονιους μέν, ὑπὸ προθυμίας καὶ ἐκπλήξεως ὡς εἰπεῖν ἐκ γῆς τε καὶ ταύτης Λακωνικῆς καὶ ἐς τὴν ἑαυτῶν πολεμίαν οὖσαν ἐκ γῆς ἐναυμάχουν. Ἀθηναίους ἀπὸ νεῶν ἐπεζομάχουν. Clearly Athenians did not launch a naval attack in the strict sense of the word but were conducting a land fight though being in their own vessels.

Chapter Seven Point Two

The Grand Strategy of Sparta

In order that a complete and thoroughgoing strategic analysis of the Peloponnesian War may be compiled, it is necessary to explore the strategies pursued by the opponent states, though emphasis will here be placed upon the grand strategy of Sparta, which eventually proved victorious, despite some of its drawbacks.

The Peloponnesian War is often considered as a conflict between a naval power (Athens) and a land power (Sparta). However, matters are more complicated. It is sufficient to say at the outset that Sparta, though fundamentally a land power, was at some point forced to build up a strong navy, so that she might face Athens on an equal footing at sea.

The *History of the Peloponnesian War* is unique, inter alia, because it fleshes out what was to become in the years which followed the main forms of strategy in international politics. Two forms of strategy were largely employed in the course of the great war between Sparta and Athens which constitute the basis of modern strategic studies, namely the strategy of nullification and the strategy of exhaustion. The strategy of nullification, on the one hand, aims at utterly destroying the military forces of the opponent state(s), whereas the strategy of exhaustion uses other methods, such as traditional battles, economic embargos, and naval blockades for example, so as to bring about the eventual subjugation of the enemy. It is noteworthy that the campaigns of Napoleon pose the paradigm example of the strategy of nullification in modern history. Similarly, von Clausewitz, in his book *On War*, developed a theory of war which is to a great extent based on this very strategy.[1]

Sparta pursued a strategy of nullification, whereas Athens followed the strategy of exhaustion. Although, under the leadership of Pericles, Athens pursued the strategy of exhaustion, in the Sicilian expedition Athens adopted the grand strategy of nullification.

The conflict as between Lacedaemon and Athens was much the product of two opposing and entirely different domestic structures of city-states, each of which had its own peculiarly interesting constitutional government. The constitution of Sparta, on the one hand, was an amalgamation of monarchy, aristocracy, and limited democracy, often overall regarded as a rather oligarchic governmental system. It certainly did not acquire the flexibility of the mechanisms of the Athenian constitution, which was, by definition, a democracy. The main reason which often explains the aristocratic character of the Lacedaemonian constitution may be found in the fact that the Dorians, having subjugated the local population of Helots, had to be wary of the constant possibility of a Helot revolt in the interior of the Peloponnese.

The strategic culture of the Lacedaemonians is eloquently reflected in the speech of their allies, the Corinthians:[2]

> Besides, surely we if anyone have the right to level complaints against our neighbours, especially when such large differences are at stake—and ones to which you are quite insensitive in our view. You seem never once to have analysed these Athenians, to see just what sort of people you are going to be set up against nor how totally different they are from yourselves.[3]

Contrary to the innovative constitution of the Athenians, the Spartan constitution was very much conservative. The pivotal role played by the elderly members of the senate in the constitutional life, though securing stability in politics, was the main reason for this conservativism. Further, as already mentioned, the constant danger posed by the Helot population forced the Lacedaemonians to be perpetually careful to prevent a revolt which would upset internal affairs of their city. As a result, the foreign policy of Sparta was fundamentally dictated by the conservative character of the city's constitution.

It is important to reflect upon the strategies of both Athens and Sparta just prior to the outbreak of the Peloponnesian War, in order to comprehend the continuity of the policies that the two cities pursued respectively in wartime. Athens, on the one hand, managed to build up a strong navy, which controlled the Aegean islands, and subsequently formed a mighty empire. Consequently, she was the one to lead the struggle of the Greeks against the Persians, though one should not forget that some of the most decisive battles of the Persian Wars were those of Thermopylae and Plataea, which were absolutely the outcome of Lacedaemonian efforts and sacrifices on the battlefield. The expansionist Athenian strategy succeeded, at the end of the Persian Wars, to exert absolute control upon the city allies, many of which were placed under taxation (φόρου υποτελείς) on a regular basis. Sparta, on the other hand, though having proved to be the power which effectively and virtually liberated Hellas in the struggles against the Persians (one's attention, of course, should always be directed to the field of the battle of Marathon 490 B.C. and the glorious navy battle of Salamis 480 B.C., which were predominantly the product of Athenian valor), chose to withdraw from the leadership of Greece as soon as the Persian Wars came to a conclusion. As a result, at the outbreak of the Peloponnesian War, Athens was a pure empire, having founded its power upon a strong navy as well as close trade relations with her neighbors and subservient city-states, whereas Sparta was merely the head of a league, which was fundamentally based on huge military power.

Let us now examine closely the strategies of the opponent states in view of the then prevailing balance of power and the international environment of the day. Firstly, it is essential to stress that the naval power of Athens, as well as its flourishing economy, would guarantee that the city, if not invincible, could definitely not suffer a defeat at a large-scale confrontation with Lacedaemon. It was evident in the words of Archidamus uttered before the Spartan assembly (ἀπέλλα) that the grand strategy of Sparta, had at the time, reached a deadlock. While the power of Athens was dramatically rising, the immediate effect being that the interests of the Lacedaemonian allies were severely damaged and thus a fundamental pillar of Spartan security and foreign policy was undermined, Sparta did not acquire the means to face, let alone eliminate, the sources of Athenian might, that is, her navy and economic wealth. It is necessary to mention in this regard that, according to the statements of Thucydides himself, Athens, though having suffered severe losses by the end of the so called "first Peloponnesian War" (445 B.C.), managed to strengthen her economy resources,[4]

> The Spartans exercised their leadership not by making allies subject to tribute but by taking good care to ensure that they were governed by oligarchies and served Spartan interests exclusively. The Athenians, by contrast, ruled by taking possession of the ships of allied cities over time, except for those of Chios and Lesbos, and by imposing fixed taxes on all these. Their own military resource available for this war was therefore greater than it had ever been when the alliance against Persia was intact and at the height of its power.[5]

Following Archidamus, the problem of the rise of Athenian power, and therefore the existing threat posed by it against the security and well-being of Lacedaemon, could not be faced and resolved immediately. Sparta should first make the necessary steps in order to improve the balance of power. Apart from strengthening ties with her allies within the Peloponnesian League, Lacedaemon ought to have made sure that she entered into new alliances, inviting even the Persians themselves, who might potentially provide what Lacedaemon lacked, that is money and a formidable navy, both of which were at the disposal of her rival city-state.[6]

> I am certainly not proposing that we turn a blind eye, however—that you just let them harm our allies and do nothing to arrest their schemes. But make no move to arms just yet. Instead, send a formal complaint to them without explicitly indicating whether we intend to go to war or make concessions, and then let us use the time to get our own forces ready by acquiring new allies, both Greek and foreign, to add to our naval or financial resources (since no one could blame people in our situation—the target of Athenian designs—if we seek salvation by attaching to our cause not only Greeks but also foreigners). At the same time we should be making our own preparations.[7]

Unfortunately, Archidamus was not successful in trying to persuade the assembly, which at the end pursued the argument of ephor Sthenelaidas. Sthenelaidas did not attempt to subvert any of the arguments of Archidamus, but merely argued that the acts of injustice done by the Athenians against the Peloponnesian League should be met powerfully, and that the only powerful response was war. He characteristically said:[8]

> The Athenians spoke a great deal but I have no idea what they meant. They had a lot to say in praise of themselves but at no point did they deny that they are wrongdoing our allies and people of the Peloponnese. They may have been good against the Persians in the past but now they are bad as far as we are concerned, so they deserve a double dose of punishment for changing from good to bad. We, however, are the same now as we were then and the "prudent" thing for us to do is not look on while they do down our allies nor put off punishing them in return, any more than the allies can put off their suffering. Others have money and ships and horses, but we have good allies and we must not betray them to the Athenians. Nor should the matter be settled by lawsuits and speeches when the damage is not a matter of words; but we must hit back quickly and with all our might. And don't let anyone tell you that at a time when we are being wronged the proper thing to do is to have a discussion. It is for those who are about to wrong us who ought to be having the discussion— and a long one at that. Vote for war then, as the reputation of your city of Sparta demands, and do not let the Athenians grow any stronger. Let us not abandon our allies, but with the gods on our side let us advance on the wrongdoers.[9]

The two Lacedaemonians surely differed in their estimation of the balance of power. Archidamus, though he did not explicitly preclude war, suggested that Athens was becoming more powerful than Lacedaemon in certain important respects. He was simply saying that Lacedaemon should first strengthen herself and then move on towards organizing war campaigns against the Athenians. It seems that the majority of the Lacedaemonians, including of course Sthenelaidas, still firmly believed that Lacedaemon was the mightiest state in the Greek world. It goes without saying, however, that both Sthenelaidas and his audience were very emotional at the time and placed emphasis upon defending the sacred land of Lacedaemon along with her customs, standing by the long-held principles with which they had been saturated. The grand strategy of Sparta was destined to pay the price of this consideration, though, again, one should always keep in consideration that the Lacedaemonians would naturally fight for their realm and way of life whatever the cost might have been. Sthenelaidas and his followers supposed that the war would end shortly and that the Lacedaemonian invasion into Attica would have been a matter of a few weeks or months. The subsequent events proved that they were at fault as regards their hopes, suppositions, or overoptimism; Athens did not surrender after a series of Lacedaemonian attacks, and conversely Lacedaemon had to sustain heavy losses because of abrupt, well-planned, and fierce operations of the Athenian navy.

The balance of power seemed to alter after the destruction of the Athenian fleet in Sicily in 413 B.C. Apart from her obvious advantage, that is, superiority in terms of land armed forces, Sparta was now to acquire mighty war vessels, whereas Athens was at the brink of total decadence. Further, the Persians commenced providing economic support to Lacedaemon. Pisander, the Athenian politician, characteristically addressed his compatriots: [10]

> This is not going to happen unless we govern ourselves more prudently and restrict office to fewer people than now, so that the King comes to trust us; unless we stop consulting more about our constitution than about our salvation in the present situation (we can always make some changes later if there is anything we don't like); and unless we recall Alcibiades, who is the only man alive able to bring this off. [11]

The Persians not only did not pursue a different policy, which would probably favor the Athenians, but enhanced the position of Lacedaemon by succoring her the more. Consequently, the balance of power changed dramatically and shifted to the benefit of the Lacedaemonians and to the detriment of the Athenians.

With regard to the political objectives of the two major opponent states, Athens, on the one hand, had limited objectives under the leadership of Pericles, aiming merely at maintaining the status quo, and Sparta, on the other, had unlimited objectives, that is, in fact, the disintegration of the entire Athenian empire. Taking into account the strategy culture of Lacedaemon this must have been a novelty in the experiences of the Lacedaemonians. It has already been pointed out that Athens used a strategy of exhaustion, whereas Lacedaemon pursued a strategy of nullification. This strategy was particularly offensive, and face-to-face war on land was its main element, though naval operations were not of course precluded, but in certain circumstances were deemed imperative.

This very strategy was particularly favored by Archidamus, who, however, reckoned that Lacedaemon in the particular circumstances did not have the means to implement such a strategy; hence he suggested that further preparations were a must. On the contrary, Sthenelaidas firmly supported the same form of strategy; but believed that his city did have the means at its disposal to pursue it at least by land.

The objectives of the strategy of Athens, it is necessary to stress, altered drastically in 415 B.C., when the Athenians undertook to launch a military expedition in Sicily. Athens decided to materialize unlimited objectives, aiming at expanding her empire over the whole of the Greek world. This shift in the objectives of Athenian policy dictated simultaneously that the strategy used correspondingly should conform to these objectives. Consequently, a strategy of nullification was at the forefront of Athenian military practices at the beginning of the Sicilian campaign.

The Sicilian expedition, though, ended up with the defeat of the Athenians, to a large extent due to the fact that the Lacedaemonians had militarily intervened, having secured significant help on the part of Alcibiades and having virtually put in practice their strategy of nullification. Having completed their large-scale military intervention in Sicily, the Lacedaemonians took up arms and engaged in further fighting within Greece itself. At the same time, allies of Athens revolted; the immediate result of which fact was that the Athenian empire disintegrated and witnessed deterioration of its real power. Athens, however, in an attempt to retain the remnants of its empire, kept pursuing the strategy of exhaustion. Since the Athenians had to face up to the Lacedaemonian threat against their naval power, they constantly set as a central objective of their policy and strategy naval battles against the Spartans. The outcome was that not only Lacedaemon but Athens too was eventually pursuing the grand strategy of nullification.

As regards the means used by Lacedaemon in the implementation of its grand strategy, it need be said that the threat of the use of military force was one example of such means. Archidamus, especially, employed very often this method or tool of strategy. Noteworthy are his words towards the Lacedaemonians:[12]

> If they then pay any heed to our representations, so much the better. But if not, after two or three years have passed we shall be better equipped to take them on, if that is what we decide to do. And perhaps when they see the level of our preparations and see that these match our claims they might be more inclined to compromise, while they still have their land intact and can make decisions about valuable property that still exists and is not yet ruined. Think of their land just as a hostage—and the better cultivated it is the better the hostage. We should spare it as much as possible instead of driving them to desperation and making them harder to manage.[13]

This method, which might otherwise be termed as high diplomacy on the part of the Lacedaemonians, aimed at forcing the Athenians to come to terms. For instance, the Spartans by means of ultimatum told the Athenians that they wished to see peace and tranquility on condition that the latter would set free the Greek city-states which were members of the Athenian empire.[14] The Lacedaemonians were optimistic that through this method they would be capable of achieving their aims on the grounds that Lacedaemon was an extremely mighty land power. Therefore, in the event of an invasion into Attica (which practically ensued) she could either force the Athenians to come out of their walls and fight, in which case the latter would almost certainly be defeated by the well-trained Lacedaemonian infantry, or the countryside of Attica would be devastated (which actually took place after repeated interventions). The events in 446 B.C. when the Athenians were forced to capitulate was a precedent which strengthened all the more the conviction of the Lacedaemonians. However, the Athenians did not act in the same way as they did in 446 B.C., as they did not yield to the Lacedaemonian ultimatum and demands. One could suggest that the Lacedaemonians had not properly foreseen the future developments in the war, but still they were successful in ravaging the countryside of Attica. The consequences of this act will be demonstrated immediately afterwards.

Also, it seems that the Lacedaemonians did not on this occasion show sufficient comprehension of historical facts in that they made the wrong comparisons right before the outbreak of the war. In 446 B.C., Athens indeed sought to come to terms with Lacedaemon, but in 432 B.C. the political circumstances were far different. In 446 B.C. Athens lost serious battles in Greece and simultaneously she faced an imminent revolution in Euboea. The Athenian effort for a creation of an empire based on land forces in mainland Greece did not succeed and Athens recognized the mere fact that its empire was destined to be constrained within the geographical limits of the Aegean Sea. In 432 B.C., by contrast, Athens was not obliged to come to an agreement since she had enhanced her empire through accepting new members into the Athenian League.

The Lacedaemonians did not confine themselves to the threat of the use of force in order to fulfill their political objectives. As it has been shown, through the advice of Archidamus they did consider the need to strengthen their navy and economy, despite the fact that they took the plunge to go to war immediately at the end of the congress at Lacedaemon and the convincing argument of Sthenelaidas the ephor.

Furthermore, Lacedaemon employed even more means to attain her political objectives in the war against Athens. A central tenet of the grand strategy of Sparta was the attempt to maximize the cost of the war and its consequential losses for the state of Athens. Unlike the maintenance cost of the mighty Athenian navy, the Lacedaemonian infantry could be maintained on a relatively low cost. The Lacedaemonians were constantly prepared to go to war, so joining the infantry in its invasion of Attica was not at all costly. The same applied in the case of the members of the Peloponnesian League, the allied city-states, the citizens of which would suffer no cost in joining the Lacedaemonians in the conduct of their invasion in Attica.

Conversely, the Athenians would, in this way, have to pay a large price:

1. Attica would be devastated (the consequence of the invasion was that it was practically ruined).
2. The Athenian empire would run the risk of disintegration (which eventually ensued).
3. The Lacedaemonians would try to take advantage of any other campaign that the Athenians might plan to organize.

A relevant point, which usually remains unnoticed, is that, through these low-cost invasions by the Lacedaemonian infantry, the morale of the Athenians was seriously shaken. Apart from the economic cost that the Athenians suffered through the ravaging of Attica's fertile land, the social structure of the city was turned upside down. The farmers, who enjoyed a sentimental bond with their homeland, were forced to abandon their property and seek refuge within the then walls of Athens. It is useful to say in this context, even briefly, that the policy of Pericles not to allow the Athenians to go out and fight in the battlefield, directly confronting the Lacedaemonians, could be heavily criticized, even though it had positive results up to the end of the first phase of the war.

The cost to be sustained by Athens lay also in the continuous efforts of Sparta to cause dissolution of the Athenian empire. Lacedaemon encouraged revolts of the Athenian allies, which led to the gradual loss of membership of the allied states in the Athenian League. In fact, these moves were generated before the outbreak of the war.

The revolt at Mytilene in 428–427 B.C. characteristically forms an example of the Lacedaemonian attempts to maximize the cost to be suffered by Athens. The Mytileneans having revolted, the Lacedaemonians engaged in serious preparations to launch attacks by land and sea against Athens, at the same time manning a war fleet to succor the revolutionaries. They supposed that it would not have been possible for the Athenians to impose naval blockade in Mytilene and at the same time to conduct raids onto the shores of the Peloponnese and take every step so as to defend their own city.

Thucydides emphasizes this point well:[15]

> Such was the Mytilenaeans's speech. When the Spartans and their allies had heard them out they accepted their arguments and made the Lesbians their allies. The Spartans then instructed the allies present to prepare for the inva-

sion of Attica and told them to go immediately to the Isthmus with the quota of two-thirds of their forces. They themselves got there first and proceeded to construct shipways for the ships at the Isthmus to drag them from the Corinthian side to the sea on the Athenian side, in readiness for a simultaneous assault by land and sea. The Spartans set to with a will, but the rest of the allies were slow to assemble, being occupied with their harvesting and being in no mood for campaigning.[16]

The Athenians, through this exhibition of power, clarified that they were far from having been worn out either economically or in terms of governing an empire. However, a Lacedaemonian fleet did set sail for Mytilene. Although the island had already surrendered to the Athenians prior to the arrival of the fleet, there still existed chances for the Lacedaemonians to set it free. However, the commander of the war fleet, Alcidas, did not take advantage of the opportunities presented on this occasion and chose not to attack. In spite of his decision, it was evident that the Lacedaemonians did have the means to cause grave losses to the Athenians, but lacked the nerve to do so in this particular incident. A reason, of course, that forced the Lacedaemonians to remain idle was the fear of a Helot revolt in the interior of the Peloponnese, a parameter which constantly dictated their foreign policy.

In this context, it should be noted in passing another instance whereby it is indicated that the speeches were the means through which major decisions of strategy were made. The city of Corcyra found itself involved in an increasingly nasty confrontation with its mother city (that is, having originally established it as a colony), Corinth. The quarrel spiraled into open conflict in which the Corcyrean forces crushed those of the Corinthians. Refusing to accept defeat at the hands of its colony, the Corinthians attempted to mobilize their economic and military power, as well as that of their allies to crush their upstart colony. Fearful of the Corinthians, the Corcyreans went to the Athenians with a clear warning that they put in simple terms. Everyone in Greece knows, they argued, that war between you and the Spartans is coming. Ally with us and add our considerable naval power to that you already possess, which will ensure your naval dominance of the Greek world, when war comes, or stand aside and allow the Corinthians and their Peloponnesian allies—that is, the Spartans—to acquire our naval power and thus be in a position to challenge your control of the seas. Interestingly, ambassadors from Corinth addressed the Athenian assembly as well, and at the same time, but their arguments, that war was not on the horizon between Athens and Sparta, proved less persuasive than those of their adversaries. By a close vote, the Athenian assembly agreed to a defensive alliance with Corcyra and sent a small squadron of ten triremes to Corcyra to warn the Corinthians off.[17]

To attain the very same goal, that is the gradual disintegration of the Athenian empire, the Lacedaemonians undertook a far more decisive expedition in 424 B.C., when they sent to Macedonia and Thrace a powerful regiment under the command of Brasidas. He succeeded in bringing about the dissolution of Athenian influence in the area by using a combination of political and military methods. In this way, the Lacedaemonians hoped that the Athenians would have been obliged to come to terms.

The final method that the Lacedaemonians put in practice was to attempt to take advantage of any secondary importance campaign that the Athenians might undertake, aiming directly at preventing the latter from enjoying the benefits stemming from such military campaigns. One such case, perhaps the most typical of them all, was the role played by Lacedaemonian strategy in the Athenian expedition at Sicily, which was much inspired by the ambitions of Athenian politicians and youth alike, as Thucydides is willing to concede. In Sicily the Athenians employed their naval powers not only to strike blows against their opponent, but also to achieve their imperialist objectives, that is, to exert influence and control over the land Magna Graecia. The immediate response of the Lacedaemonians to this imperialist policy of the Athenians was, unlike previously when they used to make periodical raids, to station a mighty military garrison at Deceleia in 413 B.C. This development drove the city of Athens almost to disaster. [18]

Deceleia, remember, had been first fortified by the whole army this summer and it was later occupied by a succession of garrisons from the different cities to initiate offensives in the countryside there. This did huge damage to the Athenians and the destruction of property and the loss of life involved was one of the principal factors in their demise. Earlier invasions had been short in duration and did not prevent them from enjoying the use of the land the rest of the time: whereas now the enemy was in continuous occupation, sometimes invading with a larger force and sometimes overrunning the countryside from the garrison there and plundering it to meet their own needs; moreover Agis, king of the Spartans, was also present and was giving all his attention to the war. So the Athenians were being very badly damaged. They were deprived of access to their entire countryside, more than twenty thousand slaves deserted—a large proportion of them skilled workmen—and they lost all their livestock and draught animals, and now that their cavalry was going out every day to make raids on Deceleia and maintain guard throughout the countryside the horses suffered, some being lamed by the constant punishment from the hard ground and some wounded in battle. [19]

The aforementioned measure indicates that such methods, pursued in the context of the Peloponnesian War, verify the magnitude of the grand strategy of Lacedaemon. It must be added, in fact, that a "permanent" fortification of Deceleia was enlisted in the Lacedaemonian strategy since the beginning of the war. This was mentioned by the Corinthians in the course of their argumentation at the congress of the Peloponnesian League in 432 B.C. Another event which attests to the validity of the suggestion that such a measure had initially been incorporated in the strategic plans of Lacedaemon is that the Lacedaemonians themselves put it forward by means of a threat, in order to exert pressure upon the Athenians and force them to accept the Peace of Nicias, when this was negotiated by the opponent states. The explanation of why this measure was implemented at a rather late stage in the war may be found in the fact that the Lacedaemonians did not actually feel the need to establish a garrison in Deceleia in the course of the other phases of the war. Also, this strategic move presupposed that a large number of Lacedaemonians and citizens from the wider Peloponnesus would have had to abandon their homes and stay away for long periods, which would have been costly; in practice, it would have meant that the forces of labor of the Peloponnesian cities would have been kept busy, and so the local economies would have suffered.

Also, some remarks still need be made with regard to the strategy of Sparta as against Sicily. The help which Sparta offered the Sicilians was decisive so as to make sure that Athens would not be proved victorious. The Athenians, in view of the circumstances, had to sustain the struggle in Syracuse, repel the continuous raids of the Lacedaemonians in Attica, and face the possibility of another revolt of an ally.

The eventual defeat of the Athenians in Sicily brought their expansionist and opportunist ambitions to an end. Two additional dimensions of the Lacedaemonian strategy were the more implemented. First, the Lacedaemonian garrison at Deceleia, formidable as it was, and the raids in Attica were bringing about Athenian exhaustion. Second, the plan of Archidamus, according to which Lacedaemon would have to make alliances with other city-states and thus enhance her naval power, found its expression in that a lot of cities ran to the help of Lacedaemon. They offered money in profusion as well as war vessels. The Peloponnesian League launched a strategic plan of building up warships, and simultaneously fifty-five ships arrived from Sicily to succor the Lacedaemonians.

Perhaps the most important success, strategically, was the fact that Lacedaemon concluded an agreement and made a strong alliance with Persia. Collaboration with the satraps Pharnabasus and Tissaphernes,[20] particularly with the former, were fruitful. Even more fruitful was the coordination developed with Cyrus, who succeeded Tissaphernes. The huge economic support that Persia provided to Lacedaemon was sufficient to fortify the Greek city militarily, and, as a result, the Archidamian plan achieved its utmost success with the victory of the Lacedaemonians at the navy battle of Aigospotamoi in Hellespont.

The Athenians, on their part, did attempt to secure some help from Persia, albeit without success, since the price for it would have been for Athens to abandon and give up control of the cities of Asia Minor and surrender them to the sovereignty of Persia. It became clear that with Persia supporting fervently the Lacedaemonian ventures, the Athenians had minimal, if any, chances of winning the war.

An issue which often remains unnoticed in philological as well as strategic analyses of the *History of the Peloponnesian War* is the methods used by the two opponent states, particularly Lacedaemon, to make their respective strategies seem legitimate in the eyes of the Greeks. Legitimization of strategy both internally and at an inter-state level did have an important effect on the outcome of the war.

International or inter-state (to be more exact) legitimization of the grand strategy of Lacedaemon was significant for this great city of Peloponnesus. The allies of Athens, members of the Athenian League, came to be under the obligation to pay heavy taxes and constantly sought opportunities to set themselves free from Athenian oppression. Lacedaemon, on the contrary, was notorious for being a mighty fighter against tyranny; hence she, on occasions, subverted tyrants in various Greek city-states, including Athens. Sparta was also the leader of the Hellenes in the course of the Persian Wars, especially at some of the most decisive battles. Consequently, the Lacedaemonians presented themselves as liberators of the Greeks from the oppressive and tyrannical policies of the Athenians, thus gaining support from Greek cities.[21]

Public support in general was very much on the side of the Spartans, especially as they proclaimed that they were liberating Greece. Everyone—individuals and cities alike—was eager to lend them what support they could, by word or deed. And everyone felt that the cause suffered if ever they were not personally involved. Such was the animus most people felt towards the Athenians, some of them wishing to be freed from their rule and others fearing to fall under it.[22]

To this effect, the Lacedaemonians delivered an ultimatum to the Athenians, officially demanding that the latter set free the Greek city-states which were under her oppressive control. What was even more significant was the fact that the Lacedaemonians made it clear that they were prepared to fight militarily for this purpose. This very argument was employed systematically during the Peloponnesian War. For example, Brasidas did use this argument in the course of his expedition in northern Greece and stressed that his mission was to liberate the Greek city-states.[23]

Brasidas himself was sent out by the Spartans very much on his own wishes (and the Chalcidians were also keen to have him). He had the reputation in Sparta itself of a man who always got things done and when he went out he proved himself invaluable to the Spartans. In the present situation he caused many of the cities to revolt from Athens through the just and moderate way he dealt with them, while other places he took with the help of betrayal from within, so that when the Spartans later wanted to negotiate, as in fact they did, they had places available to transact in mutual exchanges and there was some relief of pressure on the Peloponnese from the war. And later on in the war, after the events in Sicily, it was the character and intelligence Brasidas showed at this time, which some experienced firsthand and others knew by report, that did the most to inspire enthusiasm for the Spartan cause among those who were allies of the Athenians. [24]

Apart from taking advantage of the lack of inter-state legitimization of Athenian strategy, Lacedaemon attempted to undermine this strategy in Athens internally. To this end, the Lacedaemonians launched continuous raids against Attica, which, beyond causing severe economic and social damage, led the Athenian morale to bottom out. For instance, Archidamus, being well aware of the political divisions and feuds among the Athenians, took advantage of these controversies in order to undermine the Athenian strategy, in the course of the Lacedaemonian military interventions in the land of Attica. [25]

Archidamus's motive for staying around Acharnae in battle order instead of going down into the plain during this invasion was said to be as follows: He hoped that the Athenians, who had a flourishing population of young men and were prepared for war as never before, might perhaps come out to fight him, unable to bear seeing their land destroyed. So when they did not oppose him on the Thracian plain he based himself at Acharnae, to test them out and see if they would now come out against him there. That seemed to him a good place in itself for an encampment, and at the same time the Acharnians, who represented a large portion of the citizen body (with three thousand hoplites), seemed unlikely to stand by and watch the destruction of their territory but would urge the whole people to join the fight as well. And if the Athenians did not come out to oppose him in this invasion, then he would have less apprehension in any future one about ravaging the plain and going right up to the city itself; for the Acharnians, deprived of their own property, would not be so eager to run risks on behalf of anyone else's—which would have divisive consequences for Athenian policy. That was the strategy Archidamus had in mind in being at Acharnae. [26]

The result with regard to the morale of the Athenians was evident, indeed, and given that in Athens decision-making as regards issues of foreign policy was in the hands of the Assembly of the People (Ἐκκλησία τοῦ Δήμου), it was possible for the Lacedaemonians to influence Athenian public opinion, which occasionally witnessed fluctuations on policy and strategy matters. Thucydides makes the point that after the second intervention of the Lacedaemonians and the devastation of the land of Attica, the Athenians were forced to dispatch ambassadors to Lacedaemon to negotiate some form of armistice. It seems, though, that the demands of the Lacedaemonians were excessive and were consequently not accepted by the Athenians.

Pericles, on the other hand, to his credit, managed to maintain, at least to some extent, legitimization of his strategy within the city of Athens. The

Athenians did not come out of their walls to give battles and never again sought to conclude a peace treaty. Pericles attempted to influence the political environment of Lacedaemon herself to the interests of the Athenians, a very bold venture, indeed. He did attempt to show that war against Athens would be fruitless. However, his effort had only minimal effect. In the tenth year of the war, Lacedaemon witnessed a leadership that was keen on preserving peaceful and friendly relations with Athens, but such leadership (Πλειστοάναξ) was not destined to be long lived.

Furthermore, the two opponents launched serious efforts to take advantage of the political divisions among democrats and oligarchs within most of the Greek city-states. Lacedaemon, however, was in a position to act to this end even within the city of Athens, whereas Athens could not act correspondingly since the Lacedaemonian city-state was constitutionally unpenetrable. The structures of the Spartan constitution were such that they would not allow any such intervention. Lacedaemon though managed to influence the oligarchic sentiments of a number of political groups within Athens, so when oligarchy was imposed in Athens following political conspiracy in 411 B.C., certain Athenian oligarchs tried to achieve political compromise with the Lacedaemonians. The effectiveness of Spartan strategy in this very field is attested by Thucydides himself, who admits that these constitutional developments within Athens led gradually to the fall of the city.

Conclusively, it may be said that the constant threat of the use of military force by land on part of the Lacedaemonians as well as the farsighted foreign policy of the Lacedaemonians to make peace with the Persians in combination with the tools used to legalize or legitimize their policies eventually proved the superiority and pragmatic success of the Lacedaemonian strategy.

Certain final considerations need be put forward with respect to the Spartan grand strategy, which was at the end victorious. During the first phase of the Peloponnesian War, the so-called Archidamean war (431–421 B.C.), the Spartan strategy may be said not to have attained its goals. The Lacedaemonians invaded Attica on a number of occasions devastating the land, but the Athenians were not subjugated and did not yield to any of the demands of their opponent. On the contrary, Athenian reprisals took place, culminating in the conquest of Pylos, and taking hostages of Lacedaemonian soldiers in Sphacteria. These events led the Lacedaemonian army leaders to the need to conclude peace with the Athenians at some point. The Athenians, though, did not take up the chance to negotiate and strike an agreement to their benefit. The refusal of the Athenians to agree to any such terms led the Lacedaemonians to enforce two strategic measures that, until then, they had not deemed necessary to implement: first, to launch military campaigns in northern Greece, in order to dissolve, as far as possible, the Athenian empire, and second, to threaten that they would permanently station a military garrison in Attica. These strategic measures did force the Athenians to come to an inter-state agreement and propose the Peace of Nicias (421 B.C.), the terms of which, however, did not substantially diminish Athenian military power.

The turning point to the strategic options of the Lacedaemonians came with the rise of Argos as a continental power during the Peace of Nicias (421–415 B.C.). Argos attracted many of the allies of the Lacedaemonians who had deserted the Peloponnesian League, accusing the Spartans that they had entirely neglected keeping up friendly and close relations with them. Lacedaemon decided to face the threat coming straight from Argos by engaging in direct military confrontation against it, thus putting in practice the strategy of nullification once again. In 418 B.C. the Lacedaemonians won a valuable victory against Argos at Mantineia.

The day before this battle it happened also that the Epidaurians in full force invaded the territory of Argos, thinking to find it now undefended, and slew many of those who had been left behind as guards when the main body of the Argives had taken the field.[27]

The decisive battle of Mantineia, it must be said, is the model which Clausewitz closely pursued to develop his own perspective of war. This kind of battle was fought by rule in the summer, when crops were ripe and most vulnerable to the act of arson. Not surprisingly, in Book IV, another such battle took place in Sicily, and is vividly described by Thucydides: τοῦ δ'ἐπιγιγνομένου θέρους, περὶ σίτου ἐκβολήν, Συρακοσίων δέκα νῆες πλεύσασαι καὶ Λοκρίδες ἴσαι κατέλαβον Μεσσήνην τὴν ἐν Σικελία, αὐτῶν ἐπαγαγομένων καὶ ἀπέστη Μεσσήνη Ἀθηναίων.

In 415 B.C. it became clear that Lacedaemon would most likely win the war. The expansionist foreign policy of Athens in Sicily opened up a window of opportunity for the Lacedaemonians. They commenced plundering the land of Attica and simultaneously dispatched strong military forces to Sicily, in order to succor the Syracusans and their allies in their struggle against Athenian imperialism. These Spartan actions played a grand role in bringing about the defeat of the Athenians in Sicily.

In the last phase of the Peloponnesian War, commonly known as the War of Deceleia (413–404 B.C.), it was more than evident that the Lacedaemonians were destined to be victorious. The balance of power favored them, as they had already enhanced their military capacity at sea, and could confront the Athenians by their naval forces equally powerfully as by employing their land troops. Although the Athenians managed to retain political control over Samos and Euboia, their traditional allies, and, despite the fact that, at sea, their navy did still strike a few important victories (the city though being in a state of panic), the Lacedaemonians prevailed at the most decisive battle of the war, which took place at Aigospotamoi of the Hellespont area in 405 B.C. The Spartan strategy thus fully succeeded in realizing its aims.

Notes

1. Carl von Clausewitz, *On War*, trans. J. J. Graham (London: N. Trübner, 1873).

2. Thucydides, *History of the Peloponnesian War*, 4 vols., *Loeb Classical Library* 108, 109, 110, and 169, trans. C. Forster Smith (Cambridge: Harvard University Press, 1919–1923) (hereafter cited as Thucydides), 1.70.

3. Thucydides, *The War of the Peloponnesians and the Athenians, Cambridge Texts in the History of Political Thought*, ed. Jeremy Mynott (Cambridge: Cambridge University Press, 2013), 42.

4. Thucydides, 1.19.

5. Thucydides, *The War of the Peloponnesians and the Athenians*, 14.

6. Thucydides, 1.82.

7. Thucydides, *The War of the Peloponnesians and the Athenians*, 50.

8. Thucydides, 1.86.

9. Thucydides, *The War of the Peloponnesians and the Athenians*, 52.

10. Thucydides, 8.53.

11. Thucydides, *The War of the Peloponnesians and the Athenians*, 542.

12. Thucydides, 1.82.

13. Thucydides, *The War of the Peloponnesians and the Athenians*, 50.

14. See Thucydides, 1.139.

15. Thucydides, 3.15.

16. Thucydides, *The War of the Peloponnesians and the Athenians*, 169.

17. Williamson Murray, "Thucydides: Theorist of War," *Naval War College Review*, 66, no. 4 (2013), 37.

18. Thucydides, 7.27–28.

19. Thucydides, *The War of the Peloponnesians and the Athenians*, 468.

20. See Rosaria Vignolo Munson, "Persians in Thucydides" in *Thucydides and Herodotus* ed. Edith Foster and Donald Lateiner (Oxford: Oxford University Press, 2012), 267: "[Tissaphernes] 'feared (φοβουμένου) the Peloponnesians more than the Athenians and, moreover, wanted to wear out both sides (τρίβειν ἀμφοτέρους), as Alcibiades had instructed him to do' (8.56.2), while Alcibiades wanted to appear (δοκεῖν) to the Athenians able to persuade Tissaphernes even if he was not able to do so (56.3). In the midst of this obfuscation, Thucydides once again cannot be sure, but offers his opinion: 'It seems to me (δοκεῖ δέ μοι) that Tissaphernes also wanted this result out of fear (διά τό δέος, 8.56.3). He feared (δεδιώς, ἐφοβεῖτο) that without his support the Peloponnesians would be defeated by the Athenians, or that they would defeat the Athenians on their own, or that they would ravage his country in search of sustenance (8.57.1).'" In Thucydides's judgement therefore, Tissaphernes's decision to reconcile with the Peloponnesians and stipulate a third treaty was made "with calculation and foresight of all these factors, according to his intention to equalize the Greek forces on each side" (πάντων οὖν τούτων λογισμῷ καὶ προνοίᾳ, ὥσπερ ἐβούλετο ἐπανισουν τοὺς Ἕλληνας πρὸς ἀλλήλους, 8.57.1). "*Λογισμός* denotes the careful reasoning that allows for prudent action, advocated by leaders such as Archidamus and Hermocrates (2.11.7 and 6.34.4,6); *πρόνοια*, 'foresight,' is the primary virtue of a skillful statesman, which Thucydides attributes to Themistocles." (Munson, "Persians in Thucydides," 268).

21. Thucydides, 2.8.

22. Thucydides, *The War of the Peloponnesians and the Athenians*, 94.

23. Thucydides, 4.81.

24. Thucydides, *The War of the Peloponnesians and the Athenians*, 284–285.

25. Thucydides, 2.20.

26. Thucydides, *The War of the Peloponnesians and the Athenians*, 103.

27. Thucydides, *History of the Peloponnesian War Books V-VI, Loeb Classical Library*, 141.

Chapter Eight

Greek Religion in the Politics of the Peloponnesian War

PHENOMENA OF NATURE

It is my purpose in this chapter to show that, although reports of gods, oracles, natural phenomena, and divination are not very many in the work of Thucydides, they are, nevertheless, significant, because they prove the historian's convictions and stance toward traditional religion of his era. The religion of Thucydides is indicative of his philosophical positions: it influences his *History of the Peloponnesian War* and ought to have implications on our own interpretation of his book.

In the first subchapter, emphasis will be placed upon natural phenomena, as well as social phenomena, that have a prominent role in the *History of the Peloponnesian War*. The scientific methodology of Thucydides is evident in the description and reference to phenomena of nature like earthquakes, eclipses, and, of course, the plague. As these very phenomena were seen as expressions of anger stemming from the gods by the ancient Greeks, the fact that Thucydides points out their natural causes has been used as an argument that he is himself detached from religion. It cannot certainly be doubted that Thucydides introduced the field of historical science, but simultaneously it should not be inferred that his views were all exclusively based on science and are different from those typical of the ancient Greek.

Firstly, it has been suggested that Thucydides, to quote Cochrane, "has sought a naturalistic explanation in each and every case."[1] This assumption can be denied on the basis of the facts as described by Thucydides: of the ten earthquakes, only one is accorded a naturalistic explanation, and of the three eclipses, only two. For the volcanic eruption of Aetna, for instance, no natural phenomenon explanation is provided. One cannot deny that Thucydides did have a keen interest in natural science, which he exhibited through his observations. For example, he acquired some basic knowledge of seismology.[2] He was aware of the relation between earthquakes and floods,[3] and he surely knew that eclipses were possible when the moon was full[4] and that climatic conditions were the real causes of thunders. However, he was not entirely preoccupied with explanations based on natural sciences.

Secondly, it has been assumed that natural phenomena are factors to be traced in society or that they have social effects. It is true that a lot of Lacedaemonian as well as Athenian military expeditions and political operations were influenced or even did not take place due to eclipses or earthquakes.[5] The phenomenon which Thucydidean scholars are widely familiar with is the plague.

Thirdly, there is a category called παθήματα in the terminology of Thucydides, which is not described or explained by the historian merely on the basis of natural science knowledge, nor is it stressed because of its influence upon society:

> The Peloponnesian War was prolonged to an immense length, and long as it was, it was short without parallel for the misfortunes that it brought upon Hellas. Never had so many cities been taken and laid desolate, here by the barbarians, here by the parties contending; never was there so much banishing and blood-shedding, now on the field of battle, now in the strife of action. Old stories of occurrences handed down by tradition, but scantily confirmed by experience, suddenly ceased to be incredible; there were earthquakes of unparalleled extent and violence; eclipses of the sun occurred with a frequency unrecorded in previous history; there were great droughts in sundry places and consequent famines, and the most calamitous and awfully fatal visitation, the plague.[6]

There are two such categories of the so called *pathemata*: (1) the ones that have human origins and were the outcome of the Peloponnesian War (civil war, demolition of cities, killing) and (2) those which coincided with the war but were not the result of it (earthquakes, eclipses, the plague, for example).

Gomme, commenting on 1.23.3, suggested that Thucydides in this context renders popular belief:

> Stories of earthquakes, eclipses, droughts, etc., that is, of natural phenomena occurring in a time of war and adding to the disasters, came to be believed. Whether Thucydides himself thought there might be a connection between such natural events and human actions is not clear; from the statement that eclipses were more frequent during the Peloponnesian War, it would seem that he did. Yet, eclipses are not disasters, like earthquakes, and their natural cause was known to Anaxagoras in Thucydides's youth; when in iii. 89 he gives an account of the great tidal wave, he does not think of anything but natural causes, and suggests no portent. He may therefore mean here only that popular

opinion put all these things together as inevitable accompaniments of a human disaster.

It may be the case, however, that this passage is put in this way because Thucydides wanted to prove the importance of the Peloponnesian War, and, especially that it was greater than the Persian Wars, thus rendering his work more significant than that of his predecessor Herodotus. This opinion is strengthened and well documented by the following passage:[7]

Τῶν δὲ πρότερον ἔργων μέγιστον ἐπράχθη τὸ Μηδικόν, καὶ τοῦτο ὅμως δυοῖν ναυμαχίαιν καὶ πεζομαχίαιν ταχεῖαν τὴν κρίσιν ἔσχεν. Τούτου δὲ τοῦ πολέμου μῆκός τε μέγα προύβη, παθήματά τε ξυνηνέχθη γενέσθαι ἐν αὐτῷ τῇ Ἑλλάδι οἷα οὐχ ἕτερα ἐν ἴσῳ χρόνῳ. Οὔτε γὰρ πόλεις τοσοίδε ληφθῆσαι ἠρημώθησαν, αἱ μὲν ὑπὸ βαρβάρων, αἱ δ'ὑπὸ σφῶν ἀντιπολεμούντων (εἰσὶ δ'αἱ καὶ οἰκήτορας μετέβαλον ἁλισκόμεναι), οὔτε φυγαὶ τοσοίδε ἀνθρώπων καὶ φόνος, ὁ μὲν κατ'αὐτὸν τὸν πόλεμον, ὁ δὲ διὰ τὸ στασιάζειν.[8]

Moreover, a phrase accompanying the second subcategory of παθήματα may be indicative of the fact that Thucydides, much like his contemporaries, the ancient Greeks, was indeed thinking in terms of prodigies or events with metaphysical dimension: "Old stories of occurrences handed down by tradition, but scantily confirmed by experience, suddenly ceased to be incredible."[9] Thucydides may have found impressive the fact that these stories may have said something about the intensity, frequency, or simultaneity of such natural phenomena which tradition designated as omens.

A further issue which needs to be mentioned is Thucydides's reference to the earthquake at Delos, ominous as it was in ancient Greek belief. The historian reports that there was an earthquake at Delos, for the first time in the memory of the Hellenes. This was said and thought to be ominous of the events impending.[10]

Thucydides does not openly dispute or accept the omen itself, but certainly says that it was the first time that Delos, the holy island of the Ionians, experienced such a natural phenomenon. He objectively emphasizes the uniqueness of the phenomenon,[11] if not accepting its religious connotations, too.[12]

Another issue worth considering is surely the dramatic character that Thucydides attempts to accord to natural disasters. One of the foremost examples is the plague. The opinion which is usually expressed is that the description of this catastrophe is indicative of Thucydides's strictly scientific approach to such matters. This approach has been rebutted by Parry, who has shown that Thucydides does not purport to be exclusively scientific in this regard. He has demonstrated, in fact, that the tone of Thucydides, as well as his expressions, are, in fact, dramatic. Thucydides is concerned here with showing the extraordinary character and uniqueness of the natural disaster which befell Athens, instead of providing scientific explanation. He even describes the plague as an inhuman or even superhuman visitation.[13] Some passages from Thucydides suffice to indicate that his remarks may well have been correct: a pestilence of such extent and mortality was nowhere remembered,[14] people were overcome by evil,[15] and it was a πάθος so terrible that it defied description.[16]

Indeed, there is no contradiction between Thucydides's scientific explanations and his adherence to the traditional Greek religion.[17] There is no need to deny Cornford's providential Tyche.[18] There are forty occurrences of Tyche in Thucydides's history. Seven are in Thucydides's own voice. There are twenty-eight occurrences in speeches. Demosthenes is described as τῇ τύχῃ ἐλπίσας.[19] Smyth translated the phrase thus: "Confident by reason of his good fortune."[20] With this use of Tyche, one could compare the similar use of Tyche in the description of the Athenians at Pylos: βουλόμενοι τῇ παρούσῃ . . . ἐπεξελθεῖν.[21] In the phrase τά τῆς τύχης Thucydides is analyzing the Spartans's state of mind after the events at Sphacteria, and it is necessary to leave open the question whether this phrase expresses Thucydides's or the Spartans's view on the matter. After the Mytilene debate, the Athenians send a second trireme to rescind the harsh orders carried by the first, and Thucydides observes that it was κατά τύχην that no wind prevented the second trireme from overtaking the first.[22] In order to understand the irony of Thucydides's observation one must recall his description of the mood of the first meeting of the assembly concerning Mytilene: γνώμας ἐποιοῦντο, καὶ ὑπὸ ὀργῆς ἔδοξεν αὐτοῖς.[23] This sentence recalls the distinction made in the *prooemium* to the first speech of Pericles between the *gnome* of the Pericles and *gnomai* of the people, who are liable to passion and change. The constant *gnome* of Pericles was antithetical in that *prooemium* to Tyche. There was evidence to suggest that Thucydides understood the career of Pericles in terms of this antithesis. In the Mytilene episode, the same view of the Athenian assembly reappears. The Athenians made their first decision in anger. They showed better sense the next day, but through anger they had already committed themselves to Tyche. Thucydides observes that it was only by chance that they were able to rescind their initial decision. The decision was thus contrary to what could have been surely planned.[24]

Finally, in this subsection it would, I submit, be imperative to survey an aspect of the subject in question, which is related to the effect of natural phenomena on the politics of the Peloponnesian War. In fact, this aspect is a combination of the occurrence of events of nature and the complexities of war. Better put, it is an exploration of the fortunes of war and how these influenced the outcome of political and military campaigns.

Certainly two of the most fascinating events are described in Book IV of the *History of the Peloponnesian War*.[25] They take place in relation to the Athenian expedition at Pylos. In the first instance, the reader comes across the phrase κατὰ τύχην χειμὼν ἐπιγενόμενος κατήνεγκεν τὰς ναῦς ἐς τὴν Πύλον.²⁶ Burrows notes that Thucydides does not specify in what part of the bay they took refuge, but seems to assume that the whole harbor was safe.²⁷ The phrase *κατά τύχην* is used again of the storm which forced the Athenian fleet in at Pylos. Here, it must be observed that, of the seven uses of Tyche by Thucydides in his own voice, four occur either in the Pylos episode²⁸ or in reference to Pylos.²⁹ Thucydides suggests that, after Mantinea, the Greek world attributed the Spartan defeat on Sphacteria to Tyche.³⁰ The Lacedae-monian envoys who pled for their prisoners in Athens speak of the Athenian success as *εὐτυχία*³¹ and Tyche³² and warn the Athenians about the Tyche.³³ Since Cornford, the role of Tyche in the Pylos episode has been debated by scholars. Gomme reviews the evidence (the occurrences of Tyche) and wishes to minimize the importance of chance.³⁴ But if the present interpreta-tion of chance in Thucydides is correct, that is, everything to some extent must be contrary to calculation, then chance has a large role in the Pylos episode, as well as in the whole of the *History of the Peloponnesian War*. In the same way that the decision of the Athenians to rescind their harsh decree concerning the Mytileneans carried weight finally only *κατά τύχην*, since no wind detained the trireme carrying the recision, so the conflicting recommen-dations of Eurymedon and Sophocles on the one hand and of Demosthenes on the other are finally described as *κατά τύχην*, when a storm forces the fleet to land at Pylos.³⁵ In the second place, the really impressive picture is the one which is linked with the navy battle of Pylos itself:

Ἐγένετό τε ὁ θόρυβος μέγας καὶ ἀντηλλαγμένος τοῦ ἑκατέρων τρόπου περὶ τὰς ναῦς. Ἐς τοῦτό τε περιέστη ἡ τύχη [emphasis added] ὥστε Ἀθηναίους μὲν ἐκ γῆς τε καὶ ταύτης Λακωνικῆς ἀμύνεσθαι ἐκείνους ἐπιπλέοντας, Λακεδαιμονίους ἐς τὴν ἑαυτῶν τε καὶ πολεμίαν οὖσαν ἐπ᾽Ἀθηναίους ἀποβαίνειν. Ἐπὶ πολὺ γὰρ ἐποίει τῆς δόξης ἐν τῷ τότε τοῖς μὲν ἠπειρώταις μάλιστα εἶναι καὶ τὰ πεζὰ κρατίστοις τοῖς δὲ θαλασσίοις τε καὶ ταῖς ναυσὶ πλεῖστον προέχειν.³⁶

It is astonishing, indeed, how the methods of fighting have changed in this case. The Athenians, members of a sea power, find themselves combatting on land (practically on the shore of the Peloponnese), and the Lacedaemo-nians, on the other hand, traditionally the mightiest infantry of ancient Greece, conduct a naval operation against the Athenians, who were occupy-ing a strip of Peloponnesian land. However, Gomme has produced a fierce criticism of Thucydides as regards this passage, in particular the change of roles just described, and needs to be quoted in some detail:

I should be glad to believe that Thucydides did not write this. He has already given one comment on a strange reversal of the usual Athenian and Spartan roles, only a page or two back; that was not very profound, but it was true; this

is both trivial and untrue. To wade into the sea to save your ships from being
hauled away (or to prevent a beaten enemy getting away, as at Marathon) is no
sense ἐκ γῆς ναυμαχεῖν, nor is attempting to drag away enemy enemy ships
and keeping off enemy hoplites especially ἀπὸ νεῶν πεζομαχεῖν (what that
phrase really means in Thucydides can be seen from i. 49 1–3 and vii. 62 2–4).
Nor is there anything remarkable in what was happening, nor any paradoxical
change of role.[37]

The battle itself, in my opinion, was remarkable and surely important for the
Athenians, and one could ascribe a paradoxical feature to it, if the description
of Thucydides is to be relied upon *stricto sensu*.

Another occurrence of the phrase *κατά τύχην* is in 5.37.3. Thucydides
observes of the alliance proposed to the Boeotians by the Argives that it was
κατά τύχην that exactly what the Lacedaemonians had bidden the Boeotians
seek from the Argives. One might connect this use of *κατά τύχην* with the
frequent use of *τυγχάνω* in Book V, of the presence or the absence of ambassadors, which sometimes produces results which could not have been foreseen.[38] The review of Thucydides's uses of Tyche in his own voice shows
that thrice he finds Tyche—in the places where the phrase *κατά τύχην* appears—producing results which could not have been foreseen with any great
certainty. Furthermore, in each of these places, Tyche produces a favorable
result. In three other places, Tyche refers to a concrete situation. Two of
these situations (Demosthenes's before invading Aetolia and the Athenians'
in the battle in the harbor at Pylos) are favorable to the subjects from whose
point of view the situation is stated.[39]

Furthermore, Thucydides's discussion of the events surrounding the Theban
attack on Plataea in *The History of the Peloponnesian War* underlines brilliant-
ly the role that friction and *tychē* can and do play in thwarting the best-laid
plans. At the time the incident occurs, in 431 B.C., Greece is teetering on the
brink of a long-awaited war between Athens and Sparta. The Thebans decide
to capitalize on that fact to seize their longtime hostile neighbor, the smaller
polis of Plataea. They have set the stage for a coup with meticulous planning;
they have reached out to traitors within the city who have agreed to disarm its
guards and keep the gates open. The Thebans sneak a commando force across
the Boeotian hills separating the two cities. The advance party reaches its
target and catches the Plataeans by surprise. The traitors open the gates, panic
breaks out, and the Theban raiders announce that they have seized control of
the *polis*. At the same time, in the early evening, a larger occupying force
leaves Thebes to secure the victory. Thus far everything has worked perfectly.
But then friction and *tychē* intercede. As the main force makes its way across
the hilly terrain in the gathering gloom, it begins to rain. The torches sputter,
the Asopus River swells with runoff, and the trail, increasingly muddy, slows
all movement. At times the guides lose their way in the darkness, and the force
halts in confusion. Meanwhile, in Plataea, the locals, at first terrorized by the
sudden eruption of Theban soldiers, recover their courage as they perceive

there is only a small body of the enemy in their midst. The Plataeans regain control of the gates. At that point the morale of the Theban commandos, who had been emboldened by their initial success, collapses. They realize that their reinforcements have been delayed, and the strangeness of their surroundings adds to their dismay. The Plataeans seize the initiative. Burrowing between their buildings, through the walls from building to building, and moving over the roofs, they harry their enemies and then eventually force them to surrender. In the early hours of the morning, the main party of Thebans arrives, only to find the gates of Plataea barred and their commando force either dead or prisoner. With that flawed military operation, caught up in the entanglements of friction and chance, the great war between Athens and Sparta begins. [40]

Notable also is the use of Tyche by speakers in the *History of the Peloponnesian War*. Twenty-eight occurrences of the word "Tyche" in the history are to be found in speeches. Thucydides discloses his own view of Tyche through the distribution of this word among the speeches of the various personalities and the effect of events upon the views on Tyche given by Thucydides to various speakers. The general conclusion that may preliminarily be drawn is that Athenians take a more rationalist position on the issue of Tyche, whereas others, especially Spartans, seem to be more religious or superstitious on the matter. Let us see the instances at which Tyche appears in the speeches of important personalities in the text:

1. The view of Pericles on Tyche is diametrically opposed to Archidamus's. The statement of the Corinthians on Tyche is primarily rhetorical. They warn the Spartans that, by refusing to declare war on the Athenians, the Spartans run the risk of facing a stronger enemy and thus take greater chances. Pericles's views are opposed to those of his fellow citizens in Sparta, who refresh the memory of the Spartans by mentioning the irrational (παράλογον) element of war and that, protracted, war is wont to become a matter of chance. The war did bring with it the incalculable, firstly the plague, which even Pericles referred to as τά δαιμόνια. There is also the fact of Pericles's death and the dependence of his strategy upon his own persuasiveness and consistency, a strategy which was not followed by his successors, who virtually ruined the city.

2. At the battles in the Gulf of Corinth, the Peloponnesians conceived of their defeat in the first battle in terms of Tyche, whereas they were really defeated by τ έχνη. In the second battle, Tyche does actually intervene, [41] but in such a way that the Athenians convert it to their advantage and the Peloponnesians are again defeated. On this occasion, only one could potentially assert that the view of Tyche that the Peloponnesians hold is proved wrong by events.

3. In his analysis Diodotus speaks with disdain of the unreasonable commitment to Tyche. But, ironically enough, Thucydides converts this statement into criticism of the Athenians, [42] who, having made their first decree in anger, were capable of rescinding it only *κατά τύχην*.

4. The Spartan ambassadors use "Tyche" three times. Their use corresponds to Thucydides's own use of "Tyche" in connection with the Pylos episode and his remark that, after the battle of Mantinea, the widespread opinion of the Greek world was that the Spartans had been defeated in Sphacteria by Tyche. It seems that Thucydides did not admire the campaign at Pylos from a strategic point of view. The original decision was forced *κατά τύχην* by the storm. He did not admire the tactics of the Athenian victory, which owed its success to an accidental fire. An opinion that has not been put forward so far, or at least has not come to my attention, [43] is that Thucydides stresses the element of chance in the Pylos and Sphacteria campaign, inter alia, in order to minimize the role of Cleon in the incident, against whom the historian's prejudice has been pointed out elsewhere in this monograph.

5. Hermocrates believes that intelligence is subordinate to Tyche. He argues from the perspective of Tyche for reasonable concessions in his speech before the ambassadors of the Sicilian city-states at Gela:

> For my part, as I said at the beginning, I represent the most powerful city here, more likely to think of aggression than defence. But as I contemplate the future I conclude that my city should reach some compromise: we must avoid harming our enemies in such a way that we are the more damaged ourselves, and we should avoid persuading ourselves, in some stupid fit for ambition, that we are as much the masters of fortune, which we do not control, as we are of our own plans; instead, we should make whatever reasonable concessions we can. [44]

6. In the speech of Brasidas to the citizens of Acanthus, one may trace the traditional Spartan understanding of Tyche.

7. In the Melian Dialogue, the role of Tyche appears in the arguments of both the Melians and the Athenians. The Athenians, on the one hand, who talk to the Melians recall Pericles in their disdain of Tyche, when they speak of "disgrace more disgraceful since from foolishness not from chance." [45] In the same way that reason ought to be able to control Tyche, as in the *prooemium* to the first speech of Pericles, so want of reason can inflict a greater disgrace than Tyche can. The opposing views on Tyche as between the Athenians and the Melians further denote the conservative character of the Melians, the kinsmen of the Lacedaemonians. Whereas the Athenians see mere chance,

which they connect with hope, as Pericles and Diodotus did, the Melians believe that Tyche is an expression of the gods's will and that the God is governed by justice. Therefore, the Melians largely rely on Tyche. It is noteworthy that the Melians are perhaps the only ones in the *History of the Peloponnesian War* who, in their speeches, refer to τύχη ἐκ τοῦ θείου.[46]

8. It is difficult for one to argue that the fact of the Athenian disaster and the interpretation of that disaster in terms of Tyche by Nicias and Gylippus (to recall the Sicilian expedition that ensued) confirm the Melians' belief in a divine Tyche. It is clear, though, that Thucydides attempted to provide an interpretation of the Sicilian expedition by the main actors in that incident in terms of Tyche. Chance in Thucydides sometimes means what is against calculation or reason. Hence, the Athenians suffered the consequences of their irrational policy. Thucydides reports that Gylippus reached the heights only a moment before the Athenians completed their walling constructions.[47] The words of Gylippus vividly express the theme and role of Tyche in the Sicilian incident. Before the last great battle in the harbor of the city, Gylippus observes that the Athenians ought to run their risk.[48]

9. Nicias interpreted the Athenian failure in the Sicilian expedition in terms of Tyche, most probably because that suited his own case and could act as cover for the fatal mistakes he had committed. Nevertheless, the statements of Nicias concerning Tyche are occasionally Athenian and not Spartan in character. In advising the Athenians not to undertake the expedition in Sicily, he warns them not to be overexcited by the misfortunes of their opponents but to get the better of them in planning.

Apart from the above-mentioned elements, it is important to mention, even briefly, the relevant use of the verb τυγχάνω by Thucydides. There exist various uses of the verb which clearly manifest Thucydides's conviction in the Greek Tyche. The uses can be categorized as follows: (1) coincidence, (2) τυγχάνω with reference to vessels, and (3) τυγχάνω, which means achieving something through mere luck and not by calculation.

With regard to the first category, the use regularly and mainly refers to the presence of envoys. The meaning applies to ambassadors, whose presence cannot be foreseen by others involved in an ambassadorial incident. The regular meaning is "[ambassadors] happen to be at a place." Therefore, the use of the verb in this context implies coincidence. Sometimes τυγχάνω means "to happen by chance." The action in coincidence may have the character of irrational chance, and, in cases such as this, the verb is usually replaced by the phrase κατά τύχην. One such case is the arrival of Gylippus on the heights at Syracuse in time to prevent the Athenians from fortifying the city. Two other such cases are the eclipse of the moon which caused the fatal delay of the storm, which discouraged the Athenian army and forced it to retreat,[49] and also the wind which forced the Athenian fleet into Pylos, either of which could in no event have been expected. In a specific place, in which Thucydides states a coincidence from the point of view of Brasidas, there seems to be θεία τύχη in τυγχάνω.[50] Thucydides says that Basidas believed the capture of Lekythos to have occurred in other than mortal fashion, since there was a shrine of Athena there and Brasidas had happened (ἔτυχε) to announce a reward to the first man on the wall.[51]

As regards the second category, the common use of the verb with reference to ships should perhaps be understood as a subcategory of coincidence. The conditions of sailing were such that it was not certain that a warship would appear at a specific time and location; thus the appearance would be interpreted in terms of coincidence to some extent.[52]

With regard to the third category, the verb in a syntax with a genitive case may denote good luck. Themistocles is described by Thucydides as ὁλκάδος τυχὼν.[53]

ETHICS AND RELIGION

In this section, I shall purport to prove that ethics and religion, which are intrinsically interconnected, were shared by Thucydides to the same extent as they were accepted by philosophers of classical times, tragic poets such as Aeschylus, historians such as Herodotus, and other preeminent citizens. It has been shown in my chapter on ethics and international politics that the sophists had twisted the meaning of the accepted norms of that day. Similarly, it has been asserted that Thucydides joined them in questioning traditional ethical principles. On the contrary, serious scholars on Thucydides conclude that Thucydides did realize the decadence of ethics and society in his epoch and put forth effort to stress that compliance with moral values should be the way forward. For instance, Pearson, in his discussion of morality in the era of the historian, states that Thucydides withholds judgment and confines himself to the description of the ethical standards of his times. In the course of the Peloponnesian War, friendship,[54] which is a cardinal moral principle which should govern relationships between citizens and city-states, vanished and in its place went self-interest. The conclusion of Pearson is that the historian presents the facts without making the further comment that some higher sanction, religious or otherwise, is necessary if human virtue is to be realized.[55] Gomme has also seen Thucydides as a moralist.[56] It shall be proved that this is actually the case. But, before reaching that stage, it is imperative to analyze some respectable views going to the opposite direction, notably that of Simon Hornblower, as expressed in his famous article "The

Religious Dimension to the Peloponnesian War, or, What Thucydides Does Not Tell Us."[57]

The first minor silence Hornblower introduces is the Olympic Games of 432. They are never mentioned by Thucydides, but they certainly happened: we know the names of three victors, one of them a Spartan who was victorious in the four-horse chariot event.[58] The second example comes from Book II. The Funeral Oration never mentions the *epitaphios agon* or funeral contest, which we know from the evidence of three inscribed bronze vessels to have been a feature of the funeral by the mid-fifth century. From Aristophanes's *Frogs* and Pausanias, we know that this was a brilliant and lively affair including a torch race.[59] In the midst of mentioning examples of the absence of the religious dimension from the Peloponnesian War, Hornblower makes the important point that Lowell Edmunds has proved the religious significance of monosandalism of the Plataeans, who broke out of the siege of Plataea.[60] Their reason for leaving one foot unshod, he argues, was not, as Thucydides thought, in order to get a better footing in the mud,[61] "although this quaint explanation," in the words of Hornblower, satisfied Gomme.[62] (The Spartans, also said Thucydides, march to the sound of flutes not for religious reasons, τοῦ θείου χάριν, but simply in order to keep in step.) "It has to be said," Hornblower goes on, "without disparaging other aspects of Gomme's achievement, that the problems of penetrating Thucydides' indifference to religion are made worse by Gomme's own blind spot about religion."[63]

A third example of Thucydidean silence on religion according to Hornblower is Thucydides's utter failure to mention the amphictyony. The nearest he comes to the word is the epic and untechnical περικτιόνων, used in a sacred context (iii. 104. 3) about the island neighbors of Delos. Contrast, with Thucydides's silence, some statistics about Herodotus: Herodotus mentions the amphictyonies five times. Moreover he mentions the amphictyonic delegates called the Pylagoroi.[64] Hornblower also reports that Plutarch, for instance, who knew something about Delphi, got hold of a story that Sparta in the 470s tried to expel the medising states from the Delphic amphictyony, the "international" organization (twelve tribes, twenty-four votes) that controlled the affairs of the sanctuary.[65]

A fourth example is that Thucydides is of no help on the issue of the control of the Nemean Games.[66] The story has to be pieced together from scraps like Pindaric scholia. It is no good saying that the political importance of the sanctuaries must have been eclipsed in the time of the classical superpowers.[67]

Further, Hornblower spots the absence of the religious dimension in the context of the position Athens held in the *pentekontaetia*. Apollo Pythios was not the only Apollo: there was Apollo Delios, the god of Ionian Delos, an island that for Thucydides (i. 96. 2) is merely the ταμεῖον or treasury of the

league, but surely there was more to it than that. Delos was a great Ionian
religious center, although it is possible that Athens was having it both ways
because Delos had a religious appeal not just for the Ionian but for some of
the Dorian leaders in Athens's empire.[68]

I am quoting verbatim from Hornblower's article two more examples,
which are regarded as of importance:

> An aspect Thucydides does not mention is the well-attested myth that the
> festival of the Delia was founded by Theseus himself: Plutarch Theseus xxi.
> So Theseus was not quite forgotten in the 420s.[69] The Athenian hero was not
> purely local but had a pan-Ionian role that could be turned to imperial advan-
> tage.[70] Second, there was Eleusis and the myth of the Athenian benefaction of
> corn to Greece. This theme is found in the mouth of an Athenian orator in
> Xenophon's *Hellenica*. The orator is a hereditary priest of the Eleusininan
> Mysteries, who tells a Spartan audience that Triptolemos first gave the gift of
> corn to Herakles, the founder of the Spartan state, and to the Dioscuroi who
> were Spartan citizens (vi. 3.6.) Eleusis as an international cult center is not in
> Thucydides, indeed Eleusis scarcely features at all except in indirect mentions
> like the scandal of the Mysteries in book vi.[71]

It shall now be proved on the basis of the text of Thucydides that Thucydides
was actually religious and a moralist in the traditional Greek manner and that
Thucydides did regret the violation of moral principles, and religion itself for
that matter. In the event of *stasis*, the Corcyrean revolt, Thucydides mentions
that honor was popular with none, whereas enjoyment was considered both
honorable and useful. He stresses not only the open transgression of moral
principles, but the replacement of them by novel ones. The war was to be
held responsible for the fall of morality:

> In peace and prosperity states and individuals have better sentiments, because
> they do not find themselves suddenly confronted with imperious necessities;
> but war takes away the easy supply of daily wants, and so proves a rough
> master, that brings most men's characters to a level with their fortunes.[72]

Even more important are the comments Thucydides makes on religion as
such. He regards religion as a restraint, and he says that "fear of god or law of
man there was none to restrain them."[73] In the *stasis*, he writes that piety
(ευσέβεια), oaths, and divine law (θείος νόμος) were ineffective.[74] Clearly
the reference to divine law recalls the interconnection between ethics and
natural law, which is, indeed, one and the same concept. Natural law was
most sacred for the ancient Greeks and strictly complied with. By his invocation of divine law, it ought to be inferred that Thucydides was pious himself,
that he did believe in the traditional Greek deities, and that for him morality
was a code of life never to be transgressed by human beings.

Apart from the above, the historian must have adhered to the religious customs of his era as he manifests cases of sacrilege in the *History of the Peloponnesian War*. An instance occurred in Corcyra, where some suppliants, having entered the temple of Hera, committed suicide on the spot. Suppliants who were already present were either dragged from the sanctuary or slain in it, whereas others remained walled in the temple of Dionysus and there perished.[75] It is more than obvious that Thucydides should have been particularly astounded by the amount of acts of sacrilege observed, the violation of traditional religion and the correlative ethical values in the course of that fierce war. His regret of this immorality is also evidenced by phrases that he carefully uses in his history: χαλεπά[76] and κακόν[77] are employed to depict the revolt in Corcyra and the surrounding circumstances of the strife.

The incident of the debate between Plataeans and Thebans is notorious in the history by Thucydides not so much for its importance in military affairs, but for its moral and religious connotations. Gomme has commented aptly on this: "The fall of Plataia was of little military importance, and had not much effect on the issue of the war . . . but all its circumstances illustrated the mores of men at war in a most vivid way, and for that reason Thucydides treats it at such length and in so impressive a manner."[78] The preface to the eventuality of the incident and the Plataeans's doom is the speeches which both parties delivered, both stressing the concept of justice as a principle that should be enforced in their respective cause. It could not be easy to sympathize with the argument of the Thebans that they should be able to avenge themselves against the Plataeans,[79] not so much because Greek law dictated that suppliants be spared,[80] but because justice, objectively judged, favored the cause of the Plataeans in this particular case. It ought to be recalled that, in ancient Greek law, vengeance meant exactly the punishment of wrongdoing on someone who was considered to deserve it and was much blessed by religion itself. The principle itself had religious ramifications, since by exacting revenge a person or the state was implementing the gods's law and was acting in accordance with the gods's wishes. The speech of the Thebans is devoid of unfair accusations and sophistic arguments. It appears, in their view, that the wrongful act as it were committed by the Plataeans was that they did not choose to be led by Thebes, but welcomed the leadership of Athens. Clearly the choice of the Plataeans went against the political interests of the Thebans. Sophistic argument in the speech of the Thebans manifests itself most prominently where the Thebans hold that participation of the Plataeans in the Persian Wars, which was indeed most decisive and a proof of valor, is considered unimportant whereas medism of the Thebans is rendered an excuse, because the oligarchs were in power bearing responsibility for this act.[81] Thucydides, through his presentation of the Theban arguments, attempts to show their immoral tone. The only point which the Thebans could

seriously make was that the Theban prisoners were massacred by the Plataeans, an issue which they stretch too much.

The Plataeans, on the other hand, refresh the memory of the reader that
they defended Hellas in her struggle against the Medes, and remained loyal
to the Athenian League (later empire), thus fulfilling a moral obligation.[82]
Their statement is vivid: "And if we refused to revolt from the Athenians at
your bidding we were not in the wrong; for they helped us against the Thebans when you held back. After that it would not have been honourable for us
to desert them."[83] The Plataeans rely on moral obligation. They have done
what they saw as their duty and expect that the Lacedaemonians will do the
same, if not else, on grounds of honesty; hence, "beware lest men repudiate
an unseemly sentence passed upon good men still better and resent the dedi-
cation in the common temples of spoils taken from us, the benefactors of
Hellas."[84]

It should not be surprising that Thucydides accurately and objectively
reports what the Plataeans said, which was full of ethical and religious concepts. Justice (δικαιοσύνη) being the foremost moral value, the speech of the
Plataeans is full of such values. Similar words came up: δίκαιος, ἀγαθός,
ἀρετή.

The terminology of religion here employed is all the more impressive:
invocation of the gods,[85] oaths,[86] and temples.[87] At the point where they seek
to be given a right to be tried fairly they link the concept of fairness and
justice with religion, indeed principles that are interconnected and bear identical meanings. A point relevant to the Theban speech is that that too is full of
expressions that denote adherence to justice and morality, from the Theban
side, though the decision of the Lacedaemonians will be based on state
interest only. The Thebans, not the Lacedaemonians, put the male population
to death and reduced children and women to slaves.

Furthermore, the events at Delion are such that they manifestly prove the
religious character of Thucydides. Briefly the facts, though reported elsewhere in this monograph, were as follows: in Boeotia, at Delion, there is a
temple dedicated to Apollo, which the Athenians had occupied in the course
of their invasion in Boeotia, clearly pursuing an imperialistic policy.[88] The
Boeotians launched an attack against the Athenian infantry and were successful in recapturing Delion. At the arrival of the Athenian herald, who sought
to recover the dead bodies of the Athenian soldiers, the Boeotians denied the
request, because they claimed that the Athenians had violated Greek law and
custom in polluting the sanctuary of the god Apollo and using the sacred
water of the temple. Therefore, the Athenians were asked to leave the temple
at once. The reply of the Athenians was that they had not hurt the sanctuary,
but only used it for defensive purposes.

It seems that both sides disregard religious beliefs since the pollution of
the sanctuary by the Athenians and the refusal of the Boeotians to return the

dead so these could be buried form violations of religious practices of classical Greece. The Athenians in particular show contempt for the religious
practices and customs through their actions, and surely do not properly use
sacred practices in their speech in their effort to make sure that justice is done
with respect to their acts. They are aggressors in the words of Pagondas, and
this view seems to be shared by Thucydides.[89]

Gomme has commented interestingly on these events, relying initially on
the text of Thucydides, and it is worth quoting him:

> Finding that the Athenians had answered their charge of sacrilege . . . they (the
> Boeotians) now varied their ground, and tried the Athenian request in this
> manner: "if, as you say, you are not in our country, but in your own, then you
> can bury your dead without asking permission of us: but if you are in our
> country, then first go out of it, and afterwards you shall have your dead." The
> Boeotians knew all the time that this was merely vexatious; for the Athenians
> could not bury their dead without their leave, whether the ground which they
> occupied belonged to Attica or Boeotia—Arnold. This is true: the Boeotians
> were wholly in the wrong according to universal Greek custom (contrast the
> behavior of Brasidas at Torone, 114.2); but it is not the whole truth. The point
> of the Boeotian reply lay in its reference to the Athenian claim to Delion as a
> *permanent* conquest, and hence the reversion of the sanctuary to their care;
> after the battle this must have seemed to the Boeotians an impudent claim, and
> they answer, "if you are *masters* of this territory which you have won by the
> sword, come and get your dead."
>
> The argument of the Athenians that they fortified the temple in self-de-
> fense, however, is obviously not based in reality, and, therefore, it is not easy
> for one to take side with them. They have no restraint in misusing religious
> practices so as to achieve their political goals. As Thucydides put it, "anything
> done under the pressure of war and danger might reasonably claim indulgence
> even in the eye of the god."[90]

ORACLES AND THUCYDIDES

Thucydides is supposed to have regarded oracles, which are inseparably
linked with religion, as a kind of superstition and not to have accepted them
outright. As it shall be proved herein, views to this extent are not correct,
given the evidence in the *History of the Peloponnesian War*. On the contrary,
it may well have been the case that Thucydides was not critical of oracles but
endorsed them wholeheartedly in much the same way as Herodotus, Plato,
and others did in the classical epoch.

Oracles were notoriously ambiguous and this was an article of Delphic
belief, which was accepted outright as mere fact by ancient Greeks. The
responsibility for proper interpretation of the oracles, though, lay with the
person that sought for and received the oracle and prophecy. Although there
exist innumerable examples in ancient Greek literature of such oracles, suf-

fice it here to mention by way of prelude only a couple that can be traced in the history by Herodotus: the oracle received by Croesus,[91] and Themistocles's interpretation of the wooden walls on the eve of the invasion of the Persians in Greece.[92]

It went without saying that in cases of misinterpretation of oracles, blame was to be cast on the one who misinterpreted them. This was actually Thucydides's attitude too, and when he mentions ambiguous oracles his focus is on their interpretation, not so much their content.

In the first place, evidence coming from the history by Thucydides to prove the above statements is as follows: Cylon inquired at Delphi how he could become tyrant of Athens and received the answer "on the grand festival of." Cylon assumed that the festival in question was the "Olympia" in the Peloponnesus, and his attempt was not successful. Thucydides commented upon this fact: "Whether the grand festival that was meant was in Attica or elsewhere was a question which he never thought of, and which the oracle did not offer to solve. For the Athenians also have a festival which is called the grand festival of Zeus."[93] Whereas the ambiguity of the present oracle is manifest (τό τε μαντεῖον οὐκ ἐδήλου), Thucydides does not emphasize that. He, instead, takes side with the oracle in this context. He would not have mentioned that, according to the oracle, alternatively interpreted, the festival in question takes place in Attica, had he not considered that misinterpretation lies with the person that sought the prophecy. He in fact clearly denotes that Cylon misinterpreted the oracle: νομίσας . . . οὔτε κατενόησε.[94]

In the second place, Thucydides poses that the poet Hesiod was killed in the precinct of Nemean Zeus in Locris although he had received a prophecy that he would die in Nemea. It should not be assumed that Thucydides presents this incident so as to emphasize the ambiguity of oracles. The exact terminology used in Greek by Thucydides shows the coincidental character of the fact reported and not the inconsistency of the prophecy: ἐν τοῦ Διὸς τοῦ Νεμείου τῷ ἱερῷ, ἐν ᾧ Ἡσίοδος ὁ ποιητὴς λέγεται . . . ἀποθανεῖν, χρησθὲν αὐτῷ ἐν Νεμέᾳ . . . παθεῖν.[95]

Not surprisingly, this kind of oracle that refers to places may also be found in Herodotus. Cambyses had received an oracle that he would die in Agbatana. Although he assumed that this was the big city of Persia, the oracle prophesized his death at Agbatana of Syria.[96]

A third example that can be reported as proof that Thucydides did believe in oracles, and that this ought to be seen in the context of his wider religious convictions, is the case of Alcmaeon. When he had murdered his mother, Alcmaeon was told by Apollo that he would find no release from his troubles until he discovered a place which had not been seen by the sun at the time he had committed the act of murder. Having spotted the deposit of Achelous the river, Alcmaeon realized that this was the place meant by the oracle and settled there successfully.[97] Thucydides is very lucid in this passage. He mentions that Alcmaeon understood (κατενόησε) the oracle (ὁ δ᾽ ἀπόρων, ὡς φασι, μόλις κατενόησε τὴν πρόσχωσιν τοῦ Ἀχελῴου . . .), which is implicit in the fact that Thucydides thought the oracle conveyed a clear message that had to be grasped and that Alcmaeon did grasp it.

A fourth paradigm example occurs with the Pelasgian plot which was inhabited in the necessity of war. There existed an oracle which did forbid its inhabitation and predicted disaster for the day that it would be inhabited. These are the comments of Thucydides:

> And in my opinion, if the oracle proved true, it was in the opposite sense to what was expected. For the misfortunes of the State did not arise from the unlawful occupation, but the necessity of the occupation from the war; and though the god did not mention this, he foresaw that it would be an evil day for Athens in which the plot came to be inhabited. [98]

It may be safely inferred from the above statements that Thucydides firmly believed in oracles and was not different from his contemporaries in this regard.

Notes

1. N. Cochrane, *Thucydides and the Science of History* (Oxford: Oxford University Press, 1929), 16.

2. See A. W. Gomme, *A Historical Commentary on Thucydides* (Oxford: Oxford University Press, 1956).

3. Thucydides, *History of the Peloponnesian War*, 4 vols., *Loeb Classical Library* 108, 109, 110, and 169, trans. C. Forster Smith (Cambridge: Harvard University Press, 1919–1923) (hereafter cited as Thucydides), 3.89.

4. Thucydides, 2.28.1, 7.50.4.

5. Thucydides, 1.101.2, 4.56.2, 6.95.1, 8.41.2, 5.45.4.

6. Thucydides, 1.23: "All this occurred together with this war. It was began by the Athenians and the Peloponnesians having dissolved the thirty-years' truce which they had made after the taking of Euboea.

7. Gomme, *Historical Commentary on Thucydides*.

8. Thucydides, 1.23.1–2: "The Persian War was the greatest action of earlier times, yet that was speedily settled in two battles at sea and two on land. But the present war lasted a long time and in the course of it Greece was afflicted with sufferings unprecedented in any comparable period of time. Never before were so many cities captured and laid waste—some by barbarians and others by Greeks fighting wars among themselves (and some of these cities went on to be resettled with new inhabitants after they had been captured). Never before were so many men made exiles, never before was there so much slaughter—some in the course of the war itself and some as a result of internal conflicts" (Thucydides, *The War of the Peloponnesians and the Athenians, Cambridge Texts in the History of Political Thought*, ed. Jeremy Mynott, Cambridge: Cambridge University Press, 2013, 16).

9. Thucydides, 1.23.1–2.

10. Thucydides, 2.8.3.

11. The same may be said of his reference to the earthquake at Cos, which is presented as the greatest remembered (Thucydides, 8.41.2).

12. See Williamson Murray, "Thucydides: Theorist of War," *US Naval War College Review* 66, no. 4 (2013), 33: "One might even suggest that Thucydides, like Clausewitz, possessed a modern sense that nonlinear factors determine the course of events. His universe is one where uncertainty, ambiguity, and friction, as well as incompetence, dominate the actions of men. Moreover, the impact of *tychē* renders nearly all great events and decisions contingent: on personalities, on the relations and interrelationship between and among statesmen and military leaders, on the impact of the unforeseen or the unpredictable, and on the ability, among a host of other factors, of a single individual, even at the lowest level, to retard or thwart the best-laid plans. In particular, the competence, or more often the incompetence, of individuals plays an unpredictable role in the unfolding of history's course. Moreover, unexpected second- and third-order effects add to the difficulty of executing any strategy, whether political or military. Finally, as US forces rediscovered in both Iraq and Afghanistan, the enemy always 'gets a vote.' Again, it is not that Thucydides spells out this atmosphere of chance, ambiguity, friction, and uncertainty but that they suffuse his account of everything from diplomacy to combat."

13. A. Parry, "The Language of Thucydides' Description of the Plague," *Bulletin of the Institute of Classical Studies* no. 16 (1969): 110.

14. Thucydides, 2.47.3.

15. Thucydides, 2.51.5.

16. Thucydides, 2.50.1.

17. A story from Plutarch which denotes the coexistence of religion and science in the ancient Greek world is one which concerns Pericles in connection with the sophist Anaxagoras, an extract of which is laid down here: "These were not the only advantages that Pericles gained from his association with Anaxagoras. He seems also to have learned from his teaching to rise above that superstitious terror which springs from an ignorant wonder at the common phenomena of the heavens. It affects those who know nothing of the causes of such things, who fear the god to the point of madness and are easily confused through their lack of experience. A knowledge of natural causes, on the other hand, banishes these fears and replaces morbid

superstition with a piety which rests on a sure foundation supported by rational hopes." (See Plutarch, *Lives Volume III: Pericles and Fabius Maximus*, Loeb Classical Library 65, Cambridge: Harvard University Press, 1916).

18. See F. C. Cornford, *Thucydides Mythistoricus* (London: Routledge, 1965).

19. Thucydides, 3.97.2.

20. Herbert Weir Smyth, *Greek Grammar* (Cambridge: Harvard University Press, 1959).

21. Thucydides, 4.143.

22. Thucydides, 3.49.4.

23. Thucydides, 3.36.2.

24. Lowell Edmunds, *Chance and Intelligence in Thucydides* (Cambridge: Harvard University Press, 1975), 178.

25. See above the chapter on the grounds of war for advanced reference to the element of chance in the events at Pylos.

26. Thucydides, 3.1.

27. A. W. Gomme, *A Historical Commentary on Thucydides*, Volume III (Oxford: Oxford University Press, 1998), 438. "It is almost universally agreed that Sphakteria is the island now called Sphagia (a name which it also had in antiquity: Plato, *Menex.* 242 C; Strabo, viii. 4. 2, p. 359), that 'the harbor' is the bay of Navarino, or part of it, and that Pylos is the rocky peninsula now known as Palio-Navarino (the modern town of Neokastro or Pylos being on the south shore of the bay, opposite the southern end of Sphakteria); it is the only possible place in 'what was once Messenia.' But, as is well known, there are several serious geographical errors in Thucydides's account; these are best described in Grundy's paper in J.H.S. xvi, 1896, I, with an excellent map. . . . Thucydides, though he knew the harbor was large (13.4), clearly did not realize how large it is—much the largest in Greek waters, including south Italy and Sicily— nor, what is more important, that it was a bay and could not properly be described as a harbor at all; for it is deep, apt to be very choppy with northerly or southerly winds, and only in its northeast corner offering suitable landing ground for triremes: on its west side the eastern shore of Sphakteria offers only one small place for landing, and the southern and eastern shores of the bay, though low, are rocky. It is the perfect harbor for modern ships, with their deep draught and imperviousness to choppy seas, but an 'arm of the sea,' and not a very sheltered one at that, for triremes. For the conditions of the naval battle of 425, with some fifty or sixty vessels on either side, it provided ευρυχωρία almost as well as the open sea (13.3)."

28. Thucydides, 4.3.1, 4.12.3, 4.14.3. See the excellent comments of Simon Hornblower, *A Commentary on Thucydides Volume II* (Oxford: Oxford University Press, 1996), 152: "κατά τύχην χειμών επιγενόμενος: 'it so happened that a storm came on.' So begins a chain of events and actions which Th. represents as accidental or spontaneous even when (it is reasonable to suppose) they were not. F.M. Cornford, *Thucydides Mythistoricus* (London: Routledge, 1907), 88 n.2 notes that in the present passage we have κατά τύχην, 'by chance' rather than the weaker verbal form ἔτυχε 'it happened that,' which can just be a way of saying that an event occurred. Thus, says Cornford, 'the note of accident is clearly sounded.' Maybe, but unlike of some of what follows, the storm was a genuinely fortuitous event. See also next in J. Roisman, *The General Demosthenes and his Use of Military Surprise* (Stuttgart, 1993), ch. 3, 'Pylos and its lessons' argues that Demosthenes's planning and intelligence, in the technical military sense, were good, but that his predictions came true 'to a large part because of luck' and Spartan mismanagement."

29. Thucydides, 4.55.3.

30. Thucydides, 5.75.3.

31. Thucydides, 4.17.4, 4.18.4.

32. Thucydides, 4.18.3.

33. Thucydides, 4.18.4, 4.18.5.

34. Gomme, *A Historical Commentary on Thucydides*, Volume III, 488–489.

35. "When Gomme says that the Spartans' absorption in a festival, the arrival of the Messenian vessels, and the Spartans' omission to block the entrance to the harbor are matters of coincidence but not of chance, he misunderstands the Thucydidean concept of chance, which includes anything unforeseen or unforeseeable. If a coincidence was unforeseen or unforesee-

able, it was a matter of Tyche or chance. In any case, Gomme must admit that there were events which were really accidental" (Edmunds, *Chance and Intelligence in Thucydides*, 179).

36. Thucydides, 4.14.5. "In the great tumult that followed each side adopted the traditional naval tactics of the other: the Spartans, in their excitement and consternation, were effectively fighting a sea battle from the land; while the Athenians, who had the upper hand and wanted to press their good fortune as far as they could while it lasted, were fighting a land battle from ships" (Thucydides, *The War of the Peloponnesians and the Athenians*, 243–244). See here again the apt comment of Simon Hornblower and his reference to Macleod, *A Commentary on Thucydides Volume II* (Oxford: Oxford University Press, 1996), 166: "ἐς τοῦτό τε περιέστη ἡ τύχη ὥστε Ἀθηναίους μὲν ἐκ γῆς τε καὶ ταύτης Λακωνικῆς ἀμύνεσθαι ἐκείνους ἐπιπλέοντας: 'It was a strange turn of fortune: the Athenians were preventing the Spartans who were attacking them by sea, from landing on the Lakonian coast.' On the 'heavy emphasis' here see Macleod, *Collected Essays*, 142, comparing vii. 75. 7, an important para., full of antitheses and strongly underlined reversals. In particular the remnants of the Athenian fleet after the Sicilian disaster are there described as reduced to operating on land only, no longer sailors but out of their element. Macleod suggests that Th., in the present section, already has the events at Syracuse in mind."

37. Gomme, *A Historical Commentary on Thucydides*, Volume III, 452. Gomme further adds: "Apart from the well-known case of Marathon, Thucydides has already described, in a straightforward way, just such another fight, near Naupaktos, in ii. 90. 6. There the Peloponnesian fleet was the victor, and would have hauled off Athenian ships if the Messenians had not waded into the sea in full armour to prevent them; there had been at least this paradoxical element, that the Peloponnesians had won a battle at sea and were trying to follow it up. Here there is nothing unexpected at all."

38. Thucydides, 5.22.1., 5.30.5, 5.44.1, 5.46.5.

39. Edmunds, *Chance and Intelligence in Thucydides*, 180.

40. The description of and remarks about this affair are by Williamson Murray; hence he is quoted verbatim for the sake of full accuracy: "Thucydides: Theorist of War," 34.

41. Thucydides, 2.91.3: ἔτυχε.

42. Edmunds, *Chance and Intelligence in Thucydides*, 183.

43. The only passage where mention is in passing made on the probable prejudice against Cleon, regarding particularly the accidental fire, is Edmunds, *Chance and Intelligence in Thucydides*, 184, fn: "Contempt for Cleon may be at work here: Plut. (*Mor.* 856B) says that it is a sign of malignity in an historian when he describes a deed as done μὴ φρονίμως ἀλλ' εὐτυχῶς." Of course, criticism was originally raised by Plutarch in his *Ethics*, as Lowell refers to Plutarch in his statement.

44. Thucydides, *The War of the Peloponnesians and the Athenians*, 272: 4.64.1. I should say that I am not agreed with the view put forward by Edmunds in this context: "Thucydides apparently wanted to characterize the shrewd leader of democratic Syracuse, who was so Athenian in other ways, as the opposite of the first man of democratic Athens in the matter of tyche and gnome. Hermocrates is moderate in the traditional, pious way in recognizing and stressing essential limitations to human competence. We have seen how the figure of Nicias suggests an interpretation of the Sicilian disaster in terms of tyche. The figure of Hermocrates also serves to keep present in the reader the antithesis in which Pericles and Archidamus conceived of the war and to suggest the victory of the traditionally moderate understanding of tyche" (*Chance and Intelligence in Thucydides*, 185). It is well established that Thucydides admired the leadership of Hermocrates, an issue that has been raised and analyzed in the first chapter of this book. Hermocrates in the two passages quoted was only saying that war is sometimes ruled not by men, but by the power of chance. On the victory of the traditional understanding of Tyche fully, I agree with Edmunds's view. See also the interesting comment of Simon Hornblower on a relevant but slightly different though important issue in his *A Commentary on Thucydides Volume II: Books IV–V.24* (Oxford: Oxford University Press, 1996), 226: "το δὲ αστάθμητον του μέλλοντος: 'the inscrutable future.' Th. in the mouth of Hermocrates, is reminding us of Athens' success so far in the book, and warning us that the pattern is about to change." In the comment of this passage, however, Simon Hornblower, contrary to his statement elsewhere in his commentary that one cannot safely infer the views of

Thucydides through the speeches, here clearly makes a remark indicating that speeches, here that of Hermocrates, can at least occasionally lead us to safe conclusions about Thucydides's convictions and opinions.

45. Edmunds, *Chance and Intelligence in Thucydides*, 186.

46. Simon Hornblower, *A Commentary on Thucydides*, Volume III, 242: "ὅμως δὲ πιστεύομεν τῇ μὲν τύχῃ ἐκ τοῦ θείου μὴ ἐλασσώσεσθαι: 'we trust in divine fortune not to be worsted.' Canfora's n. argues well for this interpretation, which takes τύχη ἐκ τοῦ θείου as equivalent to the Herodotean θείη τύχη (see e.g. Hdt. 5. 92γ3). So too Deininger 1939, 31. Cf. σωζούσῃ τύχῃ ἐκ τοῦ θείου at 112.2. The usually favoured tr. is that of e.g. Hobbes 'for fortune, we shall be nothing inferior, as having the gods on our side.' On this view, here rejected, ἐκ τοῦ θείου is taken with ἐλασσώσεσθαι not with τύχῃ. It is notable that both uses of divine fortune (here and at 112) are in the mouths of the Melians, who throughout speak in more traditional terms than their opponents. (J. Griffin, *CQ* 48 (1998) 58 n. 66 observes that the Melian Dialogue is 'conducted in very different terms' from e.g. the Plataean Debate, with its 'tragic' appeals to the rights of suppliants, graves of ancestors, altars of gods etc. It would be more accurate to say that it is 'conducted by the Athenians in very different terms.')"

47. Thucydides, 7.2.

48. Thucydides, 7.67.4: Οὐ παρασκευῆς πίστει μᾶλλον ἢ τύχης. Thucydides, 7.68.1: Τύχην ἀνδρῶν ἑαυτὴν παραδεδωκυῖαν.

49. Thucydides, 7.50.4. See Hornblower, *A Commentary on Thucydides*, Volume III, 642: "ἦν γάρ τι καὶ ἄγαν θεισμῷ τὲ καὶ τοιούτῳ προσκείμενος: 'for he was rather excessively given to divination and that kind of thing.' This is one of Th.'s most famous judgements, and it is long held back. He sketched in the personality of the bold risk-taking Alkibiades much earlier in the Sicilian narrative (6. 15). The slower Nikias is suitably slower to be characterized, and we will not be told about his wealth or his moral deserts until ch. 86, at the moment of his death. For 'and that kind of thing' cf. the very similar 2. 47. 2 (the plague), 'oracles and that sort of thing,' μαντείοις καὶ τοῖς τοιούτοις, and 5. 103. 2, the scoffing Athenians of the Melian Dialogue on 'prophesy and oracles and the like, which ruin men with hope' μαντικήν τε καὶ χρησμοὺς καὶ ὅσα τοιαῦτα μετ'ἐλπίδων λυμαίνεται."

50. Edmunds, *Chance and Intelligence in Thucydides*, 190.

51. Thucydides, 4.116.2.

52. Thucydides 1.104.2, 1.116.1, 2.31.1, 2.93.2, 4.9.1, 4.104.5, 8.79.2, 8.91.2.

53. Thucydides, 1.137.2.

54. Indeed, friendship is a central principle in Aristotle's *Nicomachean Ethics*. See Lionel Pearson, "Thucydides as Reporter and Critic," *Transactions and Proceedings of the American Philological Association* 78 (1947): 37–60.

55. Certainly, attainment of virtue, and especially of justice, considered by Aristotle as the strongest and most important moral principle, is the main thesis of the *Nicomachean Ethics*.

56. These views are also strongly shared by Nanno Marinatos in *Thucydides and Religion* (Konigstein: Hain, 1981).

57. Simon Hornblower, "The Religious Dimension to the Peloponnesian War, or, What Thucydides Does Not Tell Us," *Harvard Studies in Classical Philology* 94 (1992), 169–197. Simon Hornblower, humbly puts forward, much to his credit, that "I shall try to show that Thucydides seriously understated the religious aspect of the war he set himself to describe. But in this area as in so many others we can often do no more than correct Thucydides out of Thucydides. That is *we* choose to play up what he chose to play down. Our justification for doing this, a perilously arrogant justification, consists in the little we know about Greek religion" (170).

58. Hornblower, "The Religious Dimension," 170. Hornblower, however, mentions that the contrast with Thucydides's handling of the 428 Olympic festival, four years later, is very marked: that event was turned by the Spartans into a strongly anti-Athenian occasion.

59. Hornblower, "The Religious Dimension," 171. See in this regard my commentary of the Funeral Oration above, at which the religious element of the oration is duly stressed.

60. See also W. R. Connor, "City Dionysia and Athenian Democracy" in *Classica Medievalia Dissertationes* xi (Copenhagen: Museum Tusculanum Press, 1989).

61. On this point I am agreed with Hornblower.

62. Hornblower, "The Religious Dimension," 172.

63. Hornblower, "The Religious Dimension," 172.

64. Hornblower, "The Religious Dimension," 176.

65. Hornblower, "The Religious Dimension," 175.

66. On this issue see D. M. Lewis, "The Origins of the First Peloponnesian War" in *Classical Contributions: Studies in Honour of M.F. McGregor*, ed. G. S. Shrimpton and D. J. McCarger (Locust Valley: J. J. Augustin, 1981), 71.

67. Hornblower, "The Religious Dimension," 179.

68. Hornblower, "The Religious Dimension," 182.

69. Hornblower, "The Religious Dimension," 185.

70. See further, R. Parker. "Myths of Early Athens" in *Interpretations of Greek Mythology*, ed. J. Bremmer (London: Routledge, 1987), 187.

71. Hornblower, "The Religious Dimension," 185.

72. Thucydides, 2.53. See Simon Hornblower, *A Commentary on Thucydides Volume I: Books I–III* (Oxford: Oxford University Press, 1991), 326: "καὶ τῶν οὐδὲν πρότερον κεκτημένων, εὐθὺς δὲ τακείνων ἐχόντων: 'and those who had nothing immediately inherited their property.' A revealing comment, with its implication that a category of 'new rich' suddenly emerged; this may be relevant to the changes in Athenian political attitudes which some have detected in the later 420s . . . θεῶν δὲ φόβος: 'No fear of Gods . . .' Note that, in what follows, there is no implication of punishment in an afterlife; see Dover, *Greek Popular Morality* (42. 4n), 267, who, also, as we have seen, notes (266) that the Funeral Oration says nothing about the afterlife."

73. Thucydides, 2.53.4. See, however, the view of Hornblower, *A Commentary on Thucydides Volume I: Books I–III*, 325: "καὶ ἱερῶν καὶ ὁσίων: 'sacred and profane.' For the word ὅσιον, which can sometimes mean 'sacred,' and sometimes as here 'profane' (because it is permitted by, or forbidden by, the gods, but instead belongs to the purely human sphere of men), see the interesting article by G. Eatough, 'The Use of ὅσιος and Kindred Words in Thucydides,' *AJP* 92 (1971), 238 ff. He shows that Th. avoids ὅσιος when making authorial judgements, and that on the few occasions when he allows speakers to use it and related words they are 'inoperative,' that is, the values they represent do not affect the situation or they are being used to mask true facts and intentions. Eatough has identified a genuine Thucydidean habit and offered valued analysis of individual passages, but I do not at all agree with the general conclusions he reaches about Th.'s own attitudes (see iii. 82. 8n on εὐσεβείᾳ, where the particular interpretation, also, seems to me faulty)."

74. Thucydides, 3.82.

75. Thucydides, 3.81.5. Similar events happen in Book II: "Sacred areas were full of corpses, burial customs were not observed, and men became careless of everything sacred or profane" (Thucydides, 2.52. 2–3). Only a man with deep religious convictions would emphasize the disregard of religious values and so painfully present the impiety of the people in those days.

76. Thucydides, 3.82.2.

77. Thucydides, 3.82.5. See the impressive opinion of Simon Hornblower, *A Commentary on Thucydides* Volume I–III (Oxford: Oxford University Press, 1991), 478: "The importance of this section for the student of Th.'s own opinions cannot be exaggerated. It is the most substantial expression of direct personal opinion in all Th., and whatever its obscurity it cannot simply be dismissed as a 'less successful' vehicle for Th.'s own views than the speeches, which are not a vehicle for his views at all. (Other sections like the *Archaeology* and the Plague description imply strong views, but they are more obliquely expressed.). *Idem*, 479: Th. describes with dazzling if (for the reader or hearer) uncomfortable virtuosity the changes in values brought about by the *stasis*. Then at 82.8 'he makes a fresh start, returning to the cause of it all' (Macleod, 128). A cause which he identifies as greed and ambition. Ch. 83 begins with a statement of frank personal regret and concludes with some reflections about the different fates of the clever and the less clever. This represents something of a return to the particular: see Gomme on 82.3, n. on ἐστασίαζε etc, whose formulation—a progression in ch. 82 from Corcyra, to Greece, to universal experience, then back to *stasis* in Greece and its particular characteristics (and, we might add, back to Corcyra at 85.1)—is valuable but a little mechanical. After

all, the phrase 'in the cities' occurs at intervals through this long chapter, in paras. 2, 3, and 8, and it might be better to see it as an analysis of *stasis* in Greek cities, punctuated by universal remarks like the beginning of para. 8, and prompted by Corcyra which never quite lost sight of: see 8n. on η μετά ψήφου ἀδίκου."

78. Gomme, *Historical Commentary on Thucydides*, 539.

79. See Thucydides, 3.67.1.

80. See Thucydides, 3.58.3.

81. See Thucydides, 3.62.2.

82. See Thucydides, 3.55.3.

83. Thucydides 3.55.3. The words they use indicate that they aspire to ethical values: καὶ προδοῦναι αὐτοὺς οὐκέτι ἦν καλόν.

84. Thucydides, 3.57.2.

85. See Thucydides, 3.59.2. See, though, the interesting comment of Hornblower, *A Commentary on Thucydides Volume I–III*, 452–453: "ὁ δὲ νόμος τοῖς ῞Ελλησι μὴ κτείνειν τούτους: 'Greek custom does not allow the suppliant to be put to death.' But the Plataeans had themselves put some Theban prisoners to death, ii. 5. 6 and n. there for the Plataians' reasons for passing over this point completely. (The Thebans of course rub the point in (66. 2–3) without, however, relating it as specifically as they might have done to the Plataians' present situation; though the comparison is implicit in the echo of this passage at 66.3 (see n. there) and the statement at 66.4 that the Plataians, not the Thebans, are the real criminals.) For the 'law' here invoked, see Macleod 108f; it is clearly a very different and weaker sort from the law at 56.2, which was hardly more than a generalization about human nature. In any case the Thebans will claim at 67.5 that the particular terms of the Plataians' surrender override their status as suppliants."

86. See Thucydides 3.59.2. But see the view of Hornblower on this, *A Commentary on Thucydides Volume I–III*, 453–454: "θεοὺς τοὺς ὁμοβωμίους . . . 'by the gods whom the Greeks worship at common altars.' For the very heavy concentration of religious words in this section compare Kleokritos at Xen. *Hell.* Ii.4.20ff, a highly emotive appeal of civic unity at the time of the political troubles after the end of the Peloponnesian War."

87. See Thucydides 3.57.1, 3.58.5.

88. The campaign of Delion and the military circumstance there is well commented on by Gomme: "The military situation was that Delion, supplied with food from Oropos which was firmly in Athenian hands (cf. ii. 23. 3, iv. 99), should form a strong point, an ἐπιτείχισμα (i. 142. 3–4 n.), from which harassing raids could be made into Boeotian territory, as later into Attica by the Peloponnesians from Dekeleia, and, if possible, support given to revolutionary movements in Boeotian cities (76. 5). For this purpose a garrison would be left in Delion, but the main Athenian army was not needed; it therefore was returning home, and waited for Hippokrates to join it. It had marched out to prevent the Boeotians from interfering with the occupation and fortification of Delion; it had no intention, if it could help it, of engaging the enemy forces in open combat, and besides hoped that they were distracted. The great mass of the ψιλοί were for home anyway, because they had completed the task allotted to them—the rapid building of the wall (94. 1). They would only be a hindrance in a battle, if there had to be a battle; and Pagondas saw to it that there should be one. By way of contrast compare the purely conventional picture of light-armed troops in Plutarch, Phok. 12.3" (Gomme, *A Historical Commentary on Thucydides*, Volume III, 559).

89. See Thucydides, 4.90.1–2.

90. Thucydides, 4.98.6: "πᾶν δ'εἰκὸς εἶναι τὸ πολέμῳ καὶ δεινῷ τινι κατειργόμενον ξύγγνωμόν τι γίγνεσθαι καὶ πρὸς τοῦ θεοῦ: 'The god would surely forgive offences committed under the constraint of war or some other extremity.' Critics have pounced on the speciousness of the argument: the Athenians are not in Boiotia (see 76.4: Delion in Tanagraian territory) as a result of some involuntary lapse: they are invaders. . . . The Athenian appeal to what the god would 'surely' or 'very probably' (παν εικός) do resembles the pathetic language of Nicias at vii.77.4" (Hornblower, *A Commentary on Thucydides Volume II: Books IV–V.24*, 313).

91. Herodotus, *The Persian Wars*, 4 vols., *Loeb Classical Library* 117–120, trans. A. D. Godley (Cambridge: Harvard University Press, 1920–1925)(hereafter cited as Herodotus), i. 91.

92. Herodotus, vii. 142–143.
93. Thucydides, 1.126.4–6.
94. See Thucydides, 1.126.4–6.
95. Thucydides, 3.96. But on this see the opposite view of Hornblower, *A Commentary on Thucydides Volume I: Books I–III*, 511–512: "ἐν τοῦ Διὸς τοῦ Νεμείου τῷ ἱερῷ, ἐν ᾧ Ἡσίοδος ὁ ποιητὴς λέγεται ὑπὸ τῶν ταύτῃ ἀποθανεῖν, χρησθὲν αὐτῷ ἐν Νεμέᾳ τοῦτο παθεῖν: 'at the temple of Nemean Zeus, where the poet Hesiod is said to have been killed by the inhabitants in fulfilment of an oracle which foretold that he should die at Nemea.' The point being that there was much more famous Nemea in the Peloponnese. See Marinatos, JHS 101 (1981), 139, who denies that Th.'s intention was to discredit an oracle which did after all come true in a sense, and compares the oracle about Kambyses dying in Agbatana, Hdt. Iii.64 (he died not at the famous Agbatana in Media but on obscure place of that name in Syria) . . . . See also Veyne (ii. 17. 2n) for a very confident statement that Th. believed in oracles like the present one. But on 'is said' here see Westlake (i.13. 2n.), 359, who does not think that Th. wished to express skepticism about the story (which he thinks comes from a source different from that used in the surrounding narrative), and that Th. 'may have been influenced by his customary uneasiness about oracles.'

"It seems to me that the present instance is hardly revealing, one way or the other, about Th.'s belief or disbelief in oracles (unlike the Pelargikon oracle at ii.17 or the 'Dorian War' at ii.54, nothing hangs on it). It does have this much in common with the Eurytanian reference, that Th. uses it to spice the narrative. (Cp. The colourful ch. 104, which relieves a long section of military writing)."

96. Herodotus, *The Persian Wars, Volume II*, iii. 64.
97. See Thucydides, 2.102.5
98. Thucydides 2.17.1-2.

Chapter Nine

Metaphysics in the History of Thucydides and Herodotus

A Comparative Study

SUPRANATURAL INTERFERENCES IN HERODOTUS

In the previous chapter, it has been proved that Thucydides was, in fact, very much religious. In contrast to Thucydides, against whom unfair criticisms have been raised as to his stance towards religion, Herodotus has always been regarded by modern scholarships in the classics as a historian who not only firmly accepted traditional Greek religion, but was deeply influenced by it.

In this section I shall purport to present a few cases whereby the religious convictions of Herodotus are particularly evident.

The first example will be King Xerxes's decision to invade Greece. Herodotus may be viewed as a composer of a basic plan of Greeks fighting against non-Greeks. Having excluded mythical accusations espoused by a Persian about who is guilty of having started the controversy and animosity between Greece and Persia (Europe and Asia in the wider sense) by committing the first acts of injustice,[1] Herodotus refers to the man whom "I *myself know* to have first begun to commit *unjust acts against the Greeks*" [emphasis added].[2] Clearly the man implied is Croesus and the Greeks are justifiably presented by Herodotus as fighting against Persian imperialism. Justice, divine and human, is on the side of the Greeks throughout the work of Herodotus in so far as they are being attacked (on immoral–imperialistic grounds), and the attacking side is to be seen as committing acts of violence and injustice. One of the work's two guiding motifs, then, is the Greeks's *just self-defense* against *wrongful aggression.*[3] The other motif that permeates the whole work is to be found in the sentence immediately following. Herodotus mentions "equally (*ὁμοίως*) small and large cities of men. For the majority of those that were large in times past, have become small; but those large in my time were small in the past. Knowing then that human prosperity (*τὴν ἀνθρωπηίην εὐδαιμονίην*) nowhere stays in the same condition, I shall mention both in equal fashion."[4] The word immediately following is "Croesus," the name of the man whose life will paradigmatically demonstrate the motif of the instability of human affairs, and who erroneously believes from his sufferings to have learned enough to be able to manipulate the "wheel of human affairs that, while turning, does not allow the same people always to be fortunate."[5]

The instability of the human condition is (as the case of Lydian Croesus demonstrates) a motif that transcends national boundaries. It often overlaps with another cardinal principle which may be termed as supranatural, that is, events or acts attributed to fate or divine interference. When the divine makes itself felt in the war of Greeks and non-Greeks, it will usually take the side of the Greeks, not only because their enemies perpetrate unjust acts upon them, but also because the excessive character of their enemies' endeavors transgresses the limits the divine has set to humans.[6]

Xerxes initially is not inclined to go to war against Greece, but his intention is to pursue his deceased father Darius's plan of suppressing the Egyptian revolt. However, an appearance of a ghost changes the route of political matters. The first change of mind of Xerxes happens only before departing for Egypt, when pressures are exerted upon him to launch a military expedition against Greece.[7] Mardonius, a cousin of Xerxes, was particularly influential. He led the previous expedition against Greece, which had failed when the Persian fleet was shipwrecked at Mount Athos and the army was severely beaten. He seeks to exact revenge upon the Athenians[8] for defeating the Persians who invaded Attica at Marathon.[9] He says: "You should move in revenge against Athens], in order that a good reputation be attached to you by men, and someone later beware of campaigning against your country."[10] Herodotus, in revealing the real motives of Mardonius, writes that "he was eager for military enterprise and himself wished to be the satrap of Greece."[11] Another set of people also sought the support of Xerxes: The Peisistratidae sent envoys to Susa in the hope of receiving support and to be reinstalled as tyrants in the city of Athens. They brought along an interpreter of oracles, called Onomacritus, who constantly reiterated oracles before Xerxes. He particularly promoted an oracle that predicted that Hellespont was destined to be bridged by a Persian man.[12] This was, indeed, the doom of Xerxes, as it later appeared.[13] In the histories, crossing a body of water often has the symbolical meaning of overreaching, beginning with Croesus crossing the Halys and immediately starting a scorched earth war against the Syrians "who were not guilty of anything" (*οὐδὲν ἐόντας αἰτίους* 1.76.2).[14]

When he returned from Egypt, Xerxes, in an address to the royal council, explains that he will stick to the arguments he had heard from the elders and that he would launch an invasion against Greece. He is presented as pressured when he refers to rivalling his ancestors by enlarging the power of Persia through winning reputation and conquering a more productive country, while at the same time avenging his country on the Greeks.[15] Herodotus makes Xerxes repeat the arguments of Mardonius clearly in an effort to stress Xerxes's fallacious considerations in deciding to go to war. This is particularly evident when Xerxes adopts the exhortation of the interpreter of oracles, Onomacritus, that a Persian will bridge the Hellespont. Up to this point, the interpreter of oracles may have been correct, but the sequence did not favor the Persians. Echoing Mardonius, Xerxes wants to conquer and burn Athens as a punishment (7.8β.3; singling out Athens, of course, also serves the reputation Herodotus bestows on this city). Beyond that, his ambition covers the Peloponnesus (and the rest of Europe). So we shall render the boundaries of our land coextensive with the heavenly realm of (7.8γ.1). The sun-god (to Greek readers, Helios is not just "the sun") will not look down on any country that shares a boundary with ours. This clearly is *hubris*, disregarding any moral standards: "In this way those who are guilty towards us will bear the yoke of slavery as well as those who are innocent" (7.8γ.3). Xerxes's attitude matches that of Croesus after he crossed the Halys River.[16]

Others present in the court kept silent and did not dare put forward an opinion opposite to the one placed before them. Only for a moment though.[17]

Silence breaks when Artabanus, uncle of Xerxes, introduces empirical reality and attempts through his arguments to convince Xerxes that an expedition against Greece would be calamitous. He recalled that he advised Darius not to undertake a military expedition against the Scythians, yet he did not listen, returning home having lost many competent men of his army.[18] Also he mentions that the formidable Persian army was defeated at Marathon by the Athenian infantry. As to the bridging of Hellespont, Artabanus says that the Persian army, if defeated, runs the risk of inducing the Greek navy to set sail to the Hellespont straits and put on fire the bridges that would enable Xerxes's safe return to Persia along with his soldiers. Artabanus warns Xerxes not to undertake such a dangerous campaign in the absence of a necessity to do so.[19] Xerxes, outraged, would not listen and condemns Artabanus to not take part in the campaign.

At night, Xerxes was vexed by the view of Artabanus. The appearance of a ghost, a handsome man, in the form of vision as soon as Xerxes fell asleep, was the factor that led to the change of his mind. What makes this dream look more natural than supranatural is that worries had kept Xerxes from sleeping, so they were perhaps carried over into his vision. Next morning,

Xerxes called his council and apologized for having changed his decision, which he attempted to excuse on the basis of his youth. He also asked Artabanus to forgive him for the burst of anger. During the following night, though, the dream emerged again, on this occasion with a threat that the son of Darius would fall from eminence to unimportance,[20] if he would not undertake the military expedition against Greece. The scared Xerxes called his adviser Artabanus and admitted that he spoke vain words to him (ἐπέων ματαίων 7.15.1), but said that, although he desired to remain faithful to the advice of Artabanus, he was not able to do so because of the vision he saw. To find out if it is a god who ordered him to undertake the campaign, he wanted Artabanus to put on the king's outfit, sit on his throne, and sleep in his bed, to see if the same vision appears to him also.[21]

Artabanus, however, said to Xerxes: "But these things are not divine, my son" (ω παι, 7.16β.2). He explained that dreams usually reflect what one is concerned with during the day, and that, over those days, they had dealt very much with the military campaign to Greece. This explanation may, of course, be correct in certain cases, but not necessarily in every case. The divine origin and purpose of dreams is an issue that has been discussed extensively in the Greek world and elsewhere.[22] Indeed, in the end, the vision appeared to Artabanus, too, and therefore its divinity was confirmed. This eventuality foresaw the devastating result the military campaign would have for Persia. The words used in the vision by the phantom, "what is destined to happen," ascribes a metaphysical quality to Herodotus's work. Artabanus now acknowledged a divine impulse, believing that a god-driven ruin was overtaking the Greeks. As a result he changed his opinion.

The second example comes from the Persian Wars as reported by Herodotus and Pausanias.[23]

The description goes that an unknown hero (called Ἐχετλεὺς) turned up in the course of the battle of Marathon and succored the Greeks to repel the Persian invasion. Historically this hero is not mentioned anywhere, and his existence among Greek heroes occurs after the battle at Marathon. In that battle, Echetlaeus appeared suddenly in the Greek camp, dressed in an armor with which the Athenians were not acquainted and was holding an ἐχέτλη instead of a weapon. This weapon was employed to kill many Persians. When the battle came to end, this man disappeared from the very spot that he had previously turned up, and no one knew anything about him. The Athenians consulted the oracle at Delphi in order to find out who this man was and the oracle said to them that they should worship Echetlaeus the hero. Driven from gratitude the Athenians indeed officially instituted his worship and this hero cult was from then on firmly consecrated. The victory at the battle of Marathon seems to have amazed the Athenians themselves. Many of them allegedly stated that they saw heroes fighting side by side with them and for their cause.

OATHS IN THUCYDIDES AND HERODOTUS

The oath provides a body of legal analysis inherent in ancient Greek histori-cal writings. By way of introduction in this section I shall confine the com-parative study to a single comment: Herodotus mentions only the gist of international or inter-state oaths, whereas Thucydides transcribes every sen-tence of some treaties of his era. He amazes the reader when he at times records the names of each signatory party to a treaty, for instance, seventeen Spartans and seventeen Athenians.[24] The purpose, therefore, in this sub-chapter is to examine where and how Thucydides and Herodotus mention oaths in their histories. Oaths, being solemn religious, legal, and political agreements, are certainly of historical and moral importance. Sworn state-ments as to truth or future action witnessed by higher powers deal with significant matters at stake in the ancient Greek world. Greek oaths were included in judicial proceedings of the city-state, inter-state diplomacy, and even interpersonal relations. Greek oaths consistently promise something for future performance with an invocation to the gods to punish the swearer if the promise is not sincerely kept.

In Thucydides, oaths are essential in public compacts. Swearing alliances, treaties of peace, and armistices are indicative of the historian's adherence to moral values. It must be mentioned inter alia that Thucydides describes the failures of Hellenic political systems in the Peloponnesian War—intra-state, inter-state, among alliances, and in contentious diplomacy with barbarians.[25] He quotes verbatim oaths in certain Peloponnesian War agreements, specific guaranteeing rituals described in detail, because apart from his religious con-victions that welcomed these solemn agreements, these precise oaths (bind-ing though they were supposed to be, μέγιστοι ὅρκοι) were often violated. Thucydides lays down oaths usually in the context of military alliances, the typical kind of treaties between states. The report of oaths falls into three main categories:

1. Report of a few successful and effective oaths or international oath rituals. The ratification of the Delian League is one such example, whereas a second example is posed by the Athenian symmachies with the Thessalians and Argives, in which oaths of reciprocal assistance and loyalty are sworn.[26]

2. Report of violation of traditional and old oaths between city-states and within the states themselves. Negotiators with Lacedaemon constantly refresh the memory of the Lacedaemonians by reference to oaths wit-nessed by the gods. The Plataeans, Corinthians, and no less the Athe-nians are afraid that the Lacedaemonians will betray what they had pledged for the sake of their political expediency. Conversely, the Lacedaemonians raise accusations against others for transgressing

their oaths.[27] The case of Plataea is typical of the violation of oaths underpinning an inter-state Greek symmachy. In this siege of the Plataeans by the combined forces of Spartans and Boeotians, Thucydides describes the negotiations which followed the Theban attack on Plataea, the four years of the Lacedaemonian siege as such, and the eventual capitulation of the city. First comes the arrest of some guerrillas by the Plataeans, upon which Boeotian country people asserted that the Plataeans had sworn not to kill prisoners of war, if the Boeotians left intact their fields. Then the Peloponnesian infantry arrives in support of the Thebans, their allies. Thereupon, the Plataeans remind Archidamus and the Lacedaemonians of the Panhellenic oaths of Plataea sworn fifty years before the events at stake. The Lacedaemonians, however, repel these accusations and proceed with sieging the city. Before the attack, King Archidamus invokes the gods and heroes of Plataea in a prayer that Thucydides reports directly and fully. In his appeal for divine support, that is, publicly asserting the justice of his cause, he claims that the Plataeans already deviated from their oath.[28] Thus Archidamus applies broken oaths in his attempts to justify to his fellow Spartans, their assembled allies, and the even larger Hellenic publics the breaking of the Persian War's *spondai*, and the present invasion. This attempt to cancel Sparta's oath to protect Plataea does not persuade many.[29] The Plataeans surrender two years later. Another debate erupts between Spartans, Plataeans, and Thebans with regard to the Greek oaths that were uttered before the battle of Plataea in the course of the Persian Wars. Following the Plataean speeches, Pausanias offered sacrifices in 479, at the agora of Plataea, and he stipulated that the city-state would be independent and subject to no act of aggression. The Lacedaemonians, however, reckon that they are not any more bound by their agreement with the Plataeans.[30] So they raze the city to the ground. Ten years later, nevertheless, the Lacedaemonians understand and admit their erroneous position and guilt in having violating their oaths in the case of Plataea.

Thucydides laments the transgression of the Greek traditions of faith. He mentions that there was no firm meaning of words or sufficiently terrifying oath.[31] He describes this situation as criminality or κακοτροπία. Patriotic sentiments and the traditional sanction of rituals that promote civic and smaller group solidarity shriveled in Corcyra[32] during the *stasis*. Thucydides strongly presents the decline of Greek oaths in the course of the Peloponnesian civil war. In the case of Corfu he deplores the violation of oaths in a particularly vivid manner: "And oaths, if somewhere in fact any reconciliation occurred, held strong between the parties for the moment in the face of immediate difficulty when they had no other resource."[33]

Another typical case of oaths violation simultaneously indicating that swearing was in fact employed as means of persuasion is provided in the expedition of Brasidas in northern Greece. Although his campaign was successful and proved the mightiness of the military organization of Lacedaemon, and despite the fact that the Lacedaemonians relied on their fame for honoring their oaths, Thucydides presents that the Lacedaemonians under the command of Brasidas backed down from their oaths on this occasion.[34]

Further, at the capture of Lacedaemonians as prisoners of war after the events at Pylos, the Lacedaemonian authorities stipulated a one-year truce. This agreement made Brasidas, who was campaigning in northern Greece, furious. It is noteworthy that soon after the death of Brasidas and Cleon another one-year armistice was concluded along with the Peace of Nicias in 421 B.C.[35] Under the terms of the Peace of Nicias, the Lacedaemonians agreed, having sincerely uttered oaths, that they would return Amphipolis. This oath was eventually not respected, which indicates that at the time the Lacedaemonians and other Greeks were not firm in their oath practices.

3. There is a third division in the accurate report of Thucydides, which describes defaulting on oaths. This is indicative of the fact that Thucydides transcribed official documents in every political detail. For instance, he fully quotes the treaty of alliance between the Athenians.[36] His report comprises the political and military clauses of their alliance which was supposed to last for a hundred years. Then he describes exactly who swears the oath, the person that is expected to administer and implement it in the signatory city-states, and even the process of sacrifice accompanying the treaty.[37]

As regards the deficiencies of the oaths as such, it need be said that the manipulation of oath, to the extent that this actually occurred, has been marked by Thucydides as an attribute to be deplored about oath practices in classical Greece in the course of the Peloponnesian War. Although Thucydides presents men as having the conviction that the gods enforce oaths,[38] an opinion that he may have shared himself, too, he is pragmatic in that in his history men compile and implement the oaths. After their severe defeat on the island of Sphacteria, the Lacedaemonians aptly make the point of deficiency immanent in the conventions, particularly when these are concluded under duress, that is, pressure exerted upon the defeated party by the winner in a military confrontation: "Only generous conditions can end serious enmities, not forcing a trapped opponent to swear to a disadvantageous treaty."[39] Also other oaths included in conventions clauses were designed to help city-states evade implementation of onerous obligations. This was the case with Camarina: "Men created let out clauses, such as the Corinthians," "if the god and heroes do not prevent."[40] To stay faithful to one's oath and to the gods, to be εὔορκοι in Delphic terms, always remained subject to each sovereign state's self-serving interpretations.[41]

Notes

1. Herodotus, *The Persian Wars*, 4 vols., *Loeb Classical Library* 117–120 (Cambridge: Harvard University Press, 1920–1925) (hereafter cited as Herodotus), 1.2.1.
2. Herodotus, 5.3.
3. Hans-Peter Stahl, "Blind Decisions Preceding Military Action" in *Thucydides and Herodotus*, ed. Edith Foster and Donald Lateiner (Oxford: Oxford University Press, 2012), 133.
4. Herodotus, 1.5.3.
5. Stahl, "Blind Decisions Preceding Military Action," 133.
6. Stahl, "Blind Decisions Preceding Military Action," 133.
7. See Herodotus, 7.5–6.
8. Herodotus, 7.5.
9. Herodotus, 6.113.
10. Herodotus, 7.5.2.
11. Herodotus, 7.6.1.
12. Herodotus, 7.6.4.
13. See Xenophon, *Hellenica, Volume I: Books 1–4, Loeb Classical Library* 88, trans. Carleton L. Brownson (Cambridge: Harvard University Press, 1918): ζεύξας τόν Ἑλλήσποντον, διωρύξας τὸν Εὖρον.
14. Stahl, "Blind Decisions Preceding Military Action," 135.
15. Herodotus, 8a.2.
16. Stahl, "Blind Decisions Preceding Military Action," 136.
17. "Of course, flatterer Mardonius had got what he wanted, but at the same time Herodotus had again pointed to the flaws in the one-sided information on which Xerxes' decision is based. He further unmasks the Persian Empire's ruthlessness when Mardonius enumerates the great nations subjected by Persia that 'have committed no acts of injustice against the Persians.' The more reason there is in his eyes to take revenge against the Greeks 'because they started the wrongdoing' (7.9.2). Mardonius here contradicts his literary creator's value judgments both by overlooking the ever-present danger of overreaching and by ascribing wrongdoing to the Greeks, who, after all, acted within the context of defending their freedom against unjust aggression—Herodotus' first major topic" (Stahl, "Blind Decisions Preceding Military Action," 136).
18. Herodotus, 10α.2.
19. See Stahl, "Blind Decisions Preceding Military Action," 138: "Divine jealousy and human pride in one's superior social status were addressed also by Solon the sage when he in vain warned Croesus about the instability of human prosperity (1.32.1, 9). Not only was Solon, though dismissed by Croesus as foolish (ἀμαθέα 1.33), proven right by the ensuing development, but he had also expounded the historian's own basic 'knowledge' about the instability of human prosperity."
20. Herodotus, 7.14.
21. Herodotus, 7.15.
22. The conversation's sequence is interesting: "But if this thing does have a share in the divine, you were right to say that it ought to appear to me, too (after all I was the original opponent of the campaign [7.10] who persuaded you to call it off). Let the vision appear also to me whether dressed up in your clothing or not: it will not be so stupid as to mistake me for you, going by my dress. But what we must find out now is this: whether it will hold me of no account and deem me not worthy of its visit, whether I am dressed in my own clothing or yours, but will not come to me: for if it will continue to come, I myself too would certainly say it is divine. Since you insist that I sleep in your bed all right, let it appear to me, too, but up to then I'll stick to my present opinion" (16γ.2).
23. See Herodotus, *The Persian Wars*, Volume I; Pausanias, *Description of Greece, Loeb Classical Library* (Cambridge: Harvard University Press, 1918).
24. Thucydides, *History of the Peloponnesian War*, 4 vols., *Loeb Classical Library* 108, 109, 110, and 169, trans. C. Forster Smith (Cambridge: Harvard University Press, 1919–1923) (hereafter cited as Thucydides), 5.19.

25. Donald Lateiner, "Oaths: Theory and Practice in the *Histories* of Herodotus and Thucydides" in *Thucydides and Herodotus*, ed. Edith Foster and Donald Lateiner (Oxford: Oxford University Press, 2012), 170.

26. Thucydides, 1.102.4, 5.38.3.

27. Thucydides, 2.72, 5.30.1.

28. Thucydides, 2.71.4, 2.72.1, 2.73.3.

29. Lateiner, "Oaths: Theory and Practice in the *Histories* of Herodotus and Thucydides," 173.

30. Thucydides, 3.68.1 (ἔκσπονδοι); See the article in the Transactions of the American Association for confirmation of Echetlaeus.

31. Thucydides, 3.83.2.

32. Lateiner, "Oaths: Theory and Practice in the *Histories* of Herodotus and Thucydides," 174.

33. Thucydides, 3.82.7: καὶ ὅρκοι, εἴ που ἄρα γένοιντο ξυναλλαγῆς ἐν τῷ αὐτίκα πρὸς τὸ ἄπορον ἑκατέρῳ διδόμενοι ἴσχυον οὐκ ἐχόντων ἄλλοθεν δύναμιν.

34. Lateiner, "Oaths: Theory and Practice in the *Histories* of Herodotus and Thucydides," 175, makes the point well: "Spartans traded on their reputation for integrity when offering oaths. Thucydides reports Brasidas's shrewd liberation propaganda in northern Greece. A good speaker for a Spartan (4.80.2), Brasidas informs various dithering and anxious Thraceward subjects of other powers that the Spartan authorities had sworn oaths to respect and defend the autonomy of rebels from Athenian oppression (4.86.1, 87.1, 88.1: ἦ μὴν ἔσεσθαι ξυμμάχους αὐτονόμους). Thucydides judges Brasidas' persuasive performances . . . in the region as simply attractive lies (88.1: τὸ ἐπαγωγὰ εἰπεῖν; 108.5: ἐφολκὰ καὶ οὐ τὰ ὄντα λέγοντος). Whether or not they had sworn such oaths, the Lacedaemonian authorities sent out harmosts or governors contrary to those oaths (132.3). Having breached their allies' autonomy, they perjured their oaths. This distinction between sworn oath promise and already intended discrepant actions exemplifies Thucydides's attraction to his fundamental word-deed antithesis" (175).

35. See Thucydides, 4.118, 5.18.

36. See Thucydides, 5.47: εὐθὺς δι' ὀργῆς εἶχον.

37. See Thucydides, 5.47.8–11: ὀμνύντων τὸν ἐπιχώριον ὅρκον ἕκαστοι τὸν μέγιστον κατὰ ἱερῶν τελείων. Ὁ δὲ ὅρκος ἔστω ὅδε.

38. Thucydides 5.30.3: θεῶν γάρ πίστεις ὀμόσαντες.

39. Thucydides, 4.19.2.

40. Thucydides, 5:30: ἢν μὴ ἡρώων κώλυμα ἦ.

41. Lateiner, "Oaths: Theory and Practice in the *Histories* of Herodotus and Thucydides," 177.

Epilogue

As it has been stated in the prologue of this book, my aim has been, on the one hand, to demonstrate that the history by Thucydides establishes the existence of international law in classical Greece. On the other hand, the purpose has been to prove that the *History of the Peloponnesian War* has influenced contemporary international law and political thought. Some concluding comments should definitely be useful.

The meaning of Thucydidean political realism is a peculiar one, and it has been, I believe, adequately interpreted in chapter 1. Many are the deductions from this kind of realism, which is surely different than the realism of Machiavelli. It is sufficient here to recall the message that the Melian Dialogue sends to contemporary policy makers and international lawyers, apart from the strategic studies connotations that underlie the history: "Χρήσιμον ὑμᾶς μὴ καταλύειν τὸ κοινὸν ἀγαθὸν," the Melians respond. Which is the common good? What is meant by this expression? Clearly here the Melians imply the common law, the international and inter-state law of ancient Greece. It is meant that the weak or weaker state also has the right to evoke international law and demand its implementation. It is noteworthy that the Melians do not use the word πρέπον (must), but χρήσιμον (it is useful). The utilitarian character that they ascribe to law is surely not accidental. They express themselves in the language of interest and political expediency, the only language that could potentially have persuaded the Athenians. Here, Thucydides remarkably identifies law (δίκαιον) with interest (ξυμφέρον). Law is the only real interest to the Athenians and the Melians like. The monumental book of Thucydides constitutes a blend of international law and international politics. International law and international politics should be seen as forming part of one and the same order.

It is evident that almost all modern forms of the law of war, both the justifications of war as well as the law of armed conflict, have largely been drawn from the history by Thucydides. Self-defense of states and humanitarian intervention originate in the war between the Athenians and Lacedaemonians, ably described by Thucydides. Book IV of the *History of the Peloponnesian War* may at first sight be said to pose an example of self-defense in international law, particularly of protection of nationals abroad, this being a facet or category of self-defense of states. On its way to Sicily, the Athenian fleet was met with a sea storm, which forced the ships to seek refuge in the Peloponnese (Pylos). Since the war between Athens and Sparta was at its height, the Athenian navy members were arrested by the Lacedaemonians. Cleon, the Athenian demagogue, forcefully urged the Athenian assembly to make a military campaign to prevent their fellow citizens from being massacred. The incident may be described as an operation to save nationals abroad (since the Athenian prisoners of war were not subjects of the Spartans). In modern international law UN Charter Article 2(4) provides for the following: "All members shall refrain in their international relations from the threat or use of force against the territorial integrity or political independence of any State, or in any manner inconsistent with the purposes of the United Nations."[1] However, self-defense of states is a commonly accepted exception to the general prohibition of the use of force as embodied in the UN Charter. Article 51 of the charter stipulates that "nothing in the present Charter shall impair the inherent right of individual or collective self-defence if an armed attack occurs against a member of the United Nations, until the Security Council has taken the measures necessary to maintain international peace and security. The military operation at Pylos can also be viewed as a paradigm example of unilateral humanitarian intervention, if by extension of the doctrine of self-defense one accepts the existence of a similar right of intervention for humanitarian purposes. The speech of General Demosthenes again lays down the premises and criteria of humanitarian intervention.

The law of armed conflict, otherwise called humanitarian law of armed conflict or humanitarian law, clearly forms part of the *History of the Peloponnesian War*. Legal rules governing the conduct of opponents in the battlefield were not of a rudimentary form, but, in fact, were sufficiently developed. If it cannot be said that these rules have influenced the formation of rules of equivalent value in modern international law, it could certainly be deduced that they stood firmly in their own right as an aspect of classical Greek international law. One can certainly conclude that rules governing prisoners of war and monuments of culture existed and were observed in classical times. Noteworthy is the fact that the oracle of Delphi usually exerted a powerful influence on matters of armed conflict and dispute resolution. This fact proves beyond doubt that the oracle at Delphi served also as an organization for the settlement of inter-state or international disputes in ancient Greece, much like modern international organizations purport to resolve international conflicts through the process of mediation, arbitration, negotiation, and conciliation.

The intense diplomatic activity of ancient Greeks is demonstrated by the fact that the history is full of instances of conclusion of treaties between the Greek city-states. These have been carefully excerpted and written down in this monograph in a separate chapter. Simultaneously their political background along with the relevant chronologies have been diligently laid down for the objective reader who would like to study these interesting legal practices. It is astonishing that some treaties in the history are almost identical with conventions in modern international law both in terms of phraseology and content. What is certainly absent from the overwhelming majority of modern treaties and needs to be spotted here is that ancient treaties perpetually included clauses through which the Greeks paid honor to their deities and called for their protection. Further, and equally importantly, they were committed to carry out the provisions of the treaties by reference to oaths specifically spelled out in the treaties in question (*Σπονδὰς ἐποιήσαντο Ἀθηναῖοι καί Λακεδαιμόνιοι καί οἱ ξύμμαχοι κατά τάδε, καί ὤμοσαν κατά πόλεις*, being a typical example). Even though on a number of occasions these oaths were transgressed, the mere fact of their inclusion in treaties by way of legal clauses denotes that ancient Greeks were instilled with an ethos that has clearly faded away in the modern world of politics.

The role of personalities has duly been analyzed in the present monograph. At this point, there are only three issues that I would like to stress from the funeral speech of Pericles. Firstly, Pericles stresses that the populace is also especially obedient, not only to local magistrates and laws, but to the unwritten laws which governed all human behavior.[2] Again, this contravenes the statement of Lowell Edmunds that "the fact that Pericles says nothing of the gods in the Funeral Oration is an indication of his humanism."[3] Edmunds's statement is contradicted the more by the Periclean reference to recreation and religious festivals, which strengthens the opinion that Pericles's religious belief or at least affinity to the traditional Greek religion was actually intense: *ἀγῶσι μέν γε καί θυσίαις διετησίοις νομίζοντες*. It is to be noted that the expensive public buildings on the Acropolis for which Athens was notorious are excluded here—they do not serve recreational purposes.[4] Secondly, "in the knowledge that your happiness is your freedom and your freedom your courage, do not shrink the dangers of war" (*καί τὸ εὔδαιμον τὸ ἐλεύθερον, τὸ δ' ἐλεύθερον τὸ εὔψυχον κρίναντες, μὴ περιορᾶσθε τοὺς πολεμικοὺς κινδύνους*).[5] Formally, the words recall those of Archidamus: "We are courageous because self-control derives from a sense of honor and courage from self-control."[6] Thirdly, Pericles depicts the Athenian democratic constitution as encompassing the virtues of meritocracy and justice: "By merit, each man, according as his particular ability is recognized, is advanced in public life—not by lot but by virtue" (κατὰ δὲ τὴν ἀξίωσιν, ὡς ἕκαστος ἐν τῷ εὐδοκιμεῖ, οὐκ ἀπὸ μέρους τὸ πλέον ἐς τὰ κοινὰ[7] ἢ ἀπ᾽ ἀρετῆς προτιμᾶται). Again, it seems that modern constitutions of the world, though they make constant references to democratic principles and moral values, do not in every case make sure that meritocracy is safeguarded through proper legal machinery and efficient administrative institutions. Furthermore, surprise has often been expressed that, except for a general phrase or two in the Funeral Oration, Pericles says nothing of the artistic and literary accomplishments of Athens in her greatest period, or, what amounts to the same thing, that he was so absorbed with her material and political achievements, which the war in some sense terminated, as to overlook her cultural achievements, which the war did not affect. These criticisms present Thucydides as a materialist who crassly misjudged in what sphere Athens's greatest triumphs lay.

The reader cannot miss the fact that the Peloponnesian War presents similarities with classical Greek tragedy. Athens, a superpower of classical times, is driven to total catastrophe, in particular after her defeat in the area of Hellespont, mainly because the foreign policy of the city was in the hands of arrogant demagogues who thought they could accomplish things that were, in fact, impossible or unjust. This reminds us of divine justice exacted upon the unrighteous (sometimes also through successful human effort), who violate human and divine laws, in ancient Greek tragedy.[8] Truly, it is this human effort that makes justice possible, even in the context of the Peloponnesian War. Humans tend to seek the assistance of the deity in certain circumstances, especially when they struggle to enforce justice in its various facets. However, in this world, the fight for international justice is truly, fundamentally, and substantially our own.

Notes

1. UN Charter 2(4).

2. Interesting in this regard is the view put forward by J. Finley Jr., late professor of Greek at Harvard University: "All this is not to say that he may not have believed in the gods. He mentions disbelief as a symptom of social disintegration and goes out of his way to praise the high character of the pious Nicias. He simply did not believe that the gods intervened in the working out of the political forces which he thought operative in history. One could even say that his work was a kind of Greek tragedy in which the operation of these human forces is substituted for that of divine forces" (*Thucydides*, Cambridge: Harvard University Press, 1942, 312).

3. Lowell Edmunds, *Chance and Intelligence in Thucydides* (Cambridge: Harvard University Press, 1975), 67.

4. Thucydides, *The Peloponnesian War Book II, Cambridge Greek and Latin Classics*, ed. J. S. Rusten (Cambridge: Cambridge University Press, 1990), 148.

5. Thucydides, *History of the Peloponnesian War*, 4 vols., *Loeb Classical Library* 108, 109, 110, and 169, trans. C. Forster Smith (Cambridge: Harvard University Press, 1919–1923) (hereafter cited as Thucydides), 2.43.4. The reasoning is "happiness is freedom, and freedom is bravery [so as to be happy, be brave]" (Thucydides, 171). "Μὴ περιορᾶσθε τοὺς πολεμικοὺς κινδύνους: περιορᾶσθε means to watch from the sidelines [without participating]" (Thucydides, *The Peloponnesian War Book II*, 171).

6. Thucydides, 1.84.3.

7. As to the Athenian practice of choosing most magistrates in a yearly lottery, which was often considered a major defeat of Athenian democracy, see W. K. C. Guthrie, *The Sophists* (Cambridge: Cambridge University Press, 1971), 319 no. 3. The real power, as noted by Pericles, was wielded by men of distinction, notably the στρατηγοί.

8. See, however, the view of Finley in *Thucydides*, 324: "In particular, it would be incorrect to believe that when Thucydides describes the Athenians as led by error to overconfidence and final ruin he is simply setting forth the old process of divine retribution known from tragedy, whereby ὕβρις, insolence, ends in ἄτη, disaster. For it is exactly here that the larger social forces which Thucydides saw at work in his own times and thought would be repeated in the future take the place of the gods in History" (324).

Appendix I

Further Reading

Adcock, F. E. *Thucydides and His History*. Cambridge: Cambridge University Press, 1963.

Allison, G. *Destined for War*. Boston: Houghton Mifflin Harcourt, 2017.

Andrewes, A. "The Opposition to Perikles." *Journal of Hellenic Studies* 98 (1978): 1–8.

Badian, E. *From Plataea to Potidaea: Studies in the History and Historiography of the Pente-contaetia*. Baltimore: Johns Hopkins University Press, 1993.

Bruce, I. A. F. *An Historical Commentary on the Hellenica Oxyrhynchia*. Cambridge: Cambridge University Press, 1967.

Brunt, P. A. *Studies in Greek History and Thought*. Oxford: Clarendon Press, 1993.

Buckler, J. *The Theban Hegemony, 371–362 B.C.* Cambridge: Harvard University Press, 1980.

Cartledge, P. *Sparta and Lakonia*. London: Routledge, 1979.

Cartledge, P., and D. Harvey (eds.). *CRUX, Essays Presented to G. E. M. de Ste Croix on his 75th Birthday*. London: Duckbacks, 1985.

Cobet, J. "Herodotus and Thucydides on War," in *Past Perspectives: Studies in Greek and Roman Historical Writing*. Ed. I. S. Moxon, J. D. Smart, and A. J. Woodman. Cambridge: Cambridge University Press, 1986. 1–18.

Connor, W. R. *The New Politicians of Fifth Century Athens*. Princeton: Princeton University Press, 1971.

Connor, W. R. "A Post-Modernist Thucydides?" *Classical Journal* 72 (1977): 289–298.

Crane, G. *Thucydides and the Ancient Simplicity: The Limits of Political Realism*. Berkeley: University of California Press, 1998.

Culham, P. "The Delian League: Bicameral or Unicameral?" *American Journal of Ancient History* 3 (1978): 27–31.

de Ste Croix, G. E. M. *The Class Struggle in the Ancient Greek World*. London: Duckworth Publishing, 1981.

Dewald, C. *Thucydides' War Narrative: A Structural Study*. Berkeley: University of California Press, 2005.

Dover, K. "The Palatine Manuscript of Thucydides." *Classical Quarterly* 4 (1954): 76–83.

Dover, K. *Thucydides*. Oxford: Clarendon Press, 1973.

Edmunds, L. "Thucydides' Ethics as Reflected in the Description of Stasis." *Harvard Studies in Classical Philology* 79 (1995): 73–92.

Fairchild, W. D. "Evidence of Improvised Speaking in Thucydides." *Classical Bulletin* 53 (1975): 4–8.

Fornara, C. W. "On the Chronology of the Samian War." *Journal of Hellenic Studies* 99 (1979): 7–19.

Fornara, C. W. *Translated Documents of Greece and Rome, i. Archaic Times to the End of the Peloponnesian War.* Cambridge: Cambridge University Press, 1983.

Fraser, P. M., and E. Matthews (eds.). *Lexicon of Greek Personal Names, i. The Aegean Islands, Cyprus, Cyrenaica.* Oxford: Oxford University Press, 1987.

Gomme, A. W. *The Greek Attitude to Poetry and History.* Berkeley: University of California Press, 1954.

Gomme, A. W. *More Essays in Greek History and Literature.* Oxford: Oxford University Press, 1962.

Graham, A. J., and G. Forsyth. "A New Slogan for Oligarchy in Thucydides III.82.8." *Harvard Studies in Classical Philology* 88 (1984): 25–45.

Harding, P. *Translated Documents of Greece and Rome, ii. From the End of the Peloponnesian War to the Battle of Ipsus.* Cambridge: Cambridge University Press, 1985.

Hill, G. F., R. Meiggs, and A. Andrewes. *Sources for Greek History 476–431 BC.* Oxford: Oxford University Press, 1951.

Hunter, V. J. *Past and Process in Herodotus and Thucydides.* Princeton: Princeton University Press, 1982.

Jones, N. "The Topography and Strategy of the Battle of Amphipolis in 422 B." *California Studies in Classical Antiquity* 10 (1977): 71–104.

Kagan, D. "The Speeches in Thucydides and the Mytilene Debate." *Yale Classical Studies* 24 (1975): 71–94.

Kennedy, P. M. "The First World War and the International System." *International Security* 9 (Summer 1984): 7–40.

Kennedy, P. *The Rise and Fall of the Great Powers.* New York: Random House, 1987.

Macleod, C. *Collected Essays.* Oxford: Oxford University Press, 1983

Macleod, C. "Form and Meaning in the Melian Dialogue." *Historia* 23 (1974): 385–400.

Macleod, C. "Reason and Necessity: Thucydides III,9,14, 37–48." *Journal of Hellenic Studies* 98 (1978): 64–78.

Macleod, C. "Thucydides on Faction (3.82.83)." *Proceedings of the Cambridge Philological Society* 25 (1979): 52–68.

Macleod, C. "Thucydides' Plataean Debate." *Greek, Roman and Byzantine Studies* 18 (1977): 227–246.

McGregor, M. F. "The Politics of the Historian Thucydides." *Phoenix* 10 (1956): 93–102.

Meiggs, R. *The Athenian Empire.* Oxford: Oxford University Press, 1972.

Meiggs, R., and D. Lewis. *A Selection of Greek Historical Inscriptions to the End of the Fifth Century BC*, rev. ed., Oxford: Oxford University Press, 1988.

Meritt, B. D. "The Samian Revolt from Athens in 440–439 B.C." *Proceedings of the American Philosophical Society* 128 (1984): 123–133.

Meritt, B. D., H. T. Wade-Gery, and M. F. McGregor. *The Athenian Tribute Lists*, 4 vols, Cambridge: Harvard University Press, 1939–1953.

Meritt, B. D., H. T. Wade-Gery, and M. F. McGregor. "Democracy in the Allied Cities," in *The Athenian Tribute Lists, vol. 3.* Ed. B. D. Meritt, H. T. Wade-Gery, and M. F. McGregor. Cambridge: Harvard University Press, 1950.

Morrison, J. V. "Preface to Thucydides: Rereading the Corcyrean Conflict (1.24–55)." *Classical Antiquity* 18 (1999): 94–96.

Nye, J. "Neorealism and Neoliberalism." *World Politics* 40, no. 2 (1988): 235–251.

Orwin, C. "The Just and Advantageous in Thucydides: The Case of the Mytilenaian Debate." *American Political Science Review* 78 (1984): 489–494.

Osborne, M., and S. Byrne (eds.). *Lexicon of Greek Personal Names, ii. Attica.* Oxford: Oxford University Press, 1994.

Osborne, R., and S. Hornblower (eds.). *Ritual, Finance, Politics: Athenian Democratic Accounts Presented to David Lewis.* Oxford: Oxford University Press, 1994.

Page, D. L. *Further Greek Epigrams.* Cambridge: Cambridge University Press, 1980.

Parker, R. *Miasma: Pollution and Purification in Greek Religion.* Oxford: Oxford University Press, 1983.

Parker, S. T. "The Objectives and Strategy of Cimon's Expedition to Cyprus." *American Journal of Philology* 97 (1976): 30–38.

Rawlings, H. R. *The Structure of Thucydides' History*. Princeton: Princeton University Press, 1981.

Rawlings, H. R. "Thucydides on the Purpose of the Delian League." *Phoenix* 31 (1977): 1–8.

Rhodes, P. J. *Commentary on the Aristotelian Athenaion Politeia*. Oxford, Oxford University Press, 1981.

Rhodes, P. J. "Thucydides on the Purpose of the Delian League." *Phoenix* 31 (1977): 1–8.

Ridley, R. T. "Exegesis and Audience in Thucydides." *Hermes* 109 (1981): 25–46.

Robertson, N. D. "The True Nature of the Delian League, 478–461 B.C." *American Journal of Ancient History* 5 (1980): 64–96.

Sabin, P., H. van Wees, and M. Whitby (eds.). *The Cambridge History of Greek and Roman Warfare*, 2 vols. Cambridge: Cambridge University Press, 2007.

Stahl, H. P. *Thucydides: Man's Place in History*. London: Bloomsbury, 2002.

Taylor, A. J. P. *The Struggle for the Mastery of Europe, 1848–1918*. Oxford: Oxford University Press, 1954.

Wade-Gery, H. T. *Essays in Greek History*. Oxford: Oxford University Press, 1958.

Walbank, M. *Athenian Proxenies of the Fifth Century BC*. Cambridge: Cambridge University Press, 2009.

Westlake, H. D. "The Commons at Mytilene." *Historia* 25 (1976): 429–440.

Westlake, H. D. "Ionians in the Ionian War." *Classical Quarterly* 29 (1979): 9–44.

Westlake, H. D. "The Naval Battle at Pylos and its Consequences." *Classical Quarterly* 24 (1974): 211–226.

Westlake, H. D. "Thucydides on Pausanias and Themistocles. A Written Source?" *Classical Quarterly* 27 (1977): 95–110.

Selected Bibliography

Aeschylus. *Persians. Seven against Thebes. Suppliants. Prometheus Bound, Loeb Classical Library* 145. Cambridge: Harvard University Press, 2009.
Aristotle. *Ars Rhetorica, Oxford Classical Texts*. Oxford: Oxford University Press, 1959.
Aristotle. *Nicomachaean Ethics, Loeb Classical Library* 73. Cambridge: Harvard University Press, 1926.
Aristotle. *Politica*, Book VIII, David Ross (ed.), *Oxford Classical Texts*. Oxford: Oxford University Press, 1963.
Arrian. *Anabasis of Alexander, Books I–IV, Loeb Classical Library* 236. Cambridge: Harvard University Press, 1976.
Bockh, A. *Corpus Inscriptionum Graecarum*. Officina Academica, 1828.
Brierly, J. L. *The Law of Nations*. Oxford: Oxford University Press, 2012.
Brownlie, I. *International Law and the Use of Force by States*. Oxford: Oxford University Press, 1963.
Cicero. *On Duties (De Officiis), Loeb Classical Library* 30. Cambridge: Harvard University Press, 1931.
Cochrane, N. *Thucydides and the Science of History*. Oxford: Oxford University Press, 1929.
Cohen, D. "Justice, Interest, and Political Deliberation in Thucydides." *Quaderini Urbinati* 16, no. 1 (1984).
Connor, R. *Thucydides*. Princeton: Princeton University Press, 1934.
Connor, W. R. "City Dionysia and Athenian Democracy." *Classica Medievalia Dissertationes* xi. Copenhagen: Museum Tusculanum Press, 1989.
Connor, W. R. *The New Politicians of Fifth-Century Athens*. Princeton: Princeton University Press, 1971.
Cornford, F. C. *Thucydides Mythistoricus*. London: Edward Arnold, 1907.
de Ste Croix, G. E. M. *The Origins of the Peloponnesian War*. Ithaca: Cornell University Press, 1972.
Diodorus Siculus. *Library of History, Volume I: Books 1–2.34* , C. H. Oldfather (trans.), *Loeb Classical Library* 279. Cambridge: Harvard University Press, 1933.
Dover, K. *Greek Popular Morality*. Berkeley: University of California Press, 1974.
Doyle, M. "Thucydides: A Realist?" in Richard Ned Lebow and Barry S. Strauss (eds.), *Hegemonic Rivalry from Thucydides to the Nuclear Age*. Boulder: Westview Press, 1991.
Edmunds, L. *Chance and Intelligence in Thucydides*. Cambridge: Harvard University Press, 1975.
Finley Jr., J. *Three Essays on Thucydides*. Cambridge: Harvard University Press, 1967.
Finley Jr., J. *Thucydides*. Cambridge: Harvard University Press, 1942.

Fliess, P. J. *Thucydides and the Politics of Bipolarity*. Baton Rouge: Louisiana State University Press, 1966.

Foster, E. *Thucydides, Pericles, and Periclean Imperialism*. Cambridge: Cambridge University Press, 2010.

Foster, E., and D. Lateiner (eds.). *Thucydides and Herodotus*. Oxford: Oxford University Press, 2012.

Gilpin, R. "Peloponnesian War and Cold War," in Richard Ned Lebow and Barry S. Strauss (eds.), *Hegemonic Rivalry from Thucydides to the Nuclear Age*. Boulder: Westview Press, 1991.

Gilpin, R. *War and Change in World Politics*. Cambridge: Cambridge University Press, 1981.

Gomme, A. W. *A Historical Commentary on Thucydides*, Volume III. Oxford: Oxford University Press, 1956.

Goodrich, L. M., and E. Hambro. *Charter of the United Nations: Commentary and Documents*. Boston: World Peace Foundation, 1946.

Gray, V. *Xenophon on Government, Cambridge Greek and Latin Classics*. Cambridge: Cambridge University Press, 2007.

Gustafson, L. (ed.). *Thucydides' Theory of International Relations*. Baton Rouge: Louisiana State University Press, 2000.

Guthrie, W. K. C. *The Sophists*. Cambridge: Cambridge University Press, 1971.

Harris, D. *Cases and Materials on International Law*. London: Sweet and Maxwell, 1991.

Herodotus. *The Persian Wars*. A. D. Godley (trans.). *Loeb Classical Library* 118. Cambridge: Harvard University Press, 1920–1925.

Hignett, C. *A History of the Athenian Constitution to the End of the Fifth Century B.C.* Oxford: Oxford University Press, 1952.

Homer. *The Odyssey of Homer*. New York: HarperCollins Publishers, 2007.

Hornblower, S. *A Commentary on Thucydides Volume I: Books I–III*. Oxford: Oxford University Press, 1997.

Hornblower, S. "The Religious Dimension to the Peloponnesian War, or, What Thucydides Does Not Tell Us," *Harvard Studies in Classical Philology* 94 (1992): 169–197.

International Court of Justice Reports. The Hague: International Court of Justice, 1980.

International Legal Materials. American Society of International Law, 1976.

Jennings, R. "The Caroline and McLeod Cases." *American Journal of International Law*, 32, 1938.

Kagan, D. *The Outbreak of the Peloponnesian War*. Ithaca: Cornell University Press, 1989.

Kareklas, I. *Διεθνεσ Δικαιον Και Ελληνικοσ Πολιτισμοσ* [*International Law and Greek Civilization*.] Athens: Sideris Publications, 2012.

Lateiner, D. "Oaths: Theory and Practice in the *Histories* of Herodotus and Thucydides," in E. Foster and D. Lateiner (eds.), *Thucydides and Herodotus* (Oxford: Oxford University Press, 2012).

Lauterpacht, H. *International Law and Human Rights*. London: Praeger, 1950.

Lewis, D. M. "The Origins of the First Peloponnesian War," in G. S. Shrimpton and D. J. McCargar (eds.), *Classical Contributions: Studies in Honour of M. F. McGregor* (Locust Valley: J. J. Augustin, 1981).

Liddell, H., and R. Scott. *A Greek-English Lexicon*. Oxford: Oxford University Press, 1940.

Losada, L. *The Fifth Column in the Peloponnesian War*. Leiden: Brill, 1972.

Low, P. *Interstate Relations in Classical Greece. Morality and Power, Cambridge Classical Studies*. Cambridge: Cambridge University Press, 2007.

MacGregor, M. "The Genius of Alkibiades." *Phoenix* 19, no. 1 (1965).

Marinatos, N. *Thucydides and Religion*. Konigstein: Hain, 1981.

Mearsheimer, J. *Conventional Deterrence*. Ithaca: Cornell University Press, 1983.

Meiggs, R., and D. Lewis. *A Selection of Greek Historical Inscriptions*. Oxford: Oxford University Press, 1969.

Morgenthau, H. *Politics among Nations*. New York: Knopf, 1967.

Munson, R. V. "Persians in Thucydides," in E. Foster and D. Lateiner (eds.), *Thucydides and Herodotus*. Oxford: Oxford University Press, 2012.

Mynott, J. (ed.). *Thucydides: The War of the Peloponnesians and the Athenians, Cambridge Texts in the History of Political Thought*. Cambridge: Cambridge University Press, 2013.

Murray, W. "Thucydides: Theorist of War." *Naval War College Review* 66, no. 4 (2013).

Orwin, C. *The Humanity of Thucydides*. Princeton: Princeton University Press, 1997.

Parker, R. "Myths of Early Athens," in J. Bremmer (ed.), *Interpretations of Greek Mythology*. London: Routledge, 1987.

Parry, A. "The Language of Thucydides' Description of the Plague." *Bulletin of the Institute of Classical Studies* no. 16 (1969): 106–18.

Pearson, L. "Thucydides as Reporter and Critic." *Transactions and Proceedings of the American Philological Association* 78 (1947): 37–60.

Plato. *Republic, Loeb Classical Library* 276. Cambridge: Harvard University Press, 2013.

Plato. *The Republic*, Sir Desmond Lee (trans.). London: Penguin Classics, 1987, 2007.

Plutarch, *Lives Volume IX, Demetrius and Anthony, Loeb Classical Library* 101. Cambridge: Harvard University Press, 1920.

Plutarch. *Lives Volume III, Loeb Classical Library* 65. Cambridge: Harvard University Press, 1916.

Plutarch. *Lives, Volume IV: Alcibiades and Coriolanus. Lysander and Sulla*. Bernadotte Perrin (trans.), *Loeb Classical Library* 80. Cambridge: Harvard University Press, 1916.

Roisman, J. *The General Demosthenes and His Use of Military Surprise*. Stuttgart: Franz Steiner Verlag, 1993.

Root, E. "Opening Address at the Seventh Annual Meeting of the American Society of International Law April 24, 1913," reprinted in *American Journal of International Law* 453 (1913).

Rusten, J. S. (ed.). Thucydides, *The Peloponnesian War Book II, Cambridge Greek and Latin Classics*. Cambridge: Cambridge University Press, 1990.

Schlatter, R. (ed.). *Hobbes' Thucydides*. New Brunswick: Rutgers University Press, 1975.

Smyth, H. W. *Greek Grammar*. Cambridge: Harvard University Press, 1959.

Stadter, P. A. (ed.). *The Speeches in Thucydides*. Chapel Hill: University of North Carolina Press, 1973.

Stahl, H. "Blind Decisions Preceding Military Action," in E. Foster and D. Lateiner (eds.), *Thucydides and Herodotus*. Oxford: Oxford University Press, 2012.

Tesón, F. R. *Humanitarian Intervention*. Leiden: Transnational Publishers, 1988.

Thucydides. *History of the Peloponnesian War*. C. F. Smith (trans.). *Loeb Classical Library* 108, 109, 110, and 169. Cambridge: Harvard University Press, 1919–1923.

Tod, M. N. *A Selection of Greek Historical Inscriptions* I. Oxford: Oxford University Press, 1947.

UK Foreign Office Policy Document no. 148, United Kingdom Materials in International Law 1986, 57 *British Yearbook of International Law* 614, 1986.

Waltz, K. *Theory of International Politics*. Boston: Addison-Wesley, 1979.

Walzer, M. *Just and Unjust Wars: A Moral Argument with Historical Illustrations*. New York: Basic Books, 2015.

Westlake, J. *Individuals in Thucydides*. Cambridge: Cambridge University Press, 1968.

Xenophon. *Anabasis, Loeb Classical Library* 90. Cambridge: Harvard University Press, 1998.

Xenophon. *The Constitution of the Lacedaemonians, Xenophon* Volume VII, E. C. Marchant (trans.), *Loeb Classical Library* 183. Cambridge: Harvard University Press, 1925.

Xenophon. *Hellenica, Volume I: Books 1–4*. Carleton L. Brownson (trans.), *Loeb Classical Library* 88. Cambridge: Harvard University Press, 1918.

Index

About the Author

Iacovos Kareklas got his BA and MA degrees in law from Cambridge University, Magdalene College. At the University of Cambridge, where he studied on a Cambridge Commonwealth Trust Scholarship jointly with a British Foreign Office Bursary, he won first prize in the de Smith Mooting Competition of the Cambridge University Law Society, of which he is a life member. He was particularly keen on public international law as well as on constitutional law and theory.

He holds a PhD in international law from London University (London School of Economics and Political Science). He specialized in all aspects of public international law and every aspect of the Cyprus problem. He conducted sustained and in depth research in the Foreign Office Archives with regard to the critical phases of the Cyprus question. During his doctoral program, he was a teaching assistant in subjects of his specialization.

In the academic year 2003–2004 he was a postdoctoral fellow at the department of government, Harvard University. He did postdoctoral studies in international politics theory with special reference to the use of military force and emphasis on classical antiquity under the worldwide distinguished political scientist, professor Stanley Hoffmann. At Harvard, he also taught the course *Classical Theories of International Relations*. In the year 2004–2005, Dr. Kareklas flew to Boston again and was appointed postdoctoral fellow at Harvard's Center for Middle Eastern Studies. In 2006 and 2007 he was elected fellow of the faculty of law (Honour School of Jurisprudence) in the University of Oxford, where he specialized in the philosophy of law.

As of 2013, Dr. Kareklas is an associate professor in the Republic of Cyprus, a rank at which he was unanimously elected. He teaches international law, philosophy of law, constitutional law, and international politics.

He spent a year as researcher in the Institute of Commonwealth Studies (ICS) of London (2001–2002), the British Institute of International and Comparative Law (2003), and the Oxford Centre for Criminology (2006). He has given lectures in English and American Universities as well as various political organizations. He is the author of a number of books and articles in the fields of his specialization. In 2014 he founded an original series (of which he is the editor), namely Studies in International Law and International Politics (in Greek), published by the preeminent law publisher Sakkoulas in Athens.

www.ingramcontent.com/pod-product-compliance
Lightning Source LLC
Chambersburg PA
CBHW021428110726
47901CB00008B/2346